The LAW
and the PUBLIC'S
HEALTH

health
administration
press

Kenneth R. Wing

The LAW
and the PUBLIC'S
HEALTH

SECOND EDITION

Health Administration Press
Ann Arbor, Michigan   1985

Library of Congress Cataloging-in-Publication Data

Wing, Kenneth R., 1946–
   The law and the public's health.

   Includes bibliographies.
   1. Public health laws—United States. I. Title. [DNLM: 1. Public Health—United States—legislation. WA 33 AA1 W7L]
KF3775.W5   1985   344.73′04   85–8563
ISBN 0–910701–08–3   347.3044

Health Administration Press
School of Public Health
The University of Michigan
1021 East Huron
Ann Arbor, Michigan 48109
(313) 764-1380

Contents

Preface to the
Second Edition

I wrote the first edition of this book in 1974 as an introductory text for law and law-related courses in schools of public health and medicine. Since that time I have found that it also had been used in schools of nursing and pharmacy, as supplemental reading in law school courses, and even as a reference for practitioners in both the health and legal fields.

My primary audience, however, remains the same as it was in the first edition: students and others with some expertise in the delivery of health care, but little or no background in law. My principal objective is to describe the law and the legal system in a manner that is tailored to the needs of students and practicing health professionals and that will help them understand the legal constraints within which they pursue their various endeavors and the legal controversies in which they are likely to become involved.

Thus this is not a treatise on "health law"—whatever the meaning of that overused term—or any attempt to catalogue the principles of law that affect the delivery of health care. There are other works, including some intended as textbooks, that attempt to do so, and some of these can be useful in supplementing the material presented in this book. I highly recommend, for example, Tom Christoffel's *Health and the Law*. It is an excellent reference for both students and teachers.

But after ten years of teaching I am convinced that the principal need of my students is not a treatise or compendium of legal principles but an overview of those principles that serves as an introduction to the law and the legal system and to both the theoretical and the practical determinants of legal decision making.

I have, therefore, followed in this book an approach that outlines the general principles of law most applicable to the delivery of health care and that analyzes specific applications of those principles that represent important health policy questions in their own right, but, most importantly, represent good illustrations of the manner in which American law is interpreted and applied.

There are, of course, a variety of ways in which these materials should be supplemented, just as there are a variety of methods by which they could be taught. With regard to additional reading, I have listed in the end notes following each chapter the additional materials that I have most frequently used for my own preparation and for teaching purposes. With regard to teaching methods, I have found that my students prefer a heavy dose of current events woven into these materials; I have also found, usually to the initial chagrin of my students, that it is very helpful to supplement the readings with some "hands-on" exposure to legal research. And, as these materials suggest, I generally prefer the case method of analysis, as do most of my students—at least so long as I abandon some of the Socratic overtones I apparently inherited from my legal education.

Beyond these few observations, my instinct is that teaching technique depends in large part on the particular students and the particular setting of a course. It is as much a product of the eccentricities of the instructor as it is of any pedagogical principle. My only firm commitment is to design my course not by topics covered, for the reasons outlined above, but according to a checklist of objectives against which I periodically measure my teaching and classroom activities. Again with primary reference to students in public health or medical school courses, I think the essential elements of an introductory education in law should include the following:

1. a thorough and realistic understanding of the law and the legal system, particularly the structure and function of the various legal decision-making processes

2. a familiarity with the substance of American law, including a basic understanding of important legal principles

3. the ability to sort out legal controversies and define relevant and critical legal issues in the application of these principles

4. the ability to understand how those issues are likely to be resolved

5. the ability to seek out, communicate with, and evaluate legal counsel

These are the skills and aptitudes that I believe are necessary for practicing health professionals and that are therefore the proper objectives of introductory courses in their education.

As all of the above should suggest, I am firmly convinced that a course or book designed to explain the law and the legal system in a manner that is useful to health professionals is in large part an explanation of American civics. In fact, with each year that I teach, I find that I spend increasingly more time on the structure and function of legal decision-making processes and the other materials covered in chapter 1. The so-called "checks and balances" between the various branches of government deserve particular attention. They define, after all, the distribution of power among the components of government and shape the outcome of many health policy controversies. But even the basic structure and workings of those branches, as elementary as that sounds, generally need considerable attention. In this regard, I have found it useful to supplement both my readings and my classroom activities with a variety of field experiences, visits to legislative and administrative bodies, judicial hearings, and the like.

At the risk of repeating myself, I think that an understanding of these decision-making processes and how they relate to one another is critical to an understanding of the principles of law and their application to the delivery of health care; and I think the development of this understanding should be the primary focus of any introduction of health professionals to the law. With this in mind I have rewritten these materials in the second edition.

Introduction to the Second Edition

Kerr White, writing in the introductory article to the *Scientific American's Life and Death and Medicine* in 1974, began with the question: "Why, at this time, are medicine and the provision of health care rapidly becoming a major focus of debate in almost every industrialized society?" White cited as one reason the enormous costs of delivering health care. He also found the explanation inherent in the tremendous technological advances in medicine that have developed through the last few decades; these advances, he argued, have created the potential for tremendous progress, but also have presented us with some unprecedented difficulties, among them the need to readjust our political and social institutions in light of this potential and the need to make the difficult policy choices created as a result.

A decade later, I still find that White's analysis captures the essence of our present social and political circumstances. Ours is not a single problem or dilemma, though the cost of delivering health care continues to be a dominating concern. Nor do our current circumstances constitute a single and immediate crisis—as so many observers have insisted. What we face today is a series of tremendously difficult, interwoven, and above all conflicting problems. We must somehow constrain the ever-inflating costs of health care, but we must do so not as a nation with a community of purpose but as state and federal taxpayers, individual consumers, purchasers of insurance—perspectives from which costs can be as easily shifted as contained, and from which social commitment and self-interest are frequently distinguished and just as frequently confused. And while addressing the problem(s) of containing cost, we must also address our competing needs to maintain the access to and the adequacy of that care, needs that, again, break down into conflicting demands of various perspectives and that complicate both the understanding of our problems and the formulation of appropriate resolutions.

Thus our present political problem is better characterized as a series of dilemmas of growing importance than as a crisis; and these dilemmas are hardly likely either to be resolved immediately or resolved to the satisfaction of more than a fraction of the nation at any one time.

The relative importance of health care at this time can be best understood, as White also suggested, from a historical perspective. A few thousand years ago Hippocrates wrote what were then the most profound observations about the health of man; today it seems impossible that anyone could ever accept such inaccurate and primitive ideas. Some 150 years ago John Snow made what was at that time an incredible medical breakthrough; he counted deaths from cholera and noticed that it somehow related to the water people drank. These events mark only the beginning of the evolution of man's understanding of his health. The ability actually to treat disease or injury is even more recent. We still taunt the medical profession with the estimate by one Harvard professor that it was the year 1912 when "for the first time in human history, a random patient with a random disease consulting a doctor chosen at random stood better than a 50-50 chance of benefiting from the encounter."

The technological progress that followed in this century has been so rapid and accelerated that it is impossible to characterize anecdotally. There have been tremendous advances in our understanding of both the causes and determinants of good health and of the social and medical intervention necessary to protect and maintain it. Today we see the near miracle; and tomorrow, we are promised, it will be commonplace.

Some public health authorities argue that we are reaching a point of diminishing returns, that the accelerated progress of the last half century was our rapid resolution of the most solvable problems. The health issues of the next 50 years, chronic disease, environmentally induced ills, problems that call for both behavioral change and social restructure as much as improvements in personal health services, may be more resistant to our technological fixes. But at the least the daily accounts of heart transplants and genetic splicing, test-tube babies and sonic x-rays, continue to feed our inflated expectations of progress. And at least in this country, good medical care and adequate public health services are no longer a luxury; we can afford them and thus we expect them to be successful, more so now than in any previous generation. And when our expectations are not met we bring considerable pressure on our social and political institutions to do something to satisfy them.

This rhetoric is hardly unique to the 1980s. Similar words have been heard in political campaigns for nationalizing health insurance and other progressive programs since the turn of the century. "Adequate health care is an expectation and a right" is an echo of New Deal politics, as well as those of the Truman, Kennedy, and Johnson administrations. Indeed, liberals have always used these expectations to chart a course for our progress, a tentative but straight-line progression of our nation's health policies towards a nationalized health system and towards the assurance of access for all to adequate and high quality health care—at least through the 1970s.

By the 1970s, of course, the predicted progression, if ever accurate, would no longer be descriptive of the stalemate and retrenchment that would characterize American health policy, particularly at the national level. Our basic political circumstances did not change; indeed, the rhetoric of the debate was modified only slightly. What did change was the focus of the debate. What once sounded like a quest for the elusive national solution became one which emphasized the various and competing definitions of "the cost problem," the conflict between the need to control cost and the need to improve access and quality, the inherent dilemmas rather than the possible resolutions. Even the most basic political assumptions concerning relative equity and governmental responsibility were now questioned.

By the election of Ronald Reagan in 1980, we were charting a very different national course. Federal spending on health and health-related programs, the sustenance for public policy for at least two decades, was drastically reduced. Federal enthusiasm for planning and regulatory health programs slackened; in its stead, there was a promise of—though little movement towards—inducement of competition in health care delivery. The responsibility for financing, administering, and, ultimately, making difficult policy choices was shifted by the Reagan-era politics towards state and local government and towards private institutions.

This chapter in American health politics has yet to be completely written. But even if the apparent direction of the public reaction to the critical problems of modern health care delivery does shift to follow Reagan's lead, our primary circumstances will have changed very little. We will only have complicated the already intensive debate. It is unlikely that the relative importance of the matters at hand will be in any way reduced or that the dilemmas we face will be satisfactorily resolved.

We are in the mid-1980s at a point where the promotion of health and, in particular, the delivery of health and medical services present us with important and difficult public policy issues for which there are no readily identifiable resolutions. We have been in similar circumstances for at least two decades; we will likely continue to be so for some time to come. There is at infrequent intervals a sense that we are approaching a crisis; but there is in fact little indication that any one critical decision can or will be made.

The essay above on the nature of health policy in this country is intended to highlight the importance of an understanding of the law and of the legal system for anyone who is involved in the delivery of health care, or for that matter, for the public at large. In the most elemental terms, the rights and responsibilities relating to the delivery of health care are currently and constantly being examined, reevaluated, and altered by our legal institutions. Quite literally, new law—for better or for worse or for more of the same—is being created at an ever-increasing rate and, some would argue, in ever more complicated forms. There is little doubt that the government is inextricably involved in the delivery of health care and the maintenance of health. But where are the limits on those responsibilities and how and by whom are choices to be made? Regulatory efforts may be replaced or supplemented by efforts to stimulate competition, but the resulting mix of reform strategies only assures more controversy. Cost containment, or cost shifting, and resource allocation decisions, whether made collectively or by private decision makers, will dramatically affect the health of both individuals and communities but will surely spark considerable legal and political controversies.

All these activities involve new law, both in the sense of the alteration of the legally defined relationships between the various individual and institutional actors and in the literal sense that new laws, statutes, regulations, judicial interpretations, are constantly being made.

The law as it relates to health care must be understood by anyone who deals with the critical issues that face our nation today. If for no other reason, the law effects a set of constraints on behavior. More importantly, the law is one determinant of health and of the health care delivery system; it is a means for causing change as well as preventing it. Adjustments in the law are prerequisites for almost any change and one of the most important tools available to anyone who aspires to achieve major changes. Accordingly, the objective of this book is to assist those who are involved in the delivery of health care to understand the legal constraints within which they operate and to use the law and the legal system in an effective manner.

The Law and
the Legal System

An understanding of the law as it relates to the delivery of health care must begin with a basic and practical understanding of the legal system and the law in general. This chapter will be an abbreviated description of the American legal system and an explanation of some of the basic legal concepts that underlie that system. It is intended to establish a foundation for the material that follows and a language for explaining the substance of the various legal principles that will be analyzed.

To some readers, this chapter may appear to be no more than a basic civics lesson, only indirectly related to health policy issues, and somewhat less stimulating than some of the substantive materials that will follow in later chapters. To a large extent, such observations will be accurate, but the surprising and unfortunate truth is that a basic civics lesson is exactly what most people need, however unstimulating such a lesson might appear. The vast majority of the people in this country, including professionals involved with health care, still have major misunderstandings about the law, the ways in which our legal system operates, and the nature of legal rights.

THE MEANING OF "THE LAW"

There is no truly comprehensive way to define "the law." Aside from a few, not-worth-quoting epigrams, "the law" in its entirety has rarely been described in a meaningful, accurate manner. Nor is there any entirely satisfactory way to summarize "the law" or any part of it.

Various treatises have been written attempting to set forth in relatively short, "black letter" statements "the law" on a given subject; Prosser's *Restatement of Torts* is a prime example. There is a variety of legal scholarship, ranging from philosophical commentary on the meaning of "the law" to attempts to predict future trends and directions to thinly veiled advocacy of what "the law" should be. But these are works that are written largely for lawyers and by lawyers. They assume an understanding of the legal system, of laws, and of the reality of law in practice. However useful they are in their own context, it would be inappropriate and misleading to build an initial understanding of "the law" for our present purposes on such materials.

The fact of the matter is that "the law" on a given subject, meaning its reality and impact, is not best understood with reference to a series of short statements; nor can "the law" simply be described by a compendium of principles from which applications of these principles can easily be described in question and answer form. Certainly there are principles that can be, with qualification, extracted from the substance of "the law," and in some situations rather clearcut statements can be derived of "what the law is" and "what I can or cannot do." In most controversial situations, however, such a static synthesis of "the law" is simply impossible. This is particularly true when dealing with "the law" as it relates to the delivery of health care where, except for a few long-standing traditions that may well be resistant to change, the application of "the law" is clearly subject to considerable pressure to change. Even holding aside the practical determinants of legal decision making and considering only the theory of "the law," it would be a mistake in an introductory context to present "the law" in a manner that suggests that it can be firmly defined by a series of principles or reduced to questions and answers. That is not the character of "the law" in the broader sense; it is quite different and, in some respects, much more.

"The law" is, of course, the sum or set or conglomerate of all of the laws in all of the jurisdictions: the constitutions, the statutes and the regulations that interpret them, the traditional principles known as common law, and the judicial opinions that apply and interpret all of those laws. "The law" is also the legal profession, its prejudices and shortcomings, as well as its concepts and language. To understand what "the law" is, one must know something of what roles lawyers play and how they think, of their legalese and the means by which their counsel is sought and evaluated.

"The law" is also the legal process—the ways in which laws are made, enforced, and interpreted. From one perspective, there is the theoretical framework of this decision making that must be understood in order to understand "the law." It includes notions of the divisions of power between the various branches of government, the separate roles of trial and appellate courts, the important delineations of power made by such concepts as "substantial evidence," "rational basis," and "de novo review." An understanding of the theory of "the law" requires an appreciation of the interrelationship between statutes and regulations and the distribution of power to interpret them, the meaning and role of judicial opinions, and the underlying assumption that justice in a legal system is defined not only in terms of ultimate outcomes but also in terms of the justness of the procedures used to decide them.

At a second level, there is also a required understanding of the practical realities of legal process: the legislatures and their politics; the ofttimes ponderous judicial system; the bureaucratic tendencies inherent in both the structure and function of the executive branch. A practical understanding of legal process must include the notion that legislatures make and amend laws, but that some citizens and some institutions influence those decisions more than others. It must include a recognition of such procedural devices as trial by jury, but also it must color that recognition in light of the makeup and possible biases of juries and judges given the ways they are selected. Above all, the legal processes must be understood as having an economic component. It costs money to make, enforce, or interpret "the law." It will cost most people something—frequently more than they can afford—to enforce even their most basic rights. For large portions of the population, the legal decision-making processes are virtually inaccessible and totally overwhelming when they are caught up within them.

These are the kinds of theoretical and practical things that first must be understood in order to understand "the law" and the legal system; they can be suggested here, and some are covered in more detail in the remainder of this chapter. But they are only partially revealed by academic study. In large part they must be experienced far beyond the limits of the classroom and the textbook.

It would be a mistake to go further without reference, almost by way of apology, to the traditional barrier between lawyers and nonlawyers that makes describing or understanding "the law" even more difficult. The legal profession has for centuries done many things to surround the practice of law with a mystical aura. Much as the medical profession would have us believe that there is something almost sacred about medical judgment and that only a physician can understand it, lawyers have perpetuated the only partially justified myth that there is something called legal judgment that only someone with the proper mix of formal education, practical experience, and appropriate vocabulary can make.

It does take training to read and understand law, particularly judicial opinions, but it is not as difficult as the profession would have the lay public believe. The various rules of research must be mastered, a certain disciplined diligence must be employed, and there must be a familiarity with some underlying concepts. The more practice one has in these skills, the better. But what are often passed off as legal judgments are sometimes more accurately described as educated guesses, some of which are really experienced bluffs. It is the difference between the judgments, the guesses, and the bluffs that needs to be understood by the public, but that is often confused and obscured by lawyers with their conveniently obtuse vocabulary. "The law" is sometimes contradictory, often complex, and almost always vague. There are vast gray areas between the black and the white rules where even the best of the profession cannot read "what the law says." Some lawyers would have us believe that the abilities to decipher the seemingly contradictory nature of "the law" and to fill in the missing coloration of the apparently gray area are the quasi-mystical skills that place lawyers one step above mere mortals and "the law" beyond the layperson's understanding. We would all be better served if gray areas and legal contradictions were more often described as exactly what they are, and lawyering in terms that better reflect the important but limited abilities of lawyers.

How, then, can "the law" be best described? How can these various aspects of the law and the legal system, the theory and the practice, be accurately explained?

The approach that will be taken in this book will be to enunciate and describe the background and the general legal principles for each of a series of topics and to analyze the application of these principles to a series of critical—and only partially answered—problems concerning health and health care delivery. This description will not be in the form of a series of straightforward statements of what "the law" permits or prohibits in each problem situation. In some instances there will be rather specific declarations of what "the law" is, but in most situations it turns out that the best description admits that "the law" is little more than a series of rather vague guidelines and uncertain predictions of what legal decision makers will do the next time they are faced with a given situation. In those situations it is better to acknowledge the vagueness and the uncertainty than to impose a more certain reality that is not there. Thus the most accurate approach to an important health policy problem usually involves defining the broad legal principles that are relevant to that problem and some of the factors that are considered in the application of those principles while above all, focusing on the theory and the reality of the decision-making processes by which this strange thing called "the law" has been—and will be in the future—made, enforced, and interpreted.

LAWS: STATUTES, CONSTITUTIONS, REGULATIONS, JUDICIAL OPINIONS

What are laws?

Most people think of laws in terms of statutes. Statutes are written laws enacted by legislatures at any level of government. Before passage, pending statutes are called bills or occasionally propositions, terms which are often used inappropriately in common language when referring to an enacted statute. There are federal statutes, state statutes, and the equivalent of statutes passed by city and county governments that may be called ordinances or municipal laws. Statutes can govern any of the variety of human endeavors, ranging from the distribution of property to the spending of public funds to the definition of criminal conduct, limited only by the jurisdiction—the sphere of authority—of the legislative body that enacts them.

Statutes are only one form of law. Constitutions are also laws and are the written legal documents establishing governments. There is, of course, the U.S. Constitution, which defines the various powers of the federal government and the functions of its branches. There are also state constitutions which have comparable provisions relating to each state's government. The U.S. Constitution is often referred to as the supreme law of the land because any law, be it state or federal, that is in conflict with the Constitution is invalid. Similarly, any state law in conflict with that state's constitution is invalid.

While most people understand that statutes and constitutions are laws, it is not generally understood that regulations are also laws for most intents and purposes. A statute that relates to a complex activity may be worded in very general terms, with the specific details of the legislation not determined by the statute, but delegated to some governmental agency or official to define and enact by issuing regulations. This is very common with regard to health legislation. Good examples are the federal health benefit programs. Great portions and almost all programmatic details are left to the determination of the agency that administers the program according to appropriately enacted regulations.

The first important thing to note is that because they are authorized by statute and implemented under a statutory law, regulations are part of that law and have the full force of law. The second thing to note is that the term regulation has a very specific legal definition. Regulations must be enacted by a designated agency according to a specific process. This process may be defined in the authorizing statute or by the state or federal administrative procedures act, a statute defining procedural requirements for all government agencies. Usually there is a requirement that regulations be published in proposed form and that there be opportunity for public input or a hearing. Regulations may be invalidated if they are not enacted following the proper procedures, just as they may be held invalid if their content goes beyond their statutory mandate. Frequently there will be rules or other interpretive materials employed by government agencies that are referred to internally as regulations (incorrectly), when in fact they do not have the force of law of legally valid regulations because they have not been properly or authoritatively issued.

In theory, regulations permit a legislature to delegate authority to an administrative agency that has greater expertise in that particular area of the law. It would be cumbersome and to a certain extent inappropriate for the legislature to pass statutes that define every detail of a government program or activity. This is particularly true in the field of health where the legislatures have by statute mandated a large number of programs and agencies that require for their implementation the understanding of a great amount of technical information, as well as the resolution of difficult policy issues. Because of this, the regulations can become the most critical part of the legal basis of a governmental health program. This deference to expertise often translates into a delegation of considerable power from elected members of legislative bodies to nonelected officials and therefore it can create considerable controversy, as later chapters will discuss.

Another form of the law that may be confusing at first encounter is the judicial opinion. Appellate courts (and some trial courts) write legal opinions giving the bases for their decisions in individual cases. As all legal principles and all laws are by their nature general statements, courts have to apply these general principles to specific situations and, in effect, interpret the law by their decisions. These interpretations of law in the form of judicial opinions are recorded and published and have the force of law in the particular court's jurisdiction. The most important decisions are those of the U.S. Supreme Court, since these opinions become law for all other courts, both state and federal. In issuing opinions, courts interpret regulations, statutes, and constitutions, but also enunciate and interpret principles of law that have traditionally been applied in our legal system; these principles are generally referred to as the common law.

Thus judicial opinions can be described both as interpretations of laws and laws in and of themselves. An opinion, however difficult to decipher or summarize, is a law and has the force of law, just as a statute or a regulation. Anyone who wants to have any real feeling for the law and its applications has to know something of how these opinions are made, researched, and read. And, as mentioned above, while only an experienced expert can make the most exacting legal judgment, much of the law can be understood by nonlawyers with just a basic understanding of the law and its components. Being able to locate and understand judicial opinions is one way in which that understanding can be developed.

This is an outline of the primary forms of law: statutes, constitutions, regulations, and judicial opinions. Their complexities and the difficulty of their interpretation will become more obvious in the discussion of the substantive issues in later chapters. A certain amount of "hands-on" familiarity with these components of law and at least some experience with their research are highly recommended even while making an initial attempt to develop their meaning in the context of specific legal problems. The following is intended as a guide to such experience and suggests the kind of exercises that might be attempted.

Both federal and state statutes are codified (arranged according to subject matter) in sets of volumes or codes that are periodically amended or replaced to reflect subsequent changes. Statutes can also be found in compendiums that list all statutes in the chronological order of their enactment.

Regulations are also published according to both their subject matter and their chronological order. At the federal level they are relatively easy to find: the *Federal Register* lists all federal regulations chronologically as they are proposed and then as they are enacted; the *Code of Federal Regulations* codifies regulations according to their subject matter. State regulations are a more difficult problem; many states are seriously negligent in making regulations available in a timely fashion or, in some cases, publicly available at all.

Judicial opinions, somewhat harder to find, are published in a variety of sets, called reporters, arranged by state, region, or jurisdiction of the court, and are in chronological order. Since one is generally concerned with the subject matter of an opinion, there are techniques for locating cases by using various published indices and the case summaries and footnotes that are found preceding most judicial opinions; this is a relatively difficult art to attempt and exceedingly difficult to master.

There are some practical guides to this sort of research; the references at the end of this chapter list several that would be appropriate and useful. And, again, nothing will serve better to demystify all this than a little "hands-on" research experience. The recent computerization of legal opinions may also make this task easier for nonlawyers.

At the first encounter with some of this material, however, it may appear that the legal profession is extraordinarily preoccupied with references and cross-references and a peculiarly obscure set of shorthand abbreviations. Actually, the vast amount of materials encompassed by the law at least partially justifies this preoccupation, and a basic understanding of legal references and citations can be very useful in both understanding and finding the law.

Although statutes can be referred to by their title (if they have one), e.g., the Administrative Procedures Act or the Social Security Act, they are most often cited by the section and volume of their subject matter code; the Administrative Procedures Act would be cited as 5 U.S.C. § 1000, meaning volume (or title) five of the *United States Code* at section 1000; for state statutes, the citations are basically the same, although some state statutory citations refer to a section or chapter or title within the state code, e.g., N.Y. GEN. BUS. LAW § 352, meaning *New York General Business Laws*, section 352; CAL. WELF. AND INST. CODE, § 1400, would refer to the *California Welfare and Institutions Code*, section 1400. Statutes can also be cited by their chronological reference, e.g., Pub. L. No. 93–641 means the 641st enactment of the 93d Congress (found in several sources).

Regulations are cited similarly. For example, 42 C.F.R. § 562 is volume 42, section 562 of the *Code of Federal Regulations*. State Regulations are usually codified in the same way, e.g., 22 CAL. AD. CODE § 50000 is volume 22 of the *California Administrative Code*, section 50000.

Judicial opinions are more uniform in their citations. They will almost always be referred to by the page in the particular volume in which they appear; 183 U.S. 427 (1901) is a U.S. Supreme Court case decided in 1901 that appears on page 427 of volume 183 of the *United States Reports*. Likewise 459 F.2d 6 (lst Cir. 1972) is a 1972 case, decided in the First Circuit Court of Appeals, that can be found on page six of volume 459 of the second series of the *Federal Reporter*.

About the only real difficulty is understanding the rather complicated system of abbreviations that has developed over the years; one should also be aware of the fact that most judicial opinions are published in more than one source and that sometimes several citations to different sources of the same material may be given. In terms of actually locating the material from a citation, the only real skill is being able to transcribe the citation exactly. All law libraries have a variety of indices and references, as well as reference librarians to assist in the interpretation of citations—a service used quite frequently by lawyers as well as laypeople.

THE LEGAL SYSTEM

As has been indicated earlier in this chapter, in order to understand the law as it relates to health and health care delivery, it is important to understand the legal process and the various legal decision-making agencies.

To begin in the most elementary terms, the American legal structure is traditionally described as having three branches: the legislative, the executive, and the judicial. This description applies to the federal government as well as state government and, in most cases, local government, except where these functional branches are merged at the local level into one or two bodies. The legislative branch is usually defined as the branch that makes the law; the executive branch enforces the law; and the judicial branch interprets the law. However, that is not literally accurate. Judicial interpretations in some sense make law as well as interpret it, and the executive branch and its administrative agencies make, as well as enforce, the law through administrative regulations and other rulings. Similarly, it can be argued that the executive branch in some ways interprets laws as it enforces them, subject to the ultimate interpretation and review of the courts. In any event, this is the traditional definition of our basic legal structure: the legislature, the executive branch, and the courts, however rough the delineation of their function may be.

This traditional definition also has to be qualified by reference to the nature and function of the various administrative agencies that are, in theory, part of the executive branch of the government. They could just as accurately be described as a fourth branch of the government. Over time and with the growing complexity of American government, the enforcement of law and the administration of government programs have led to the creation of hundreds of agencies under the executive branch, some of which develop a significant amount of autonomy and do not function under the direct control of the executive hierarchy. Almost all agencies carry out quasi-legislative functions (e.g., they issue regulations) and quasi-judicial functions (e.g., they hold administrative hearings). Health may be the archetypal example: state and federal executive branches have been expanded to include the administrative capabilities to enforce a variety of health and health-related programs, from certificate of need programs to health education, from Medicaid to occupational health and safety enforcement. The practical result has been in some cases the formation of great bureaucratic institutions, with all of the good and bad implications that the term "bureaucracy" suggests. In other cases the result has been the development of fairly autonomous agencies, e.g., boards of medical examiners, neither directed by nor responsible to the chief executive. It would be difficult and probably misleading to portray the reality of American governmental function or structure solely in terms of the tripartite model that our constitutional bases imply, particularly when concerned with governmental activities relating to health and health care.

More detailed descriptions of the legislative and executive branches of government will be left to other sources, although it must be noted that a "who runs what and answers to whom" civics lesson and even a rather elemental "how a bill becomes a law" lecture are not inappropriate exercises even for students with some claim to real world experience. (Note also that chapter 7 considers in greater detail the distribution of power within the executive branch.) But to ensure that the materials that follow in later chapters are clearly understood, it is appropriate at least to outline the structure of the judicial branch of the government in the present context.

There are two separate judicial systems in the United States. In addition to the system of federal courts, each state establishes a system of state and local courts that may vary greatly from other states and that functionally overlaps with the federal judicial system.

Some states establish different courts for different kinds of legal disputes. For example, in addition to the courts of general jurisdiction (i.e., courts that hear any kind of legal dispute) a state may also have courts of special jurisdiction that deal with such things as probate, juvenile matters, and small claims. In addition, courts of general jurisdiction will usually divide administratively into divisions (or departments or sessions) handling only criminal matters, civil matters, or matters in equity.

Because of this interstate variation it is probably unwise to consider any state's judicial system typical of the rest. Speaking generically, there are basically two types of courts that make up any state judicial system—appellate courts and trial level courts. All state judicial systems have at least a supreme appellate court; almost all have intermediate appellate courts. These courts hear appeals from their trial courts. All states have many trial level courts.

Trial courts hear all cases first; they hear oral testimony, take other evidence, and interpret the law as it applies to the facts established by all the evidence. Most people are familiar with trial courts and the trial process, thanks to Perry Mason, "The People's Court," and the other offerings of the mass media, however accurate these may be. Most people are less familiar with appellate courts which only review the legal interpretations of trial courts. In essence, appellate courts consider and hear only legal arguments and generally take no evidence.

They make their decisions based on the factual conclusions of trial courts and their own interpretations of the law. Appellate courts do write opinions, and it is the opinions of appellate courts (and a few trial courts) that are reported and that become part of the law.

A trial court judge sees witnesses, hears evidence, and considers the arguments of the parties' lawyers. An appellate court hearing involves only the judge considering the arguments of two lawyers; usually nothing more is presented.

The federal judicial system consists of the U.S. District Courts, the federal trial courts; U.S. Circuit Courts of Appeals, the intermediate level federal appellate courts; and the U.S. Supreme Court, the supreme appellate court of the legal system.

The federal judicial system handles cases that involve disputes over federal law. Federal courts also handle cases involving disputes over state law, if the disputing parties are from different states. There is also something known as pendent jurisdiction, which means that if a case involves a violation of both state law and of federal law, the federal courts will decide both issues. The state court, on the other hand, has jurisdiction over all legal disputes in that state, whether the disputes involve violations of state or federal law. Therefore at times a case may be brought in either the state or the federal judicial system. If a case is brought in the state judicial system and involves federal law, in addition to the appeals to the state appellate courts there is also the possibility that the case may be appealed to the U.S. Supreme Court, since in matters involving federal law, particularly the U.S. Constitution, the federal Supreme Court is the ultimate authority.

Notwithstanding its ability to do so, when a federal court is considering a case that involves a state law, it is extremely hesitant to overrule a previous interpretation of that state's law by its own state courts, and in theory does not have the power to overrule an interpretation of the state's constitution by its own state supreme court.

The interjudicial bounds of jurisdiction, as well as the division of power within the judicial system, are critically important. In the chapters that follow, the underlying principles outlined above will be developed in much greater depth.

THE FUNCTION OF LAW: LEGAL RIGHTS

To understand that laws can be in the form of opinions, statutes, constitutions, or regulations and to understand some of the framework of our legal system is only the beginning of a conceptual understanding of the law and the law as it relates to the delivery of health care. As suggested in the introduction to this chapter, the real function of the law should also be understood.

To put the matter in terms that sound oversimplified, the basic function of the law is to establish legal rights and the basic purpose of the legal system is to define and enforce those rights. But what does it really mean to establish, define, and enforce a legal right?

For present purposes, legal rights can most usefully be defined as specific relationships among individual people or institutions that are recognized in the law and enforced through the legal system; in terms more popularly used, they are relationships that establish privileges and responsibilities among those governed by the legal system.

The essence of this definition is the notion that rights are specific relationships. They are not protected freedoms or interests held out against all the world, but a protection of one rather specific interest from the effects of another. The freedom of speech, for example, is a constitutional right assured to all American citizens—protecting most forms of speech from interference by the government. But it does not protect everyone (e.g., there is still some question whether American corporations have a freedom of speech), nor does it prohibit interference with the speech of private citizens by other private parties. In fact, most of the constitutional rights establish relationships only between citizens and the government—not among those citizens in their private capacities. Other laws, for example common law principles of tort liability or civil rights statutes, establish legal relationships which do in effect protect speech and other constitutional freedoms from interference by private parties, but neither the federal nor state constitutions do so directly.

Whether the issue is personal freedom or protection of property, the right to legislated entitlements or responsibilities to other people, it is extremely important to order those rights in terms of who is protected from whom, what relationships are established by the law, and what they protect or require. It is also important to understand that the relationships established by law are limited to those that are defined and enforced through the legal system. This means that some law, some regulation, statute, constitution, or judicial opinion, has to be interpreted to recognize such a relationship and that the legal system has to provide both for that recognition and for its meaningful enforcement.

Again, the freedom of speech provides a good illustration. According to the text of the First Amendment, "Congress shall make no law respecting an establishment of religion, or prohibiting the free exercise thereof; or abridging the freedom of speech, or of the press; or the right of the people peaceably to assemble, and to petition the Government for a redress of grievances."

That the venerable free speech clause establishes protection for all citizens not only from congressional interference but from all governmental activity is hardly clear from first glance at this text; indeed it was only after a century or more of judicial controversy, and through a liberal reading of the Fourteenth Amendment, that this First Amendment guarantee was definitely settled as extending protection from state and local government as well as from federal government activity. Or to say the same thing somewhat differently, whatever its value as a "freedom" in 1796, the free speech clause has real meaning today only because the courts are willing to interpret it to apply to specific situations and to define specific relationships between the various levels of government and individual people. Only these applications, as well as those that can be predicted or expected, should in a functional sense be considered legal rights.

Similarly, until they are enforced, or at least potentially enforceable, these relationships even if defined are only legal rights in a very limited sense of that term. The right to treatment for mental patients, discussed in chapter 3, is a particularly good illustration of this point. Although it took some years before the courts were willing to do so, it was not an intellectually demanding interpretation to find that the due process clause of the Fourteenth Amendment required that people who are committed by the state for reason of their mental illness must be treated (notwithstanding Chief Justice Burger's tirades against it). Reading American case law with even a little dose of common sense virtually requires recognizing such a relationship between the state governments and the mentally ill people they incarcerate. But providing for the enforcement of that right through the legal system, as chapter 3 discusses, has proven to be an onerous task and one that leaves the answer to the question "Do mental patients have a right to treatment?" rather difficult to answer without considerable qualification.

Thus, in order for legal rights to exist in a practical sense, there must be a specific law that defines a specific relationship between individual people or institutions; and the privileges, protections, or responsibilities of those parties must be recognized and somehow enforceable through the quixotic machinations of the American legal system.

This rather abstract discussion can be brought into better focus by its application to specific examples. The materials that follow in subsequent chapters essentially outline a series of public policy issues that have presented our legal system with difficult questions in making, interpreting, and executing American law. To understand how these questions are to be resolved, it will be necessary to sort out of the particular circumstances of each issue those legal relationships that are recognized by the law and enforceable through the legal system.

This definition of legal rights is not meant to imply that there are no other relationships that may be appropriately called rights. Certainly there are other relationships that are important and relevant to health policy issues, and these should at least be recognized in any discussion of the law as it relates to health care delivery, even if they are only to be distinguished.

First of all, some rights, meaning relationships between two or more specific entities, are enforced and defined not by (or in some cases, not only by) the legal system, but by the force of prevailing ethics. Loosely, ethics can be defined as formal principles of conduct recognized and enforced by whatever sanctions are employed by one's associates or professional peers. In many cases ethics are only nominally recognized and are not enforced in any pragmatic sense. Conversely, ethics can be vigorously enforced, and, particularly with regard to medical care providers, the sanctions available to one's professional associates can have serious personal or economic impact. Similarly, there are certain values that each of us individually feels so strongly about that we consider them "rights" despite the fact that they are not legally enforceable or enforceable under any ethical code. There is nothing more than the power of moral suasion to enforce these rights or relationships, but these moral or human rights can have powerful influences on individual behavior.

It can be helpful and ofttimes necessary in analyzing the law to speak not just of legal rights but also of their interface with these other notions. However, the materials in this book will be primarily concerned with existing, legally enforceable rights in the context of various health policy issues; and it will be important to focus on the elements of a legal right as a language to use in discussing these issues and in analyzing their implications.

PERSPECTIVES ON THE LAW

There is at least one other observation that ought to be made about the law in general before proceeding to specific topics. As these materials will illustrate, there are a number of different perspectives from which the law and the legal system can be viewed. The law can be analyzed in terms of what it is in theory—the responsibilities the law imposes or the benefits it confers, if and when it is perfectly enforced. But the law can also be considered with a firm awareness that the law is imperfectly enforced. Law enforcement is discriminatory along a number of parameters. The courts are slow to act and access to them is expensive. Many violations of legal rights go undetected and unenforced and, even when recognized, many injustices have no remedy. Thus you can evaluate the law in the most pragmatic terms: what can I get away with? Yet at the other extreme you can compare it to your own notions of right and wrong: what should the law be?

To a certain extent, the choice of perspective will depend upon the viewer's circumstances. In practice, most of us initially seek out legal counsel in terms of the justness of our cause or the legality of our conduct. Eventually, however, we either tacitly or, sometimes, explicitly adopt the "what can I get away with" posture. In an academic setting we are more often allowed the luxury of considering both what the law ought to be and what it is in terms which at least imply that we are unconcerned with the imperfections of the system that defines and enforces the law.

If it were possible to carry out a study by any even roughly scientific method to evaluate the factors that influence outcome in any legal decision-making process, it is likely that the factors most responsible for that outcome would not be either the correctness of the interpretations of the law or, for that matter, the justness of the result (holding aside the problem of defining what they are). It is more likely that the greater weight would have to be given to such factors as the relative resources available to the parties to the controversy, the preparation and competence of the parties' legal counsel, and the relative ability of the various parties to the controversy to tolerate the status quo pending the final decision. On the other hand, it is highly unlikely that many people understand that these biases have such influence on the law or that many lawyers establish such an understanding before advising their clients or their students.

As postulated in the introduction of this book, if an understanding of the law and the legal system requires an understanding of how legal controversies are resolved, and the ability to seek out, communicate with, and evaluate legal counsel, then at the least the implications of this hypothetical study must be rather thoroughly understood before the law and the legal system are evaluated and before specific applications of the law to health policy issues are examined. There is clearly a gap between "what you can get away with" and what the law would require or allow if it were perfectly enforced. That gap can be ignored, or it can be used to advantage. One can resolve to mitigate its impact, or simply accept it as an unfortunate reality. But whatever perspective is adopted, it is clearly advisable to appreciate that it exists and to understand its implications at least as well as the legal principles upon which legal decision making is theoretically based.

END NOTES

1. For a somewhat longer essay on the difficulty of "viewing" the law in a practical way, see Wing, *Science and the Law: A Muddled Interference*, in 4 PERSPECTIVES IN ETHOLOGY 225 (P. Bateson & P. Klopfer eds. 1981). (It is not necessary, however, to read the whole essay; the essence of the problem can be understood from the (in)famous poem by J. SAXE, THE BLIND MEN AND THE ELEPHANT (1850), included in full text in the preface to the essay.)

2. For a good historical account of the development of the American legal system, see L. FRIEDMAN, A HISTORY OF AMERICAN LAW (1973). For a collection of essays reflecting a more critical analysis of the legal system, see THE POLITICS OF LAW: A PROGRESSIVE CRITIQUE (D. Kairys ed. 1982).

3. There are few good accounts of the workings of the judicial system. B. WOODWARD & S. ARMSTRONG, THE BRETHREN: THE INSIDE STORY OF THE SUPREME COURT (1979) is probably the most popular insider's view of the workings of the Supreme Court. For more recent, but less critical, insight into the current Supreme Court, see THE BURGER COURT: THE COUNTER REVOLUTION THAT WASN'T (V. Blasi ed. 1983).

4. There are a number of useful works on the legislative process. The Congressional Quarterly publishes a variety of periodicals and references documenting the machinations of Congress, including, THE ORIGINS AND DEVELOPMENT OF CONGRESS (2d ed. 1982) and HOW CONGRESS WORKS (1983). For better reading (although somewhat out-dated), see E. REDMAN, THE DANCE OF LEGISLATION (1973).

5. For assistance with the techniques of legal research, M. COHEN, LEGAL RESEARCH IN A NUTSHELL (3d ed. 1978) is a good basic primer. M. PRICE, H. BITNER & R. BYSIEWICZ, EFFECTIVE LEGAL RESEARCH (4th ed. 1979) is more detailed, although probably not as useful for the first time researcher.

6. As for popular criticism of the American lawyer, there seems to be an endless variety. Even the president of Harvard University (and former dean of the Harvard Law School) has recently added his voice to the chorus of critics of the American legal profession and its role in our "litigious society." And as some indication of popular sentiment, a new consumer group was formed in 1983 under the banner of "HALT" (Help Abolish Legal Tyranny). Moreover, most bookstores have a ready supply of "how to avoid lawyers" and "why not to go to law school" books—a tribute both to prevailing public attitudes and to entrepreneurial literature.

2

The Power of the State Governments in Matters Affecting the Public's Health

This chapter and the three that follow will focus on one major set of legal rights relating to health and health care delivery: the legal rights that define the relationship between the people and their government. The present chapter will be primarily concerned with the legal rights of the state governments—generally referred to as the states' police powers—to control the personal conduct of individual people.

FEDERAL CONSTITUTIONAL AUTHORITY

The basic definition of the powers of the government at either the state or the federal level is derived from the constitutions that establish the underlying legal framework of all governmental institutions.

The U.S. Constitution sets out the enumerated powers of the federal government. All powers not granted explicitly to the federal government by the Constitution are retained by the state governments or by the people themselves. The origins of this principle are best understood from a historical perspective. The colonists who settled in America in the seventeenth and eighteenth centuries and later expanded across the continent formed governments that eventually evolved into individual states. Only later was a federal government established, first as a federation of those states and then under the federal Constitution in 1789. Additional states were added to that federal government, but in each case the territory involved was first created as a state and then allowed to join the federal union. Thus the states are the primary source of governmental power in this country; it was only through the collective agreement of the Constitution that a federal government was created with higher authority.

Understandably, the states gave up their power reluctantly and rather carefully. The Constitution very clearly enumerates those powers ceded to the federal government, and by explicit provision of the Tenth Amendment to the Constitution (adopted immediately after its ratification) the principle underlying this division of authority was codified: "The powers not delegated to the United States by the Constitution nor prohibited by it to the States, are reserved to the States respectively, or to the people." Because of this constitutional principle of delegated federal power, any federal government activity must be justified in terms of one of the enumerated powers of the Constitution.

It is worth noting, however, the manner in which this principle has been interpreted as the role of the federal government has evolved in such matters as health and social welfare, particularly since the American depression of the 1930s. As a response to an increasing political sentiment, the federal government has taken on an expansive role in the governing of the nation, most probably a far more active role than was contemplated at the time of the drafting of the Constitution. This more active role has evolved through additional amendments to the Constitution, but also through judicial interpretation of the enumerated federal powers in ever-expanding terms. For example, the explicit power of the federal government to regulate interstate commerce has been expanded to include not just the power literally to regulate commerce across state borders, but also to regulate goods after they have passed through interstate commerce as well as activities that are only indirectly related to people or goods that have previously been involved in interstate commerce. The courts have also interpreted the federal power to tax as including broad power to regulate and control whatever federal tax revenues are spent for, the so-called power of "conditional spending."

Notwithstanding these broad interpretations, however, the principle remains that the federal government must operate within its enumerated powers, and federal government activities must be justified in terms of one or more of the explicit provisions of the Constitution. This has led on occasion to considerable controversy, as will be examined in chapter 6. One need only compare the principle of enumerated powers with the active role that the federal government has developed over the last 30 years in promoting and maintaining health and health care delivery, or to various proposals for nationalized health insurance, hospital cost containment, or health personnel redistribution to see how constitutional questions could be raised. No matter what the advantages of an expanded federal role or the merits of the various proposals, each will have to be justified as being within explicit, constitutionally permissible federal governmental powers.

STATE CONSTITUTIONAL AUTHORITY

In direct contrast to the federal government's explicit powers, the state governments have extremely broad, inherent powers to act, and these rights or powers are not limited to the exercise of powers explicitly defined by the state or federal constitutions. Under the American legal system, the state governments may exercise all powers traditionally inherent in government itself.

Again in terms of history, it was groups of individuals that came to this country and formed governments that later became states. It could be argued, therefore, that it is the individual citizen that is primary, and that there are areas of human conduct that are inherently beyond the reach of the state's broad powers and withheld by the people themselves. For that matter the language of both the Ninth and Tenth Amendments imply that there are such inherent rights reserved to the people. Nonetheless, rarely has either of these constitutional provisions been interpreted to recognize the existence of any right inherent in individual people. In fact, the courts have been extremely reluctant to recognize any individual rights except those explicitly recognized by the state or federal constitutions. For all practical purposes, the only recognized inherent rights under our legal system are those of the states to govern. Moreover, these rights or powers are broadly interpreted and constrained only to the extent that they interfere with (1) the explicit powers granted to the federal government (or prohibited to the states) by the Constitution or (2) the individual rights of citizens recognized by the federal or state constitutions.

Since these state powers derive not only from constitutional provisions but also from inherent powers implied in the structure of the legal system, a state's powers to govern, known generally as its "police powers," have proven to be very difficult to delineate specifically. In the broadest usage of the term, the courts have defined the police powers to be all of the legitimate functions of government. Other courts have added some specificity, defining the police powers of the state as the powers inherent in the state to prescribe, within the limits of the state and federal constitutions, reasonable laws necessary to preserve the public order, health, safety, welfare, and morals.

The specific applications of the police powers in the context of public health laws exemplify the nature of the police powers in general.

Throughout the years, with the almost endless ways in which the state legislatures have chosen to exercise their police powers in matters relating to health, these legislative enactments and their implementation by the executive branches of the state governments have almost always been upheld by the courts as proper exercises of state authority so long as they could somehow be justified as providing for the public's health, safety, or welfare. It has also been generally recognized that this broad power of state government over matters affecting health can be delegated by the state legislatures to local and municipal governments, particularly with regard to enforcement of public health laws in the local community.

Not only have the courts interpreted the scope of the police powers rather broadly in matters relating to health, the courts also have tended to justify the validity of the police powers in terms that reflect a state interest in either the protection of the public at large or the protection of any one individual. That is to say, it is legitimate for state government to regulate the conduct of an individual where that conduct presents a risk to the health, safety, or welfare of others, but it also may be legitimate where the regulation is only for the protection of that individual. As the cases that follow will illustrate, clearly the state can act to protect any member of society from another, or even to prevent any one member from becoming a burden on others. But in some cases, the state has been allowed to act with strictly paternal motives and to protect an individual from only self-imposed harm or injury.

LIMITATIONS ON GOVERNMENTAL AUTHORITY

It should be obvious that the purposes outlined above, if taken to their extreme, could justify any number of things that would be repugnant to the traditions of American society and, as a consequence, would not be considered within the inherent powers of government as interpreted by most courts. Moreover, even when state governments are arguably within their broadly defined police powers, there are limits on the scope of their authority and the manner in which their powers can be implemented.

As mentioned above, the state cannot exercise authority in any way that has been explicitly prohibited by the federal Constitution or that conflicts with a power granted by the Constitution to the federal government; nor can the states exercise their police powers in such a way as to abridge any of the constitutionally protected rights secured to individuals by the state or federal constitutions.

It is helpful to think of these individual rights as falling into two basic subcategories: procedural and substantive rights.

When either the federal or a state government acts, even if the action is within the scope of its authority, there are still limits on how the government must act and by what means. The most important sources of these procedural limitations are the due process clause of the Fifth Amendment (prohibiting the federal government from depriving any person of life, liberty, or property without due process of law) and the Fourteenth Amendment to the federal Constitution (imposing on the states a similar requirement of due process). In most state constitutions there are similar requirements that the state provide its citizens with due process of law as well.

The specific meaning and requirements of procedural due process will be explored in a number of different contexts in this book and in great depth in chapter 3. For initial purposes, it is probably sufficient to think of due process as requiring different specific procedures depending upon the circumstances under consideration, but requiring generally that whatever the government does it must do so using what courts consider to be fundamentally fair procedures.

Substantive individual rights refer to the various individual interests that have been interpreted to be in the state or federal constitutions, primarily those in the first ten amendments to the Constitution, the Bill of Rights. Examples of these are the freedom of speech, the right to be free from cruel and unusual punishment, and the right to privacy. Where the exercise of the state's police powers causes too great an infringement on one or more of these basic individual rights, that exercise of power may be prohibited or, at least, limited.

As with so many other critical legal concepts, it is difficult to define with any specificity the exact circumstances under which government authority will be seen as abridging individual rights. Indeed, a large portion of this book will document examples of attempts to achieve just that definition. Basically, in a conflict between the state government exercising its valid police powers in matters involving health or health care and a claim that individual constitutional rights are being violated by that exercise of power, the courts must weigh the purposes of the state against the importance of the individual's rights. Defining the nature of that weighing process, literally deciding how to decide, and identifying the proper factors to consider have sparked some of the most controversial decisions in American legal history. As will be demonstrated by the decisions that follow, sometimes the interference with constitutionally protected interests can be quite severe, yet the power of the state has been nevertheless upheld. In other circumstances, where individual rights are more drastically abridged, or where the state's justification is less convincing, courts have been more willing to protect the individual and invalidate state legislative or executive action. Indeed, the willingness of individual judges to protect individual rights or defer to the discretion of state legislative or executive authority is one of the key distinctions in the identification of liberal or conservative judicial philosophies, a critical concept in understanding the manner in which individual courts are likely to interpret the states' police powers.

The archetypal case that illustrates the scope of the states' powers in matters affecting health is *Jacobson v. Massachusetts*, 197 U.S. 11 (1905).

In 1902 Jacobson refused to comply with a Massachusetts statute that required compulsory smallpox vaccination for all adults. He argued that the statute invaded his personal liberty and that

> a compulsory vaccination law is unreasonable, arbitrary and oppressive, and, therefore hostile to the inherent right of every freeman to care for his own body and health in such a way as to him seems best; and that the execution of such a law against one who objects to vaccination, no matter for what reason, is nothing short of an assault upon his person.

Jacobson's arguments fell on deaf ears in the state trial court and in his appeal to the state supreme court. Jacobson then appealed to the U.S. Supreme Court, again claiming that the state was exercising authority beyond its constitutional powers and in violation of his individual constitutional rights.

The Supreme Court denied his appeal. The Court, in terms that would be cited frequently in subsequent litigation, found that the state was very clearly within its legitimate authority:

> The authority of the State to enact this statute is to be referred to what is commonly called the police power—a power which the State did not surrender when becoming a member of the Union under the Constitution. Although this court has refrained from any attempt to define the limits of that power, yet it has distinctly recognized the authority of a State to enact quarantine laws and "health laws of every description;" indeed, all laws that relate to matters completely within its territory and which do not by their necessary operation affect the people of other States. According to settled principles the police power of a State must be held to embrace, at least, such reasonable regulations established directly by legislative enactment as will protect the public health and the public safety. . . . The mode or manner in which those results are to be accomplished is within the discretion of the State, subject, of course, so far as Federal power is concerned, only to the condition that no rule prescribed by a State, nor any regulation adopted by a local governmental agency acting under the sanction of state legislation, shall contravene the Consti-

tution of the United States or infringe any right granted or secured by that instrument.

This is one of the clearest overall summaries of the breadth of the state's power in matters involving health and the wide latitude given to the state in implementing this power. The state may enact "health laws of every description" and "such reasonable regulations established directly by legislative enactment as will protect the public health and the public safety." Within these wide bounds, the only limitations on the state's power suggested by the Court were where the exercise of power interfered with a power of the federal government or where it infringed on an individual constitutional right. There was no claim that federal power was being interfered with. As for Jacobson's claim that the statute interfered with his personal liberty and his "right to make personal decisions about his person," the Court found that in the face of the obvious public interest in preventing smallpox, these rights must be subordinated. Although there is a "sphere within which the individual may assert the supremacy of his own will and rightfully dispute the authority of any human government," the Court held:

> [T]he liberty secured by the Constitution of the United States to every person within its jurisdiction does not import an absolute right in each person to be, at all times and in all circumstances, wholly freed from restraint. There are manifold restraints to which every person is necessarily subject for the common good. "[Liberty] is only freedom from restraint under conditions essential to the equal enjoyment of the same right by others. It is then liberty regulated by law."

The decision in *Jacobson* should be juxtaposed with the Supreme Court's decision in that same term in *Lochner v. New York*, 198 U.S. 45 (1905). In that case, the Court struck down a New York statute that set a work maximum of 60 hours per week for employees of bakeries. In weighing the police powers of the state against the individual rights of the employee to sell his labor and the employer's right to buy it, the Court was extremely sensitive to the effect on the employee-employer contract and rather skeptical of the state legislature's purpose in enacting the law.

> It is a question of which of two powers or rights shall prevail—the power of the State to legislate or the right of the individual to liberty of person and freedom of contract. The mere assertion that the subject relates though but in a remote degree to the public health does not necessarily render the enactment valid. The act must have a more direct relation, as a means to an end, and the end itself must be appropriate and legitimate, before an act can be held to be valid which interferes with the general right of an individual to be free in his person and in his power to contract in relation to his own labor.

* * *

We think the limit of the police power has been reached and passed in this case. There is, in our judgment, no reasonable foundation for holding this to be necessary or appropriate as a health law to safeguard the public health or the health of the individuals who are following the trade of a baker. If this statute be valid, and if, therefore, a proper case is made out in which to deny the right of an individual, *sui juris*, as employer or employee, to make contracts for the labor of the latter under the protection of the provisions of the Federal Constitution, there would seem to be no length to which legislation of this nature might not go. The case differs widely, as we have already stated, from the expressions of this Court in regard to laws of this nature, as stated in *Holden v. Hardy* and *Jacobson v. Massachusetts, supra.*

While distinctions can be drawn between a compulsory smallpox vaccination program and a law regulating conditions in the work place, it is still difficult to view these two cases as consistently applying the same principles. The same court that was so quick to defer to legislative discretion in *Jacobson*, suggesting that the weighing of public benefits against individual liberty was largely a matter of legislative prerogative when risks to health are at stake, examined rather closely in *Lochner* both the public benefits and the rights of the individual involved, in a manner that suggested a much broader role for the judicial branch in defining the scope and extent of governmental power, even to the extent of declaring the New York law unconstitutional. Indeed, the two cases sit on either side of a key distinction: at the turn of the century the Court was what is now regarded as judicially liberal in defining its role in the protection of what it viewed as property rights; in such situations the Court did not hesitate to substitute its judgment for that of the legislature. At the same time, the Court was judicially conservative in defining its role in matters where it viewed only individual liberty at stake, and particularly where that liberty was constrained for purposes of protecting the health or safety of others. This liberal/conservative distinction is, as later chapters will illustrate, a distinction of critical importance, albeit one of some complexity.

The two cases also illustrate an important lesson in the real meaning of the police powers and the underlying issues involved in their definition. To define the scope of the police powers, the courts must in effect address two related issues. Clearly the courts must define the relationship between the state government and individual citizens, weighing the state's inherent powers against those individual rights protected by the constitutions. But implicit in this weighing of interests is a second, equally important issue. In weighing the powers of the state against the rights of the individual, the courts are also defining the scope of their own authority. By their nature, these decisions necessarily must address the distribution of power between, on one hand, the legislature and the state agencies that carry out the legislature's directives, and, on the other, the courts which through their interpretative function must decide whether to check or limit that authority. These are the essential issues underlying all of the cases considered in the remainder of this chapter, as well as those that follow in the next three chapters.

Parenthetically, neither *Jacobson* nor *Lochner* would be decided in the same way if argued in the 1980s. The judicially liberal attitude towards the protection of the type of property interests involved in *Lochner* has passed out of fashion and the case has been long since overruled. Virtually no modern court has so jealously guarded the "right to contract," and most have been willing to defer to the discretion of the legislatures in fashioning health and safety laws for the workplace. At least where there is some arguable connection between the individual conduct constrained and the health, safety, welfare, or, in some cases, the morals of other members of the public, all modern courts continue to cite *Jacobson* as controlling precedent and ignore *Lochner* and, more importantly, tend to adopt the judicial attitude taken in the *Jacobson* case. Jacobson, on the other hand, might prevail in a modern court on the facts; if recent reports that smallpox has been eradicated are to be believed, then he might convincingly argue that there no longer exists the minimal connection between a compulsory vaccination program (if a state were to implement one) and the public's health and, as a consequence, even while upholding the same principles and attitude, a modern court might well rule in his favor.

More critically, as will be examined in more detail in chapter 4, if Lochner and Jacobson were to argue their cases today, the analysis in both cases would likely follow the "rational basis/close scrutiny" rhetoric that has been developed by the courts in the last several decades.

What would surely be the same today as in 1904 are the underlying issues. In the cases that follow in this chapter and the next several, the courts are essentially addressing the difficult problem of defining the relationship between the state and the individual citizen, and in doing so, the fundamental relationship between the various branches of the government.

THE BROAD RANGE OF STATE AUTHORITY IN MATTERS RELATING TO THE PUBLIC'S HEALTH

In some circumstances, of course, the scope of the police powers is almost beyond question. At least where the state government activity is for the purpose of protecting third parties from risks created by individual conduct, virtually all courts have followed the lead of the *Jacobson* decision and quickly deferred to state legislative authority. Thus, the power of the state—should it choose to do so—to examine, quarantine, and, in some cases, treat people suspected of carrying contagious diseases, has been consistently recognized. Many types of compulsory medical examinations and treatment, e.g., vaccination of children prior to and during school attendance, have been held to be valid, as has compulsory examination of people getting married or engaging in certain occupations where they will be exposed to the public. Such treatment and examination have been held valid even in the face of religious objections arising under the First Amendment, as well as against the more general liberty arguments of the type raised by Jacobson. Likewise, the state may require compliance with fire, safety, and sanitation laws, in both private and public buildings. The state's power has also been consistently interpreted to include the power to take such health-related measures as fluoridating the public water supply (or empowering local government to do so), again under the rationale that the state police powers clearly include broad authority to protect the health, safety, welfare, or morals of the public.

Another area within which the courts have given the states a great deal of discretion is the civil commitment of certain categories of people. It has been generally recognized that the state may involuntarily confine and treat the mentally ill, the mentally retarded, drug abusers, even epileptics. Recently this authority has come under greater scrutiny by some courts, both in terms of the procedures used and the realities of the resulting confinement, as will be examined in more depth in chapter 3. But, notwithstanding these developments, there is no doubt that civil commitment, using proper procedures and within certain circumstantial restraints, is a valid exercise of the state's police powers.

THE STATE'S POLICE POWERS:
COMPULSORY STERILIZATION

In other circumstances, the extent of the police powers is far more likely to be questioned. One good example involves states that have adopted programs to sterilize people who are civilly or criminally committed. While the courts have traditionally upheld the power of the state to maintain such programs, modern courts have tended to examine the use of state power in these circumstances much more critically, and during the last 50 years the judicial interpretation of the state's power to require sterilization has virtually been reversed.

In *Buck v. Bell*, 274 U.S. 200 (1927), the Supreme Court upheld a Virginia law allowing the state to sterilize mental patients under certain circumstances. The opinion summarizes the facts and the posture of the Court at that time better than any paraphrase:

> Carrie Buck is a feeble minded white woman who was committed to the State Colony above mentioned in due form. She is the daughter of a feeble minded mother in the same institution, and the mother of an illegitimate feeble minded child. She was eighteen years old at the time of the trial of her case in the Circuit Court, in the latter part of 1924. An Act of Virginia, approved March 20, 1924, recites that the health of the patient and the welfare of society may be promoted in certain cases by the sterilization of mental defectives . . . that the Commonwealth is supporting in various institutions many defective persons who if now discharged would become a menace but if incapable of procreating might be discharged with safety and become self-supporting with benefit to themselves and to society; and that experience has shown that heredity plays an important part in the transmission of insanity. . . .
>
> * * *
>
> . . . In view of the general declarations of the legislature and the specific findings of the Court, obviously we cannot say as a matter of law that the grounds do not exist, and if they exist they justify the result. We have seen more than once that the public welfare may call upon the best citizens for their lives. It would be strange if it could not call upon those who already sap the strength of the State for these lesser sacrifices, often not felt to be such by those concerned, in order to prevent our being swamped with incompetence. It is better for all the world, if instead of waiting to execute degenerate offspring for crime, or to let them starve for their imbecility, society can prevent those who are manifestly unfit from continuing their kind. The principle that sustains compulsory vaccination is broad enough to cover cutting the Fallopian tubes. *Jacobson v. Massachusetts*, 197 U.S. 11. Three generations of imbeciles are enough.

This opinion would be remarkable enough if it were a lower appellate court and not the Supreme Court. It is even more remarkable since it was written by Oliver Wendell Holmes, otherwise known for his passionate defense of civil liberties on the Court. Sixty years later, it can be argued that our more sophisticated knowledge of the etiology of imbecility (and even the use of the term) might be used to challenge some of Justice Holmes' specific conclusions and possibly his implicit attitude. Yet the case still stands, as yet not directly overruled, and some states continue to sterilize mental patients without their consent, claiming either an interest in preventing the birth of certain kinds of people or of children whose parents would be unable to care for them.

This interpretation of the police powers to include the power to sterilize people involuntarily has been severely narrowed, however, by modern courts, both in regard to mental patients and in regard to similar laws that still exist in some states that allow involuntary sterilization of "habitual criminal offenders." Some lower state and federal courts have found state sterilization statutes to be legitimate exercises of the state police powers, citing *Buck v. Bell*, but not properly implemented. Thus where a statute failed to provide notice or an opportunity to be heard to the person whose sterilization was proposed, the law was held to be unconstitutional as a violation of procedural due process. (*See* chapter 3.) Other statutes have been struck down or modified where the standards for decision making were too vague. Another statute was held to be cruel and unusual punishment and violative of the Eighth Amendment in a case where the sterilization was apparently intended for punishment as much as for the prevention of procreation.

Despite its holding in *Buck v. Bell*, the Supreme Court later declared a sterilization statute unconstitutional in *Oklahoma v. Skinner*, 316 U.S. 535 (1942), where the state allowed the compulsory sterilization of "habitual criminals." A divided Court struggled for a rationale for its decision, with a majority holding that the statute violated the requirements of the equal protection clause of the Fourteenth Amendment in that it permitted the sterilization of anyone who was convicted on three successive felonies, but it exempted felons convicted of the violation of such "white collar crimes" as the prohibitory laws, revenue acts, embezzlement, or political offenses. (Could the members of the Oklahoma state legislature have been protecting themselves?)

And while the majority of the Court refused to directly overrule *Buck v. Bell*, at least one of the justices of the 1942 Court indicated some willingness to do so in a concurring opinion:

> I also think the present plan to sterilize the individual in pursuit of a eugenic plan to eliminate from the race characteristics that are only vaguely identified and which in our present state of knowledge are uncertain as to transmissibility presents other constitutional questions of gravity. This Court has sustained such an experiment with respect to an imbecile, a person with definite and observable characteristics, where the condition had persisted through three generations and afforded ground for the belief that it was transmissible and would continue to manifest itself in generations to come. *Buck v. Bell*, 274 U.S. 200.

> There are limits to the extent to which a legislatively represented majority may conduct biological experiments at the expense of the dignity and personality and natural powers of a minority—even those who have been guilty of what the majority define as crimes. But this Act falls down before reaching this problem, which I mention only to avoid the implication that such a question may not exist because not discussed.

Since *Skinner* and particularly in the last 20 years, most, but not all, courts that have considered the power of the state to require sterilization of mental patients, and all courts that have considered sterilization of criminals, have simply ruled that these programs are beyond the state's power. Even those courts that have allowed that compulsory sterilization could be valid under some circumstances have been quick to demand that the state follow rather rigorous procedural safeguards and have been unwilling to accept anything but convincing evidence that the sterilization can actually be justified.

The modern view of the state's police powers in this context, virtually a reversal of the holding as well as the judicial attitude adopted in *Buck v. Bell*, is probably best summarized by this quote from a 1981 decision of the Colorado Supreme Court:

> While *Buck v. Bell* has never been explicitly overruled . . . the Court in *Skinner v. Oklahoma* . . . overturned an Oklahoma statute providing for sterilization of thrice-convicted felons and established procreation as a fundamental right. The shift in judicial thinking paralleled an advance in prevailing scientific theories about retardation (citations omitted). Today, compulsory sterilization of incompetents based on eugenic theories can no longer be justified as valid exercise of governmental authority, *see In re Grady*, 85 N.J. 235, 246, 426 A.2d 467, 472 (1981), and while the Supreme Court has not considered the constitutionality of involuntary sterilization laws since *Skinner*, commentators generally have concluded that compulsory sterilization laws, no matter what their rationale, are unconstitutional in the absence of evidence that compulsory sterilization is the only remedy available to further a compelling governmental interest (citation omitted).

THE STATE'S POLICE POWERS: COMPULSORY MEDICAL TREATMENT OF CHILDREN

Another situation in which the definition of the state's police power has generated considerable controversy involves attempts by state government to require the medical treatment of children over their objections or those of their parent(s).

Under American law, minors are generally considered "incompetent" to make most legally binding decisions, including decisions to accept or refuse medical care. (*See* chapter 4 for recent developments regarding the definition of "maturity" and the age of majority.) The child's parent(s) or guardian is generally empowered to decide on his or her behalf, and the law has traditionally respected the autonomy of the family—as exercised by the parent(s)—as a constitutionally protected right. However, in situations where it is alleged that the health, well-being, or, especially, the life of a child is jeopardized, every state has legislation allowing a government agency, usually a local social services agency, to take custody of and care for the child, and to provide medical treatment over the objection of the child or the parent(s). Such legislation has been consistently upheld as constitutional. Parenthetically, courts have also upheld state legislation that provides for the criminal punishment of the parent(s) where the refusal to allow medical treatment is considered to be child neglect or abuse.

Such legislation is an example of the state acting *in loco parentis* (in place of a parent) or of *parens patriae* (the sovereign's power of guardianship over people under disability). In effect, both terms are little more than a convenient characterization of the state's police powers, the inherent powers of a state to, among other governmental functions, act as a parent to neglected or disabled people.

The guardianship may be temporary or permanent, depending upon the type of abuse or neglect. Where medical care is involved the guardianship may be little more than a fiction, existing only long enough for the guardian to consent to a single procedure.

Medical care provided to children over the objection of their parent(s) has been upheld even when the parent is not neglectful or abusive in any real sense, but merely distrustful of physicians or hospitals, and even when the objection is based on firm religious belief. For example, the courts have repeatedly ordered blood transfusions as "in the best interests" of the children of Jehovah's Witnesses despite the fact that their religious tenets forbid any such procedure. And, in a case that received considerable national attention in 1983, the courts in Tennessee had little trouble deciding to order chemotherapy for a 12-year-old child with cancer, despite her and her parents' religious objections to treatment.

Since constitutionally protected rights are involved, however, the autonomy of the family is heavily weighted in these cases, and the courts take an active role in examining the preferences of state agencies and officials. As one important consequence, most courts are reluctant to require medical treatment for a child over the objection of his or her parent(s) except where immediate action is necessary or where the potential harm is rather serious. In such circumstances courts often have considerable difficulty striking the proper balance of the state's power against the individual rights of the parent(s) and the child and defining and carrying out the proper judicial role.

A classic illustration of a "cutting edge" case is *In re Martin Seiferth*, 309 N.Y. 80, 127 N.E.2d 820 (1955). In that case a 12-year-old boy had what was described as a massive harelip and unrepaired cleft palate. It not only detracted from his personal appearance, it also severely limited his verbal skills. There was no real risk of physical harm, but the conditions represented a serious risk to his social and psychological growth. The boy's father thought that only the forces in the universe should work on one's body and that medicine or surgery would only interfere with those forces; the boy concurred in his father's opinion.

The county health department did not agree with the Seiferths' views. Under a state statute delegating authority in these matters to the county agency, the department petitioned the local court for the custody of the child for purposes of consenting to restorative surgery. After an evidentiary hearing, the trial court denied the petition. On appeal to an intermediate appellate court, the decision was reversed. The boy's father appealed to the supreme appellate court in New York.

After considering the evidence compiled by the trial court relating to the potential harm to the boy, the purposes justifying the county's proposed actions (as representative of the state), and the nature of the parent's objections, the court concluded that there was neither an emergency nor a serious threat to health or life and therefore reversed the case again, denying the petition. The court weighted heavily the fact that it was the boy, albeit a minor, who was objecting to the operation, not just the parent, and also considered relevant the fact that there would be time for the boy to change his mind as he grew older.

Clearly the specific facts of the situation were as determinative of the decision as were the legal principles that the case illustrates. Had the medical needs of Seiferth been even slightly more severe, or had Seiferth been much younger, the court could have ruled in favor of the county and upheld the state's power to intercede. In fact, of the seven members of the state's supreme appellate court, three dissented and would have voted to allow the county to take temporary custody of the boy and to have him treated. Indeed, their dissenting opinion was vigorous and clear in its view that the state could substitute its judgment for that of the parents even when no threat to life was presented:

> It is quite true that the child's physical life is not at peril—as would be the situation if he had an infected appendix or a growth on the brain —but it may not be questioned, to quote from the opinion below, "What is in danger is his chance for a normal, useful life. . . ."

* * *

> . . . [I]t is the court which has a duty to perform (citation omitted) and it should not seek to avoid that duty by foisting upon the boy the ultimate decision to be made. Neither by statute nor decision is the child's consent necessary or material, and we should not permit his refusal to agree, his failure to cooperate, to ruin his life and any chance for a nor-

mal, happy existence; normalcy and happiness will unquestionably be impossible if the disfigurement is not remedied.

* * *

The welfare and interests of a child are at stake. A court should not place upon his shoulders one of the most momentous and far-reaching decisions of his life. The court should make the decision, as the statute contemplates, and leave to the good sense and sound judgment of the public authorities the job of preparing the boy for the operation and of getting him as adjusted to it as possible. We should not put off decision in the hope and on the chance that the child may change his mind and submit at some future time to the operation.

Cases even more difficult to analyze—and to decide—have been presented to the courts by situations where the parent(s) decides to forgo life-saving medical care for infants who are mentally or physically handicapped. The basic legal principle involved is much the same; the state's police powers are broad enough to allow government to require medical life-saving treatment in the best interests of children even over the objection of the parent(s). The critical factor in these cases is not defining the controlling principle but interpreting its application. Among other things, individual judges may not view medical treatment as in the best interests of such children. Thus, at least in some jurisdictions and in some circumstances, courts have declined to intervene, but in other jurisdictions, the courts when forced to address these controversies have been willing to order continued treatment over the objection of the parent(s), arguing that a state has an interest in protecting life even under extreme circumstances. (*See* note at end of chapter.)

THE STATE'S POLICE POWERS: COMPULSORY MEDICAL TREATMENT OF INCOMPETENT ADULTS

The cases recognizing that the government has broad powers to require medical treatment for children, and the principles that govern them, suggest an even more controversial question: To what extent is the state allowed to compel medical care for people who are legally incompetent, not because they are minors, but because they are viewed as mentally incompetent because of retardation, mental illness, or a comatose condition, or are otherwise not capable of making competent decisions with regard to their own health?

The declaration that an individual is mentally incompetent and the concomitant appointment of a guardian occur in a number of situations. Acting *in loco parentis*, the state has the power to intervene in the life of any person not competent to conduct his or her own life and affairs. It may do so on the initiative of one of its own officials or at the request of a friend or relative or medical advisor of someone thought to be incompetent. The state can appoint some other person that will, as the agent of the state, make that incompetent individual's decisions. A guardian can have power over an individual or his or her property or both; the breadth of the guardian's power is defined in the court order appointing the guardian and is intended to be tailored to the needs of the incompetent person. Courts have frequently allowed the guardian's discretion to include decisions relating to the medical treatment of his or her ward.

As will be discussed in the next chapter, mental patients are usually committed under a standard that calls only for a finding that they are in need of psychiatric treatment. Thus they are not automatically considered legally incompetent. Commitment is a judicial determination that the patient is, in effect, incompetent to seek psychiatric treatment, but commitment does not require a finding of general incompetency. Before a mental patient can be given involuntary nonpsychiatric medical care, a separate incompetency proceeding must be initiated and a guardian must be appointed. The guardian would then have the choice of consenting or not (as a practical matter, the guardian almost always does consent). Similarly, an incompetency determination would have to be made following the proper legal procedures before a mental patient's control of his or her property is given to a guardian.

This power to appoint a guardian over allegedly incompetent people is the primary means by which the state provides involuntary medical care to adults under certain circumstances. Similarly, guardianship is ordinarily the procedural device used in seeking judicial approval for termination of medical treatment for people who are terminally ill but unable to make their own decisions, as will be discussed below. Clearly the state has the power to make these decisions for the incompetent. Providing for the medical care of incompetent people is little different from providing psychiatric care to mental patients, providing necessary medical care to children over the objection of their parent(s), or requiring people to submit to compulsory vaccinations. However, in these other circumstances the justification for the power over an individual is generally based on the state's authority to protect some members of society from others, e.g., to protect the society from those with contagious diseases or children from their parents. In contrast, the state's power as exercised over incompetent adults is often to protect these individuals from themselves. In some instances, the state is acting to protect someone who simply cannot act at all, as in the *Quinlan* case discussed later in this chapter.

In other cases, the state is more clearly attempting to substitute affirmatively the judgment of a state agent for that of the individual. Courts have been readily willing to deny an individual the rights to freedom, privacy, or self-determination where that individual presents the threat of dangerous conduct or risk to the health, welfare, or safety of the public. To interfere with these rights simply to protect certain individuals from themselves has not been as easy for many courts to accept. For most courts, the justification stands or falls on the reality of the incompetence. Is this really a person who is unable to make a competent choice? Or are we labeling as incompetent a choice that we cannot accept or identify with? Understandably, the courts have not always upheld the state's power to provide medical care involuntarily when the individual involved is not incompetent in the strictest sense of the term.

In a few cases, however, even competent adults have been held to fall within the scope of the police powers. As the most obvious example, courts in many jurisdictions have ordered medical treatment in the form of blood transfusions to competent adults who refuse to consent to the transfusion based on religious beliefs. In most of these cases the courts have scrupulously avoided recognizing a broad power of the state to act in the best interests of competent adults and have justified these particular interventions on the basis of special circumstances. One court justified its ruling on the grounds that the transfusion would save the life of a yet unborn child. Another court argued that by saving the parent it was protecting the interests of the dependents of that parent. Another court simply said that in an emergency the courts must first act to protect life, especially when the law is not clear. Almost every court that has squarely faced the issue of whether the state has the power to compel treatment of a competent—but arguably foolish —adult has ruled that there is no general state power to do so, yet most courts have found ways to sidestep the logical consequences of that conclusion.

A few courts, however, have been willing to recognize the autonomy of the competent individual both in theory and in practical effect. In *In re Yetter*, 62 Pa. D.&C.2d 619 (1973), the brother of a 60-year-old woman filed a petition in a New Jersey court asking that his sister be declared incompetent and that he be appointed her guardian. The purpose behind the request was to give him the power to consent for his sister to undergo diagnostic and corrective surgery. The woman was a mental patient diagnosed as a chronic undifferentiated schizophrenic. Her physician believed that she may have had breast cancer and recommended surgery, but she refused. At first she objected because of her fear that she might die. She believed, incorrectly, that her aunt had died during similar surgery. By the time the case got to court, her fears were also based on her delusions that the surgery would interfere with her genitals, that she would lose her ability to have a baby, and that her chances for a movie career would be lost.

Apparently her specific delusions were not typical of her general condition. Nonetheless, her physician regarded her as incompetent to make the decision with regard to surgery. The court was faced with the dilemma of balancing the state's powers and legitimate purposes in protecting incompetents against her individual rights to freedom, self-determination, and privacy. The court concluded:

> In our opinion the constitutional right of privacy includes the right of a mature competent adult to refuse to accept medical recommendations that may prolong one's life and which, to a third person at least, appear to be in his best interest; in short, the right to privacy includes a right to die with which the State should not interfere where there is no minor or unborn children and no clear and present danger to the public health, welfare, or morals. If the person was competent while being presented with the decision and in making the decision which she did, the Court should not interfere even though her decision might be considered unwise, foolish or ridiculous.
>
> The testimony of the caseworker with respect to her conversations with [the woman] in December, 1972, convinces us that at that time her refusal was informed, conscious of the consequences and would not have been superceded by this Court. The ordinary person's refusal to accept medical advice based upon fear is commonly known and while the refusal may be irrational and foolish to an outside observer it cannot be said to be incompetent in order to permit the State to override the decision.
>
> The obvious difficulty in this proceeding is that in recent months [the woman's] steadfast refusal has been accompanied by delusions which create doubt that her decision is the product of competent, reasoned judgment. However, she has been consistent in expressing the fear that she would die if surgery were performed. The delusions do not appear to us to be her primary reason for rejecting surgery.

The New Jersey court then concluded that she was entitled to make her competent but irrational decision to refuse surgery. The court clearly recognized the state's power over medical decisions of incompetent people, but did not extend that power to include competent people who make irrational choices.

Not all courts, however, have been willing to so boldly protect individual autonomy. In other jurisdictions, cases with virtually identical facts have been decided against the individual and in favor of state intervention.

This type of case may mark the furthest extent of the state's power over the individual in matters involving health. When the state's purpose is solely for the individual's benefit, and the individual is competent and defines his or her interest differently, most courts have ruled that the right of the individual to exercise that choice appears to be dominant. On the other hand, not all courts agree, and many courts have been quick to find exceptions to this rule and have tended to be receptive to the circular argument that any healthy person who refuses medical treatment is incompetent to choose. Indeed, it is very difficult to find any American case where an adult with the potential of productive years and capacity has actually been allowed to refuse life-saving medical treatment.

It is noteworthy, in fact, that the cases that are the clearest in their defense of the individual's right to refuse medical treatment without government interference have been those that involved either elderly or very infirm people, such as people who are terminally ill and kept alive only through extraordinary medical procedures. In these cases courts have been much more willing to recognize that the rights of the individual outweigh any interest the state may claim as justification for the continuation of medical treatment.

This factual distinction—troubling as it may be—as much as relevant legal principles may explain the decisions in the so-called "right to die" cases.

Starting with the celebrated *In re Quinlan*, 70 N.J. 10, 355 A.2d 647 (1976), there have been a series of cases in recent years that have raised the basic question of whether medical treatment can be legally terminated for people who are either physically or mentally incompetent and for whom continued treatment would be either extraordinary or, for all practical purposes, ineffective. These cases are usually raised by a petition for guardianship, requesting that the court appoint a guardian with the authority to withdraw consent for treatment on behalf of the patient.

Courts have generally analyzed these "right to die" cases in a manner consistent with the principles outlined throughout this chapter. They have examined the constitutionally protected interests of the individual and weighed them against the interest of the state in ordering continued treatment. Virtually all courts have concluded that the terminally ill patient has a right to refuse at least extraordinary medical treatment even if he or she is incapable of exercising that right, and, indeed, they have generally implied that this principle derives from the right of competent adults to refuse any medical treatment.

Under these circumstances, with regard to people who have through prior statements made clear their views on extraordinary medical care or who have executed living wills, courts have generally allowed termination of treatment in accordance with their expressed views. For others, whose views are not known, most courts have appointed guardians or empowered themselves to make a third party judgment on behalf of the incompetent, terminally ill patient.

With regard to the terminally ill patient, the reasoning of these cases is rather straightforward. There can be little interest of the state, even acting *in loco parentis*, in ordering continued extraordinary treatment, other than in the preservation of life in the strictest sense of that term. And whatever the weight of the state's life preservation interest, it could hardly outweigh the adult patient's right to exercise his or her autonomy, even where that right must be exercised by a surrogate on the patient's behalf.

Such reasoning, however, is only persuasive so long as the patient is terminally ill and beyond the reach of ordinary medical care, and, most importantly, so long as it is reasonably assumed that the patient's choice would be to terminate treatment. Where the circumstances are such that the patient's preferences are unknown and, particularly, where the treatment is characterized as "life saving" rather than "life prolonging," then both the applicable legal principles and their interpretation have proven to be far more complicated. Courts have had particular difficulty in deciding who shall exercise the rights of the patient in these situations and in outlining the factors to be considered by the surrogate decision maker in deciding whether to terminate treatment. Some courts have indicated that only a judicial weighing of the interests can fully protect the individual; others have tended to empower the family to act on the individual's behalf, reserving only a limited role for the court in reviewing the family's decision. Some courts define the relevant test as determining what the patient would decide, i.e., "substituted judgment;" others have felt that a "best interest" test must be employed. As one court pointed out, in some situations a substituted judgment test is akin to asking, "if it snowed all summer would it then be winter?"

The opinions from the various "right to die" cases have been remarkably inconsistent. Even in states where the legislature has tried to codify these principles by enacting "living will" statutes, neither the legislature nor the courts have had much success in clarifying the application of the law to any but the most obvious of situations. Thus, while the "right to die" cases have generally affirmed the importance of individual autonomy vis-á-vis the interests of the state, the application of that principle to the difficult questions raised by "right to die" cases is not clear, nor is it clear whether the application of that principle in these cases really reflects judicial willingness to respect individual autonomy as outweighing state interests; or whether other factors, tacitly or explicitly, are actually being considered.

END NOTES

1. For a full discussion of federal authority in matters relating to health and health care, see Wing & Silton, *Constitutional Authority for Extending Federal Control over the Delivery of Health Care*, 57 N.C.L. REV. 1423 (1979). For a discussion of the authority of the local government, see D. MCCARTHY, LOCAL GOVERNMENT IN A NUTSHELL (1983).

2. Beyond the basic definition of the state's police powers and an illustration of the wide discretion that definition implies for state legislatures to enact "health laws of every description," the essential question raised by *Jacobson* and *Lochner* involves the nature and kind of showing that a legislature has to make to satisfy the court that a "reasonable relationship" exists between the proposed state activity and the health, safety, welfare, or morals of the public. (This latter state interest—the morals of the public—raises intriguing although somewhat parenthetical questions. *See infra* chapter 4.)

   Jacobson suggests that a "widespread public belief" in the need for a health measure may be sufficient justification, although the facts in *Jacobson* certainly make the case for Massachusetts much stronger. It is likely, however, that a modern court would require more than a belief, and probably some sort of scientifically derived basis, for a legislative decision to undertake any program that requires compulsory medical treatment or that would otherwise directly affect individual liberty.

   One example worth considering is the justification that would be required for a compulsory vaccination program in anticipation of a "swine flu" or other modern day epidemic, particularly where the effectiveness (or safety) of the vaccine is untested or where the likelihood that the disease will become prevalent is speculative.

   The same question is raised somewhat differently where the legislature addresses a health problem by effective but overly inclusive means, e.g., a stringent highway safety law that includes a presumptive standard for intoxication set at a low level of blood alcohol. Is it reasonable—in the name of public safety—to be overinclusive, perhaps punishing unfairly some people in order to discourage others from creating risks?

3. Other examples demonstrating the breadth of the state police powers with particular relevance to traditional public health programs are discussed in F. GRAD, PUBLIC HEALTH LAW MANUAL (1973).

4. For other cases demonstrating the modern view of statutes that authorize involuntary sterilization and their constitutionality, see Stump v. Sparkman, 435 U.S. 439 (1978), North Carolina Ass'n for Retarded Children v. North Carolina, 420 F. Supp. 451 (M.D.N.C. 1976), In re A.W., 637 P.2d 366 (Colo. 1981). *Cf.* Matter of Johnson, 45 N.C. 649, 263 S.E.2d 809 (1980).

5. Two recent but very different examples of "child abuse" have drawn considerable attention. In one celebrated case, the Tennessee Court of Appeals (affirmed without opinion by the Tennessee Supreme Court) upheld the right of the state to order medical treatment for a 12-year-old girl with cancer whose parents had objected to her treatment on religious grounds. *See* Dept. of Human Services v. Hamilton, 657 S.W.2d 425 (Tenn. 1983). An even more publicized case involved the decision of the New York Court of Appeals (the highest appellate court in New York) to allow the parents of a baby with spina bifida and severe related disorders to refuse corrective surgery for some of the complications of her condition, arguably shortening the expected life of the child. Doe v. Stonybrook Hosp., 60 N.Y.2d 208, 469 N.Y.S.2d 63 (Ct. App. 1983). For a related case, see United States v. University Hosp., 729 F.2d 144 (2d Cir. 1984).

6. As noted in the last section of the chapter, one important limit on the extent of the police powers may be reached where the state action is solely for the protection of the individual—not any risk to a third party or society at large. Intriguing illustrations of the judicial attitude towards this type of legislation can be found in statutes requiring motorcyclists to wear helmets (*see, e.g.,* State v. Brady, 290 A.2d 322 (Del. Super. Ct. 1972)) or state attempts to prohibit religious ceremonies involving "snake handling" (*see, e.g.,* State ex rel. Swann v. Peck, 527 S.W.2d 99 (Tenn. 1975), *cert. denied*, 424 U.S. 954 (1975)).

But as indicated in the text, the best examples of the contemporary interpretation of the state's power to protect the individual can be found in the so-called "right to die" cases. For the most authoritative cases, see In re Storar, Eichner v. Dillon, 52 N.Y.2d 363, 420 N.E.2d 64 (1981), *cert. denied*, Storar v. Storar, 454 U.S. 858 (1981); Superintendent of Belchertown v. Saikewicz, 373 Mass. 728, 370 N.E.2d 417 (1977). For a general reference see also J. ROBERTSON, THE RIGHTS OF THE CRITICALLY ILL (1983).

It should be noted, however, that while these cases raise the power of the state over the individual in a dramatic and poignant manner, in most of these cases the underlying issue is clouded by the uncertainty of assessing whether the individual in fact wants to terminate treatment.

Most importantly, it is difficult to fully explain the modern view of the police powers in these cases or any of the other circumstances referenced in this chapter without some reference to the cases discussed in chapters 3 and 4, and particularly those cases defining the modern notion of a right to privacy and the development of the distinction between the "close scrutiny" and "rational basis" tests of legislation.

7. For references on "living will" and "natural death" statutes, see Annas, et al., *The Right to Refuse Treatment: A Model Act* , 73 AM. J. PUB. HEALTH 918 (1983). For discussion of "durable power of attorney" legislation, see Note, *Appointing an Agent to Make Medical Treatment Choices*, 84 COLUM. L. REV. 985 (1984).

3

The State's Police Powers and Involuntary Civil Commitment

In contrast to the overview of the state's police powers in the previous chapter, this chapter will focus more closely on one specific application of those powers in an effort to demonstrate further the legal rights that define the relationship between the individual and the government.

As stated previously, it has been firmly recognized that the state has broad powers to civilly commit, meaning involuntarily confine and treat, the mentally ill, as well as other categories of people such as drug addicts and the mentally retarded. This is constitutionally justified as serving the state purpose of protecting the health and safety of society as well as that of the individual involved. Nonetheless, despite the fact that commitment is clearly within the state's power, as with other legitimate exercises of the state's police powers, there are some important substantive as well as procedural limitations that the state must observe in implementing this power. This chapter will review the wide range and diversity of civil commitment procedures among the states and examine (1) the procedural safeguards that states must follow in civil commitment and (2) the constitutional limits on the nature and duration of the resulting confinement.

THE VARIOUS FORMS OF CIVIL COMMITMENT

Confinement and treatment of the mentally ill is considered "civil"; this is to be distinguished from the criminal process by which the state punishes people who have been found guilty of crimes. In theory, civil

confinement is considered more benevolent than criminal confinement, and, as a consequence, courts have tended to allow states more
discretion in fashioning their civil commitment procedures and in administering their commitment and treatment programs.

There are various kinds of civil commitment. In general, civil
commitment means the process by which people are declared in need
of treatment, confined, and treated. This basically requires a finding
that a person is mentally ill and, in most states, either dangerous to
him/herself, dangerous to others, or unable to care for him/herself.
Two other processes also result in commitments that are considered
civil. Both involve people who have been first accused of a crime.

Accused criminals may be civilly committed prior to their criminal
trial if they are found to be incompetent, meaning that they cannot assist in their defense and do not understand the nature of the proceedings against them. The justification for this confinement is that it
would be unfair to force an incompetent to stand trial when with treatment he or she might regain competency; however, it is somewhat
ironic that in the name of fairness some people are confined civilly for
considerable lengths of time purportedly to avoid the risk that they
might be confined criminally.

Civil commitment also results when an accused individual is found
not guilty of a crime by reason of insanity. Here the question is not the
presence of mental illness or the individual's present competence to
stand trial, but the mental condition of the individual at the time of the
crime. In general, if an individual is found to be unable to distinguish
between right and wrong at the time of a crime or unable to understand the nature of the act committed, he or she is technically not
guilty of the crime, even if in fact he or she did commit the crime. In
most states the defendant found not guilty by reason of insanity is then
automatically civilly committed, although the constitutionality of such a
practice has been questioned recently.

Each of these forms of civil commitment will be illustrated in
more detail in the cases that follow.

THE IMPORTANCE OF CIVIL COMMITMENT
AS A LEGAL ISSUE

As an example of the state's police powers, civil commitment dramatically illustrates the legal issues involved. On one hand, a mentally ill
person can be clearly in need of treatment or present a direct threat to
the safety of society. On the other, civil commitment involves the most
serious abridgment of individual rights imaginable—the total denial of

freedom and privacy, often for long periods of time and often under abhorrent conditions. In examining its validity, the courts must strike a difficult balance between important state purposes and constitutionally protected individual rights. But not only is civil commitment a good illustration of constitutional principles, it is itself no small problem. Estimates of the number of people hospitalized in mental institutions in this country range between 200,000 and 500,000; many of these people are involuntarily confined. That is at least the number of people in jails and prisons. Even compared with the system for providing medical care, the system for providing psychiatric services is still relatively large, and larger than many people realize. As many as 40 percent of the hospital beds in this country may be used for psychiatric patients.

What is equally important is that civil commitment also illustrates some of the inherent flaws in the American legal system. Despite the fact that important constitutional rights are at stake in civil commitment, until recently most courts have been extremely reluctant to examine either civil commitment procedures or the resulting conditions of confinement. This behavior still characterizes the judiciary in many parts of the country.

This reluctance can almost be quantified. Regardless of the literally millions of people who have been involuntarily civilly committed, extremely few decisions have ever been contested or appealed. Very few judicial opinions exist that interpret the state's power to confine mentally ill individuals through civil commitment; there were virtually none prior to 1970. Thus many critical questions regarding the scope of state power in civil commitment have been addressed only infrequently and many have yet to be fully answered.

By far the most important reason for this failure of the judiciary to play its role is based on economics. The American legal system relies heavily on a privately financed adversarial system as a means to adjudicate almost all civil and even some criminal controversies. Consequently, only people who can afford the costs of litigation have a meaningful opportunity to protect and enforce their rights. To put it bluntly, such a judicial system could hardly be expected to protect the rights of poor people, and, at least in public mental institutions, people involuntarily committed are almost always poor. Even with the advent of government-sponsored legal services programs for indigent people and public defenders for indigent criminal defendants, few states have provided adequate legal counsel to defend those who are civilly committed. Moreover, mentally ill individuals are usually precluded by their condition or by their commitment from reaching even the few legal services programs that are available for the poor.

Added to this is a general attitude on the part of lawyers and judges that mental patients are not really clients and defendants and are less deserving of their full attention.

The focus of the blame should not be entirely on the judiciary for failing to protect the rights of individuals in civil commitment. Traditionally, civil commitment statutes were rather loosely drawn, reflecting a similar lack of concern for individual rights on the part of state legislatures and a willingness to allow virtually unchecked authority for committing people to be left in the hands of state agencies and the medical profession.

The 1960s, however, brought a number of changes to the legal system that involved an increased concern for the rights of the individual with respect to government power. Among the most important developments was the recognition and enforcement of the constitutional rights of the criminally accused, particularly the right of the accused indigent individual to appointed legal counsel. Courts started examining more critically the procedures by which accused criminals are tried and confined, and attorneys became available to advocate the rights of accused people. As one related result, some courts and some attorneys brought attention to the analogous situation of the "civil" process by which people accused of being mentally ill are confined and treated.

This period of reexamination has been played out for nearly two decades, but the answers to many of the long-overlooked questions are still not fully answered. The attitudes of the courts, the legislatures, and even society in general have been only partially modified, and, of course, there is still the problem that the legal system relies heavily on financial access to it. Consequently, even the legal rights that are recognized are not always respected and enforced.

Nonetheless, in the next decade many questions that are today unanswered will be litigated, and predictably one of the results will be that the state's powers to commit civilly will be in some ways modified, both procedurally and substantively. But as mentioned in chapter 2, this reexamination of the state's powers to commit civilly the mentally ill will not be directed at the basic constitutionality of that power. Civil commitment is clearly one of the state's legitimate police powers. Rather, the thrust of recent cases has been in two tangential directions: (1) an examination of the adequacy of the procedures used in civil commitment and (2) an examination of the purposes of civil commitment in light of the realities of the resulting confinement. Each of these trends will be discussed separately.

THE CONSTITUTIONAL ADEQUACY OF
CIVIL COMMITMENT PROCEDURES

As briefly noted in chapter 2, the basic constitutional requirement for procedures is in the due process clause of the Fourteenth Amendment to the U.S. Constitution. The Fourteenth Amendment reads:

> All persons born or naturalized in the United States, and subject to the jurisdiction thereof, are citizens of the United States and of the State wherein they reside. No State shall make or enforce any law which shall abridge the privileges or immunities of citizens of the United States; nor shall any State deprive any person of life, liberty, or property without due process of law; nor deny to any person within its jurisdiction the equal protection of law.

The federal government must also provide due process in its exercise of power over individuals under the requirements of the Fifth Amendment. Similar due process provisions can also be found in many state constitutions.

The requirement that the state provide individuals with due process is arguably the single most important mandate of the Constitution. But what does it mean when specifically applied to any one of the thousands of relationships between the government and an individual? In general, due process is the requirement of basic fairness in the exercise of power by the government. In addition to what it requires substantively (*see* next section), due process requires that the government use fundamentally fair procedures in exercising its police powers. In the criminal context, for example, the requirement of due process has been interpreted to include the right to counsel, the right to jury trial, the right to remain silent when held in custody, and other procedural safeguards to insure that the procedures followed are fundamentally fair.

With regard to civil commitment, it is not as easy to specifically define what due process requires because the due process clause has not been applied or interpreted in the civil commitment context very frequently. As indicated earlier, the law had for many years neglected these proceedings, and until relatively recently few courts have addressed themselves to the various procedural issues that can be raised. Indeed, until modern courts began to look at civil commitment with a more critical eye, there was some question whether the due process clause would be applied to civil commitment at all.

Most importantly, most courts decline to view due process as requiring any fixed set of procedural steps. Rather, the specific requirements of fundamentally fair procedures depend on the specific circumstances under consideration; and the courts generally prefer to give considerable discretion to the individual states. In all circumstances, however, the requirement of procedural due process will necessitate some kind of notice to the individual involved of the reasons for the proceedings, some kind of hearing in which those reasons can be questioned, and almost always representation of the individual by legal counsel. Notice, hearing, and counsel are regarded as the foundation of the adversary system and usually the minimum requirements for fair procedures.

Before applying these elements of due process to specific situations such as civil commitment or other areas of the law, it is important to consider first why they are regarded as so basic and essential.

Notice informs the individual of the state's allegations, and gives the individual an opportunity to prepare whatever defense is available. Thus the concept of notice not only involves a communication of information, it also implies notification sufficiently in advance to allow a reasonable amount of preparation. It is obviously unfair not to tell someone what to defend against or not to allow him or her the opportunity to defend. Furthermore, the opportunity whatever it is, would be meaningless unless the affected individual is informed in advance and allowed time for preparation. The only contrary consideration is that the requirement of notice should not be inappropriate or burdensome so as to frustrate the actual purpose of the state. Obviously, prior notice may be impossible or inappropriate in some circumstances, for example at the initial stages of civil commitment.

A hearing is basically an opportunity to defend. Hearings can take a number of forms ranging from an informal discussion with the decision maker (which is all that is required by procedural due process in some situations) to a full-blown jury trial (which is required in situations where the rights at stake are very important). But whatever the form of the hearing, it is an opportunity to confront the decision maker and to advocate the interests of the accused person. In the most basic sense a hearing is a safeguard against errors. It is an opportunity to present the decision maker with evidence or argument that shows that the contemplated decision is based on incorrect information, is poorly conceived, or, possibly, is not within the legal authority of the decision maker. This is true whether the decision maker is a judge in a criminal trial or a public official in an administrative agency's hearing.

Not only is a hearing a safeguard against errors, it also serves the purpose of forcing the decision to be made publicly. Hearings are open to at least some members of the public (at the very least the individual involved represents the public). The assumption is that a decision made openly is not only better conceived and less likely erroneous, but also not as easily corrupted or abused. If the decision maker knows that the decision and the reasons for it are open to public examination, it is more likely that the decision will be made more carefully and more honestly.

Beyond that, there is also the notion that it is "just" to require that the government make decisions publicly. The Kafkaesque notion that the government could make secret decisions that affect the lives of its citizens is itself offensive to most people, apart from whether or not the decision itself is good or bad. People simply like to participate, even as observers, in things that affect their lives.

Why is legal counsel so often considered an essential requirement of due process?

Obviously a lawyer can assist the individual in a number of ways. In most situations only a lawyer can explain to the individual the relevant legal issues, and only a lawyer can make the proper legal arguments that may be available to defend the individual. Lawyers also have skills that go beyond their abilities to research and interpret the law. Lawyers are skilled in arguing and in presenting facts in their most convincing manner; anyone who has ever seen a skillful attorney cross-examine a witness can attest to that. This does not mean that all attorneys are that skillful or that some people are not able to defend themselves. However, it is important to note that the law has recognized that ours is an adversary system relying on an effective advocate for each side. Because of this, procedural due process requires that in most situations an individual can be represented by legal counsel, and in some important situations procedural due process requires that the government pay for legal counsel for people who cannot afford one.

JUDICIAL AND LEGISLATIVE REFORM OF CIVIL COMMITMENT PROCEDURES

By the 1980s, the questions concerning procedural due process and civil commitment pending before the courts largely concern the definition of the kind of notice and hearing, and the other procedural safeguards that must be followed by the state, and the discretion that should be allowed to individual states in fashioning their civil commitment procedures. These questions have only arisen, however, following a period in which more fundamental issues were litigated.

Until the last several decades, many states allowed the civil commitment of the mentally ill and other categories of people with little or no judicial oversight. In some states, the civil commitment legislation actually provided for summary procedures whereby a physician or, in some states, a public official could authorize commitment with virtually no allowance for due process procedures. In other states, where the statutorily authorized procedures did require some form of notice or hearing, these procedural protections were often neglected or simply followed in a "rubber stamp" fashion. But in the late 1960s and the 1970s, following the increased awareness of the constitutional rights of those who are civilly committed and the increased responsiveness of courts to constitutional challenges to civil commitment procedures, these practices were amended in most states. Following a series of judicial decisions throughout the country recognizing that procedural due process should apply to civil commitment—initially some states insisted that the due process clause did not apply to "civil" commitments at all —most states either chose to, or were forced to, revise their civil commitment procedures. Today virtually every state's civil commitment statute requires that civil commitment follow procedures that provide the individual some type of notice, a hearing before a judge, representation by counsel (if not appointed counsel), and procedures designed to meet the modern judicial interpretation of fundamental fairness. If a state were to allow for commitment that narrowly defined these procedural safeguards or adopted practices which ignored them altogether, it is clear that the courts would invalidate such procedures as a violation of the requirement of procedural due process.

Thus there is no doubt that the summary procedures that historically were followed in many states would be held unconstitutional should they be enforced today. If at no point before or after the actual confinement is the allegedly mentally ill individual given an opportunity for a trial-type hearing before a judge, and an opportunity to argue his or her case, then fundamentally fair procedures have not been provided. And for that hearing to be fair, the hearing would have to be preceded by adequate notice of the hearing and the nature of the proceedings. Moreover, to make the defense meaningful, the individual would have to be represented by counsel—and in a matter as crucial as civil commitment, procedural due process would require that such a right to counsel include the right to appointed counsel if the individual could not afford one. Indeed, today such an accounting of fundamentally fair procedures should seem to be so obvious that it hardly deserves attention; yet 20 years ago each of these elements would have sparked considerable and heated debate.

But while the courts, and the state legislatures following their lead, have recognized that people who are civilly committed are entitled to some form of notice, hearing, and counsel, and that the procedures must be fundamentally fair, the constitutional outlines of the procedural rights of the individual and the constitutional responsibilities of the state have been judicially interpreted only in the broadest of terms. Clearly the timing and the content of the notice, as well as the timing and structure of the hearing, can be fashioned in a variety of ways. Courts have been uniformly insistent that the state's procedures include elements of fundamental fairness, but beyond this basic principle requiring fair procedures the courts have been very reluctant to interfere with legislative discretion in designing the state's civil commitment process.

This can best be demonstrated by reference to specific civil commitment statutes and by general reference to the wide range of civil commitment practices that exist today, which have by and large received judicial approval.

The North Carolina civil commitment statute, substantially revised in the 1970s, is a good example of the civil commitment procedures to be found in many jurisdictions today. Under the North Carolina procedures, anyone can file a petition with the clerk of the state district court alleging that an individual is mentally ill (or retarded or an inebriate) and is dangerous to self or to others. If the court's clerk "finds reasonable grounds to believe that the facts are true," the clerk orders that the individual be taken into custody and issues a notice for a hearing for involuntary commitment.

The individual is then taken into custody and examined and, within ten days, a hearing is held before the district court. The individual is entitled to be represented by legal counsel, and the state will pay private attorneys (a very small amount) to represent those who are indigent. If the judge finds "clear, cogent, and convincing evidence" that the individual is mentally ill and dangerous to self or others, the individual is involuntarily confined and treated in a state institution. This confinement is subject to review every 90 days. (Note that "dangerous to self" is defined in North Carolina to include people unable to care for themselves.)

Thus while an individual subject to this statute is eventually given notice of the allegations and an opportunity to defend against them before a judge, the statute does allow for at least a temporary confinement with only minimal judicial scrutiny of the basis for it, and notice to the individual of the proceeding only after he or she is taken into custody.

Other states have struck a quite different balance between traditional due process procedures and their interest in confining and treating the mentally ill. In larger, more urban states, such as California, New York, and Massachusetts, civil commitment procedures tend to be more complex, affording more protection to the individual and even funding legal counsel and advocacy programs of one type or another.

California provides an interesting example. In order to be committed as mentally ill, a person must fall into one of three categories: the individual must be mentally ill and dangerous to others, mentally ill and dangerous to self, or mentally ill and gravely disabled, meaning unable to feed, clothe, and protect him/herself. The procedures and length of commitment for each category differ substantially.

When an individual is, in the opinion of a police officer or a mental health professional, mentally ill and dangerous to others, the individual can be involuntarily committed for 72 hours for examination. If based on that examination the individual is found to be mentally ill and dangerous, the confinement can be extended for 14 days of intensive treatment. This all occurs without any intervention by judicial process, although the procedures for examination and intensive treatment are strictly defined in terms of who can commit and on what basis and the length of the resulting confinement. Any commitment beyond 17 days —3 days of examination and 14 days of intensive treatment—requires rather elaborate judicial procedures to be followed. Moreover, at any time during the 14-day period of intensive treatment the individual may petition for judicial review of the commitment, and this review must be held within 2 days of the filing of the petition. The state law also requires that the individual receive notice of the right to contest any further confinement, the right to a trial by jury, and the right to appointed legal counsel. An additional 180 days of intensive treatment can be ordered, but only after a jury finding that the individual is still mentally ill and dangerous to others.

A similar set of procedures allows for the commitment of people accused of being mentally ill and dangerous to themselves. Again, an individual can be committed for 72 hours' examination by a peace officer or a mental health professional. If the diagnosis is confirmed by the examination, 14 days of intensive treatment can be ordered. At the end of 17 days, if the individual is still dangerous to self, an additional 14-day confinement can be ordered, but such a person can be held for only a maximum of 31 days and must then be released.

A third set of procedures is available for the commitment of people accused of being mentally ill and gravely disabled. After a 72-hour period of examination and a 14-day period of intensive treatment following the same procedures outlined above, no further involuntary confinement can be ordered. However, the state may request a court to appoint a conservator for the individual. In that case the individual is notified of the proceedings, given an opportunity to request a jury trial, and appointed legal counsel. If the trial results in the appointment of a conservator, the appointment lasts for one year and expires unless renewed by a court order based on another trial. An appointed conservator almost always exercises the authority to "voluntarily" commit the individual involved. However, an appointed conservator must place the conservatee in the least restrictive alternative, and preference is given to the conservatee's home or the home of a relative, although the conservatee may be placed in a state or private hospital. In any event, the conservatee at the end of six months may petition the court for a rehearing on his or her status as a conservatee.

Thus in California an individual alleged to be mentally ill can be held for only very short periods of time without some form of judicial or administrative review. And commitment following judicial review is closely prescribed.

Significantly, both the California statute and the more traditional North Carolina statute have survived challenges that they violate the requirements of procedural due process.

The constitutionality of the North Carolina procedures was challenged in *French v. Blackburn*, 428 F. Supp. 1351 (M.D.N.C. 1977). French was taken into custody after his mother petitioned the local court claiming that he should be involuntarily confined. He was subsequently examined by a physician who recommended that he be hospitalized. At the judicial hearing ten days later, however, the judge found that French may have been mentally ill, but that there was not sufficient evidence that he was dangerous to himself or others. French was released. He then brought a class action against the state, asking the federal court to enjoin the enforcement of the state statute, attacking the statute on a number of constitutional grounds including the argument that the statutory provisions for notice and hearing did not meet the fundamental fairness requirement of procedural due process.

The federal district court's dismissal of French's arguments on these issues provides a good illustration of the modern judicial attitude towards the requirements of procedural due process in the civil commitment context:

> The plaintiff asserts that a probable cause hearing should be held within forty-eight hours after the respondent in an involuntary commitment proceeding is taken into custody to be examined by a qualified physician. The statutory procedure of N.C.G.S. § 122-58.7 currently provides only for a final hearing on commitment within ten days after his custody unless the respondent is given a continuance which may be for up to five days at a time.
>
> Every court which has addressed this issue has held that due process demands that some sort of a hearing be held within a reasonable time after confinement or custody. These same courts vary as to the time in which such a hearing must take place. The issue before this court should not be phrased, nor should it be resolved, in terms of required days,

hours, or minutes, but should rather turn on the basis of the interests involved and fundamental fairness. The due process clause does not deal in magic numbers, but fundamental fairness.

We are of the opinion that the provision of N.C.G.S. § 122-58.7 which calls for a hearing within ten days of the respondent's custody is not unconstitutional. During this time period the respondent is receiving treatment, *id.*, § 122–58.6, which may not only aid his mental health, but which also may be necessary to an adequate and informed hearing on the necessity of his commitment. The nature of the confinement itself is limited to the humanitarian purpose of the proceedings as by the very terms of the statute, custody may not be accomplished in a jail or other penal facility but in an institution where treatment and medication are available. *Id.*, § 122–58.4(a). The ten-day period appears even more reasonable in light of the additional procedural safeguards afforded a respondent, which, among other things, gives the respondent at least two opportunities to be released prior to the hearing based upon medical examinations and the findings of the qualified examining physician. In light of the fact that the inquiry throughout the proceedings is aimed at the respondent's mental health, this Court is very reluctant to substitute another judgment in lieu of the legislature's deference to qualified medical opinion at these initial stages of the involuntary commitment proceedings.

In addition to these considerations, the Court is very much persuaded by the reasoning of *Coll v. Hyland*, 411 F. Supp. 905 (D. N.J. 1976), which held that a hearing within twenty days was constitutionally permissible. The *Coll* opinion in turn relies heavily on Logan v. Arafeh, 346 F. Supp. 1265 (D. Conn. 1972), *aff'd sub nom.*, *Briggs v. Arafeh*, 411 U.S. 911, 93 S. Ct. 1556, 36 L.Ed.2d 304 (1973), in which a three-judge court ruled that confinement on the basis of a physician's findings for a period of forty-five days pending a hearing was not unreasonably long and did not constitute a denial of due process. . . .

* * *

Plaintiff contends that the notice provision is constitutionally deficient in that it does not indicate a basis of the detention, does not set forth the standard of proof required at the hearing, does not inform him of a right to a jury trial, and does not indicate the names of the witnesses and/or physicians who will testify at the hearing in favor of commitment and the substance of their testimony. We find these assertions to be of little merit.

Due process requires that the notice of a hearing be appropriate to the occasion and reasonably calculated to inform the person to whom it is directed of the nature of the proceedings. *Mullane v. Central Hanover Bank & Trust Co.*, 339 U.S. 306, 70 S. Ct. 652, 94 L. Ed. 865 (1950). The concept of due process is not a static one and it does not mandate particular forms of procedure. *See, e.g., Mitchell v. W. T. Grant Co.*, 416 U.S. 600,

94 S. Ct. 1895, 40 L. Ed.2d 406 (1974). As stated by the Supreme Court
in *Mullane v. Central Hanover Bank & Trust Co.*, 339 U.S. at 314, 70 S. Ct.
at 657, 94 L. Ed. at 873:

> An elementary and fundamental requirement of due process
> in any proceeding which is to be accorded finality is notice reason-
> ably calculated, under all the circumstances, to apprise interested
> parties of the pendency of the action and afford them the opportu-
> nity to present their objections. [Citations omitted] The notice
> must be of such nature as reasonably to convey the required infor-
> mation, [citation omitted], and it must afford a reasonable time for
> those interested to make their appearance, [citations omitted]. But
> if with due regard for the practicalities and peculiarities of the case
> these conditions are reasonably met, the constitutional require-
> ments are satisfied.

* * *

The notice form used by the defendant to inform the plaintiff of
the proceedings against him is entirely adequate. It stated not only the
time and place of the hearing but also notified him: (1) of the purpose of
the hearing; (2) the right to counsel; (3) that he would be given the opportunity to present evidence at the hearing; and (4) that the presiding
judge would then determine whether he should be released, be committed for up to ninety days, or undergo outpatient treatment.

In light of the nature of the proceedings, we find that this procedure is reasonably calculated to inform the respondent in an involuntary
commitment proceeding of the nature and purpose of the hearing and,
therefore, is not constitutionally infirm. We can find no constitutional
mandate to notify the respondent of the burden of proof or to serve upon
him a list of witnesses and the substance of their proposed testimony.

With a similar deferential regard for the wide discretion of state
legislatures, a federal court in New Jersey has held, as noted in *French*,
that temporary civil commitment pending a full hearing before a judge
could be extended as long as 45 days. In New York, a federal district
court has ruled that an individual can be held as long as 60 days without a hearing before a judge unless the individual specifically requests a
hearing, and up to 15 days without any judicial oversight, citing *French*
as reflecting the proper judicial attitude towards the requirements of
procedural due process in the civil commitment context. On the other
hand, in Texas a state statute that allowed for 14 days' confinement
without a probable cause hearing (and also without treatment) and confinement for longer than 72 hours without notice of the allegations or
of the right to request a probable cause hearing was declared to be a
violation of procedural due process.

In all jurisdictions, the courts have required that the individual is entitled—eventually—to a trial-type hearing before an impartial judicial officer and that counsel be provided at least at the hearing itself. But the clear intent of the courts is only to insure that the procedures taken as a whole reflect modern judicial notions of fundamental fairness. Beyond that the courts have allowed each state virtually unchecked discretion in defining the procedures that the state follows in civil commitment.

This is a marked change from the attitude of the courts in previous generations when there were no judicial limitations on state discretion in civil commitment. The attitude of modern courts in interpreting the requirements of procedural due process requires at least some judicial oversight of the fairness of each state's procedures. But the courts have also attempted to delineate that role so as to allow the states considerable discretion. Thus in states where the civil commitment procedures do not realistically entail the basic notions of a hearing, notice, and counsel, the courts have been willing to step in and invalidate the statutory scheme. But beyond requiring some minimum measure of "fundamental fairness," even modern courts prefer to leave the framing of the state's procedures as a matter of legislative—and not judicial—prerogative.

JUSTIFYING CIVIL COMMITMENT IN TERMS OF THE REALITIES OF THE RESULTING CONFINEMENT

The second major trend in the recent interpretation of the state's police power as applied to civil commitment involves a more direct examination of the resulting confinement. In the last two decades, some courts—but not all—have been willing to examine rather closely the purposes justifying civil commitment in light of the terms and circumstances of the resulting confinement. Not surprisingly, these courts have in some cases invalidated the exercise of power by the state; but in doing so, they have encountered both theoretical and practical difficulties, both in marking the boundaries of their newly defined judicial role and in developing realistic mechanisms for the enforcement of their rulings.

THE APPLICATION OF SUBSTANTIVE DUE PROCESS TO CIVIL COMMITMENT

Most traditional civil commitment statutes simply allow for the commitment of people believed to be in need of treatment for indefinite periods of time. There is no explicit assurance within these statutes that the length or conditions of confinement will relate to the original purpose for the commitment or to the specific needs of the individual. Of course there is no civil commitment statute that explicitly prohibits a state that is implementing the statute from considering these factors; a state could decide administratively to implement its civil commitment statute in such a way that people are only confined for appropriate lengths of time and under conditions relating to their specific needs. Unfortunately, that has not been the case in many states. Indeed, the practice in most states has been exactly the opposite: thousands of people are involuntarily committed each year with little specification of their needs or the appropriate length for their confinement. At least until very recently, civil commitment has most often resulted in indefinite confinement in large, custodial mental institutions that are typically poorly staffed and underfunded, and under conditions not necessarily related to each patient's individual needs. Even attempts to place some mental patients in community-based facilities and the increasing effectiveness of modern psychopharmacology have not changed the basic reality of the circumstances of many civilly confined people.

This somewhat unsettling picture of the realities of civil confinement can be contrasted with the legal notion that civil commitment is a drastic deprivation of liberty and, according to legal doctrine, should be constitutionally justified only where it can be shown that the confinement will serve an overriding social purpose, primarily the concern for the patient's need for treatment. It is primarily in reaction to this contrast that many courts have developed greater willingness to question the validity of civil commitment and to examine the nature of the resulting confinement.

Parenthetically, not all courts have been willing to adopt a more active posture. Some courts still tend towards the deferential attitude that historically allowed state legislative and administrative officials virtually unchecked discretion in determining who should be confined and under what conditions. A minority of courts—and even Chief Justice Burger in several dissenting opinions—have suggested that indefinite confinement or confinement without treatment of the mentally ill or of others may be justified solely by the state's interest in protecting the public from the dangers presented by such people. Thus Justice Burger and some other judges have virtually refused to consider the conditions of the resulting confinement as relevant to the constitutionality of civil commitment. Several counter arguments make it unlikely that such a view will become widespread. First, not all people who are committed are dangerous, at least to other people. More importantly, to the extent that states justify involuntary confinement based on dangerousness alone and not on the need for treatment, the distinction between civil and criminal confinement will break down and procedural due process will likely require rather elaborate safeguards to be followed in adjudicating commitments. For that matter, while the state can obviously enact laws to protect its citizens from the acts of others, it is not yet clear whether "preventive detention" laws, laws which confine people before they commit dangerous acts, are substantively within the scope of the police power.

In any event, at least through the 1980s, most courts view treatment as the primary justification for civil commitment and do not accept social protection by itself as sufficient for civil confinement. As a consequence, there has been an increase in the willingness of many courts to examine the realities of the circumstances of the resulting confinement.

One important line of cases, demonstrating the initial willingness of the Supreme Court to examine more closely the circumstances and justification of civil commitment—and, more recently, a moderation of that trend—began with the Supreme Court decision in *Jackson v. Indiana*, 406 U.S. 715 (1972).

In the *Jackson* case, a deaf-mute who was described as "mentally defective" was charged with two counts of robbery. (The total value of the stolen goods was five dollars.) He was civilly committed after examination by two physicians and a hearing on the matter, in which he was found incompetent to stand trial on the robbery charges. Indiana law also provides for the civil commitment of insane persons (comparable with what other states call mentally ill) and the civil commitment of feebleminded persons (comparable with the mentally retarded). Both of these other processes differ in a number of ways from the process for the commitment of people like Jackson as incompetent to stand trial, including: (1) commitment under either of the other two statutes would have been according to a stricter standard of proof of the relevant mental condition; (2) release under the other civil commitment statutes would have been easier to attain; and (3) the treatment received under either statute would have been different and arguably better for Jackson.

Jackson claimed that his commitment violated his rights to due process and equal protection secured by the Fourteenth Amendment to the U.S. Constitution. The Supreme Court agreed on both issues.

In finding that Jackson's commitment was a violation of equal protection, the Court was extending to a new situation a principle previously applied in a 1967 case, *Baxtrom v. Herold*, 383 U.S. 107 (1967). In *Baxtrom*, the Court held that the state of New York had denied Baxtrom, a convicted criminal, equal protection of the law when, near the expiration of his prison sentence, he was summarily transferred after a very brief hearing from prison to a hospital for the criminally insane to serve indefinitely until considered sane. In effect he was civilly committed while a prisoner. At that time all other people civilly committed under New York state law were entitled to a jury trial; when they were committed to the facility where Baxtrom was confined, the jury was required to find that the individual was both mentally ill and dangerous. The Court said that this denial of procedural rights to Baxtrom was a violation of equal protection. A distinction based on Baxtrom's status as a prisoner is not a rational basis upon which to justify a discrimination between Baxtrom and all other people subject to civil commitment. The Court applied this logic to Jackson's situation: "If criminal conviction and imposition of sentence are insufficient to justify less procedural and substantive protection against indefinite commitment . . . the mere filing of criminal charges surely can not suffice."

In order to satisfy the requirements of equal protection, the state must show at least a rational basis for any process that deprives the committed person of substantial rights that would be available to other committed people. The Court rejected the argument by Indiana that Jackson's pending trial on the criminal charges was sufficient basis for this distinction and also rejected the argument that the commitment was only temporary, i.e., until Jackson recovered to stand trial, since based on the facts, that was unlikely to happen. (For a more detailed discussion of the requirement of equal protection, see chapter 5.)

The Court's ruling on the due process issue had even more far-reaching implications. The Court examined the proceedings used to commit Jackson and the reasons cited by the state to justify his confinement and compared them to the treatment that Jackson would receive. While withholding explicit statement or definition of the exact basis upon which commitment could be justified, Justice Blackmun, writing for the Court, very bluntly stated that Jackson's confinement violated the fundamental fairness requirement of due process, not in the procedures followed, but in the "substance" of the confinement:

> We need not address these broad questions here. It is clear that Jackson's commitment rests on proceedings that did not purport to bring into play, indeed did not even consider relevant, any of the articulated bases for exercise of Indiana's power of indefinite commitment. The state statutes contain at least two alternative methods for invoking this power. But Jackson was not afforded any "formal commitment proceedings addressed to [his] ability to function in society," or to society's interest in his restraint, or to the State's ability to aid him in attaining competency through custodial care or compulsory treatment, the ostensible purpose of the commitment. At the least, due process requires that the

nature and duration of commitment bear some reasonable relation to the purpose for which the individual is committed.

We hold, consequently, that a person charged by a state with a criminal offense who is committed solely on account of his incapacity to proceed to trial cannot be held more than the reasonable period of time necessary to determine whether there is a substantial probability that he will attain that capacity in the forseeable future.

Thus Jackson's commitment was invalidated as a violation of the substantive requirements of due process.

In the same term that the Supreme Court decided *Jackson*, it decided another case that also recognized the need to examine the purposes of civil commitment in terms of the resulting confinement. In *McNeil v. Patuxent Institute Director*, 407 U.S. 245 (1972), McNeil, originally convicted on two counts of assault and sentenced to five years in prison, was sent to a mental institution for examination and observation during his criminal sentence. The purpose was to determine whether McNeil should be confined under the Maryland defective delinquent law; in effect, it was a temporary commitment for observation prior to the defective delinquent proceedings, much like Jackson's "temporary" commitment. McNeil flatly refused to talk to the institution's psychiatrists during his confinement, and, when his original prison sentence expired, no decision to initiate the defective delinquent proceedings had been made. The state tried to extend the period of observation, and McNeil filed suit claiming his confinement was no longer valid.

The Supreme Court agreed with McNeil. Specifically, the Court held that it is a denial of substantive due process to continue to hold a person in a mental institution on the basis of an administrative decision to have the person observed. Citing the *Jackson* decision, the Court said that since this was clearly a long-term commitment (it had lasted seven years), the state must civilly commit McNeil as it would any other person, using the proper procedural safeguards, or strictly limit the confinement so that it is in reality a temporary observation.

Parenthetically, the Court took great pains to avoid deciding whether McNeil had a right to remain silent—just as a criminal defendant does—or, conversely, whether the state could interpret that silence as evidence that he was a defective delinquent. Thus the right to remain silent issue in commitment proceedings surfaced before the Court, but the Court chose not to rule on it.

The fact that these cases signaled a growing judicial interest in examining the realities of civil confinement was highlighted by Justice Blackmun's concluding remarks in *Jackson* tacitly inviting more frequent challenges to the substantive bases of civil commitment: "Considering the number of persons affected, it is perhaps remarkable that the substantive constitutional limitations on this power have not been more frequently litigated."

While *Jackson* and *McNeil* are still "good law," the notion suggested by these cases that the courts, led by the Supreme Court, are willing to examine rather closely the realities of civil confinement in terms of its justification must be qualified by the implications of the most recent decisions of the Court. First of all, as explained in more detail in the next section, it is still not clear whether the Supreme Court is willing to expand that judicial examination of state legislative and executive power to include review of the actual treatment available or rendered to people who are civilly confined; in fact, the "right to treatment" cases decided by the Court following *Jackson* may well signal at least a partial retreat from the apparent direction of the Court's judicial philosophy as exhibited in its earlier cases. Second, in its most recent related decision, *Jones v. United States*, 103 S. Ct. 3043 (1983), the Court demonstrated what has to be regarded as a marked change in its attitude towards enforcement, even in very similar situations, of the substantive due process principle enunciated in *Jackson*.

In *Jones*, the plaintiff was charged with shoplifting, but following a jury trial, found "not guilty by reason of insanity." According to the practice in the District of Columbia, he was then civilly committed indefinitely without additional proceedings. Had he not been involved in a criminal proceeding, Jones could have been civilly committed only following a judicial hearing and a jury trial on his present mental condition—not that at the time of the crime—and by a finding by "clear and convincing evidence" that he was mentally ill and dangerous to others, subject to periodic review every six months. Under the statute used to commit Jones, there were no additional procedures following his acquittal; he was subject to recommitment every six months on a finding that he was mentally ill and dangerous based on "the preponderance of the evidence" and without a jury trial. Relying heavily on the apparent implications of *Jackson* and the obvious parallels to the factual settings in *Baxtrom* and *McNeil*, Jones argued that his commitment and subsequent confinement were unconstitutional. Principally he argued that his civil commitment based on the finding at a criminal trial that he was not guilty by reason of insanity was a violation of his rights to procedural and substantive due process. In particular, he argued that any civil commitment should follow procedures similar to those followed in civil commitment of other people in the District of Columbia and should be based on findings as to his condition at present, not at the time of the crime. Further, he argued that the length of the confine-

ment, if he were to be committed based on the finding at the criminal
trial, could not be longer than the maximum penalty for the crime for
which he had been tried.

Over the vigorous objection of Justice Blackmun and two other
justices, the majority of the Supreme Court had little trouble in upholding the commitment procedures allowed by the District of Columbia statute and the continued confinement of Jones. First, the Court
held that it was not a violation of procedural due process for Congress
to allow the District to commit acquitted criminals based on the findings at the criminal trial, largely on the grounds that the District has an
"important interest in automatic commitment," presumably a reference to the time and effort required to relitigate some of the same issues settled at the criminal trial. Second, the Court found that the purposes served and the circumstances involved in this type of
commitment could justify a commitment following less rigorous procedures and a less demanding standard of proof than are used in commitments where other purposes are being served. Finally, the Court ruled
that since the purpose of this form of civil commitment was also different from that of criminal confinement, the resulting confinement could
last longer than the maximum sentence and still meet the substantive
due process requirement of fundamental fairness.

It is difficult not to read *Jones* as a partial retreat from both the
constitutional principles and the judicial attitude that were established
in *Jackson* and its companion cases, at least with regard to people who
are committed after being found not guilty by reason of insanity.
Clearly by 1984 the majority of the Supreme Court is willing to allow
considerable discretion to the state legislatures in formulating civil
commitment procedures and in dictating the terms of the resulting
confinement. The Court in the earlier cases appeared to be less willing
to allow states to confine the various categories of civilly committed
people following different procedures and more willing to require that
states conform to judicially determined notions of fundamental fairness
and equal protection. On the other hand, it is absolutely clear that the
most important constitutional principles established by earlier cases
have not been abandoned. The *Jones* opinion explicitly held that whatever procedures are followed must conform to both substantive and
procedural due process requirements; most particularly *Jones* held,
quoting the words of Justice Blackmun's opinion in *Jackson*, "the nature
and duration of the commitment must bear some reasonable relationship to the purposes for which [Jones] is committed." If anything has
changed, it is not the definition of the relationship between the state
police powers and individual rights as inherent in these principles, but
the Court's view of the judicial role in interpreting their application to

particular cases. Substantive due process requires that there be a reasonable relationship between the purpose of the commitment and the resulting confinement, just as procedural due process requires that the procedures followed must be "fundamentally fair." But the extent of the power of the courts vis-à-vis legislative and executive discretion implied by these principles continues to be a question of considerable controversy.

THE EVOLUTION OF THE "RIGHT TO TREATMENT"

The principles that define the relationship between the state and the individual, and the importance of the judicial role in interpreting that relationship, can also be illustrated by another line of civil commitment cases.

Even before the Supreme Court decided the *Jackson* case, a number of lower courts had decided cases indicating a similar interest in an examination of the purposes of civil commitment in light of the realities of the resulting confinement, holding that people who are involuntarily committed have a right to receive adequate treatment for their condition.

There have been various legal bases for these decisions. Some opinions have found a statutory basis for a "right to treatment." That is, some courts have interpreted the explicit provisions of a state's civil commitment statute or the strong implication of that statute to require that anyone committed under the statute be given adequate care while confined. Other courts have found a "right to treatment" in the provisions of the federal Constitution. The majority of courts recognizing a constitutional "right to treatment" have held that civil commitment without adequate treatment is a violation of substantive due process. Following logic similar to that of *Jones* and *Jackson*, these courts have held that it would be fundamentally unfair to deprive an individual of personal liberty based on society's concern for—or fear of—his or her condition, but not, in fact, to treat that condition. A few courts have also found that failure to treat people who are civilly committed is cruel and unusual punishment in violation of the Eighth Amendment.

The logic of the "right to treatment" cases is simple and compelling. Indeed, but for the traditional reluctance of the courts to become involved in civil commitment, there might well be a much longer history of its recognition. But even where it has been recognized, this right has not always been effectively enforced. The history of the development of this legal doctrine from its earliest recognition to the most recent pronouncements of the Supreme Court indicates that even if courts are willing to recognize such a right, they may not be willing or able to expand the judicial role to include the extraordinary measures that would be necessary to translate their legal rulings into realistic enforcement orders.

As early as 1963 the Massachusetts Supreme Court recognized that people involuntarily confined to mental institutions have a constitutional "right to treatment." In 1965 the Court of Appeals for the District of Columbia under Judge David Bazelon, who has been responsible for a number of decisions articulating the rights of the mentally ill, came to a similar conclusion. In both cases, the courts were clearly responding as much to the abysmal conditions in the mental institutions where the plaintiffs were committed, Bridgewater State Hospital in Massachusetts and St. Elizabeth's Hospital in Washington, D.C., as to the persuasiveness of the constitutional argument. Ironically, in both cases the courts were willing to recognize the constitutional "right to treatment"; yet in neither case did the court take steps to reform the institution involved or otherwise provide for the enforcement of the plaintiff's rights. (And neither patient was released from confinement.)

Following the lead of these cases, a number of other state and federal courts also recognized constitutional rights to treatment for mental patients, the mentally retarded, and other institutionalized wards of the state, again reacting in large part to the conditions in large custodial institutions. Few cases, however, were able to provide for any workable remedy. A notable illustration was the litigation that resulted in the decision in *Wyatt v. Aderholdt*, 503 F.2d 1305 (5th Cir. 1974). The factual setting in *Wyatt* was typical of the "right to treatment" cases in the 1970s. Although originally brought by a group of employees who were laid off because of budget cutbacks, the case evolved into a class action on behalf of the patients of the Alabama state mental institutions, arguing that the lack of adequate care available to them violated their constitutional "right to treatment." The factual allegations of their suit were not difficult to prove; the facilities for both the mentally ill and the mentally retarded in Alabama were largely custodial institutions, clearly understaffed and poorly supported. In the largest of the state's institutions there were 5,000 patients for whom there were only 17 physicians (3 of whom had psychiatric training), 21 nurses, 12 psychologists (only 1 of whom had a Ph.D.), 13 social workers, 12 patient activity workers, and 850 psychiatric aides. These statistics tend to obscure a number of things, including the fact that most of the physicians were involved in the administration of the hospital, not patient care. It was also found that Alabama ranked fiftieth in the nation in expenditures per patient per day. Thousands of geriatric and mentally retarded patients were indiscriminately mixed with the other mentally ill patients. The programs available for treatment were found to conform to no known minimum standards for the treatment of the mentally ill.

Based on such evidence, the federal district court judge had little trouble in finding that people civilly confined in Alabama were in fact not receiving treatment, or in accepting the plaintiff's legal argument that it is a violation of substantive due process to deny liberty to an individual through civil commitment and confinement without providing adequate treatment. But this ruling left the federal district court in a difficult position. Having ruled that the available treatment was not constitutionally adequate, the judge was faced with the prospect of defining standards for adequate treatment. This is not only technically a difficult problem; but it also puts the judicial branch of the federal government in the constitutionally and politically sensitive position of directing the state legislature to appropriate more funds and telling the executive branch of that government how to administer those funds and manage its programs. Moreover, even if the court could fashion an order doing so, it is not clear what options the court would have if the state chose not to comply with such orders. Courts theoretically enforce their orders through the powers of contempt and can even empower court officials to take control or possession of the parties' property to secure compliance. But such remedies cannot assure compliance with judicial orders even by private litigants, not to mention state agencies under federal court order.

As a consequence, the trial judge initially issued a rather conservative order. The court held that the conditions in the Alabama institutions were unconstitutional, but rather than issue a specific enforcement order, the court gave the state 90 days to develop its own plan to improve the level of care that was available.

By the time the state filed its first report, the case had drawn considerable national interest. Both the federal Department of Justice and the Department of Health, Education, and Welfare, as well as a number of advocacy groups, had joined the case on the side of the plaintiffs. At their urging, the court rejected the state's plan, and ordered that the state set standards for treatment that included (1) qualified staff in numbers sufficient to administer adequate treatment, (2) a humane physical and psychological environment, and (3) individualized treatment plans for each patient. But the court was clearly still wary of expanding the judicial role into the administration of the state's programs and gave the state several months to implement this order.

Eventually all parties agreed to a set of standards—although they were largely the work of the plaintiffs—that represented "minimally adequate treatment." These standards included elaborate specifications for the adequacy of facilities, implementation of individual treatment plans, and specific standards for staffing. The staffing standards (for one of the state's institutions) included:

— One psychiatrist for every 125 patients
— One psychologist for every 125 patients
— One physician for every 125 patients
— One psychiatric aide for every 3 to 5 patients

Alabama argued that the state should be required only to make progress towards these "goals." The plaintiffs argued that they should be implemented immediately. Eventually the court (1) ordered their implementation, (2) ordered the establishment of a human rights committee in each Alabama institution to review all research and treatment programs to ensure that the dignity and human rights of all patients were preserved, and (3) ordered that the state file a report within six months on the implementation of these orders.

Alabama appealed the decision to the U.S. Court of Appeals for the Fifth Circuit. The court of appeals heard oral argument on the case and, for reasons known only to the members of the court, waited nearly two years before issuing its decision. Finally, over four years after the original case was filed in the district court and after numerous hearings, negotiations, and reports, the court of appeals affirmed the lower court's finding that civilly confined patients have a constitutional "right to treatment" and that in Alabama that right was being violated. Referring to its earlier decision in *O'Connor v. Donaldson* (discussed *infra*) the court of appeals argued:

> [W]e held that civilly committed mental patients have a constitutional right to such individual treatment as will help each of them to be cured or to improve his or her mental condition. We reasoned that the only permissible justifications for civil commitment, and for the massive abridgements of constitutionally protected liberties it entails, were the danger posed by the individual committed to himself or to others, or the individual's need for treatment and care. We held that where the justification for commitment was treatment, it offended the fundamentals of due process if treatment were not in fact provided; and we held that where the justification was the danger to self or to others, then treatment had to be provided as the *quid pro quo* society had to pay as the price of the extra safety it derived from the denial of individuals' liberty.

The court of appeals was not, however, as secure about the manner in which the judiciary should enforce this right. Again the problem was no less than ordering the executive branch to vastly improve its administration of the state's mental health programs, and, in effect, requiring the state legislature to allocate more funding and to hire more staff. If the state did not comply, the court could only turn to extraordinary measures, e.g., holding the legislature or state officials in contempt or, literally, taking over the administration of the state programs and even selling state property—measures hardly likely to be acceptable or workable. Understandably the appellate court downplayed these possibilities:

> With respect to judicial accomplishment of the remedy, profound questions are presented regarding the scope of substantive due process and the role of federal courts in matters affecting the management of state institutions. . . .
>
> * * *
>
> The serious constitutional questions presented by federal judicial action ordering the sale of state lands, or altering the state budget, or which may otherwise arise in the problem of financing, in the event the governing authorities fail to move in good faith to ensure what all parties agree are minimal requirements, should not be adjudicated unnecessarily and prematurely. (citations omitted) Since we have now affirmed that part of the district court's orders recognizing the constitutional right to treatment, determination of good faith efforts by state authorities to ensure these rights should be made in the first instance in the district court.

For whatever reason, judicial enforcement of the order in *Wyatt* has never been carried any further. Alabama declined to appeal the case to the Supreme Court, and the plaintiffs have never pursued whatever remedial measures the federal courts might eventually have been forced to follow. Reports from Alabama regarding the state's voluntary compliance with the *Wyatt* orders have been mixed; none indicate that the quality of treatment available in the state's mental institutions has been markedly improved. (*See* note at end of chapter.)

Whatever the practical effect, the *Wyatt* decision has had a more certain effect on legal doctrine. *Wyatt* clearly held that substantive due process requires that treatment be provided for people who are civilly confined—or, at least, that conditions for adequate treatment be available. Thus, in the Fifth Circuit, what is generally referred to as a "right to treatment" has been established. On the other hand, another case from that circuit, *O'Connor v. Donaldson*, 422 U.S. 563 (1975), eventually found its way to the Supreme Court and cast some doubt on whether the Fifth Circuit's broad interpretation of the "right to treatment" will be adopted by the Supreme Court—and therefore by all jurisdictions.

At about the same time that the *Wyatt* case was being litigated, Donaldson sued the superintendent of the Florida state mental institution where he had been confined, claiming that his commitment without treatment was unconstitutional and arguing that federal civil rights statutes provide for monetary damages to be awarded where a state official violates the constitutional rights of any individual. Donaldson had been confined for nearly 15 years under circumstances where it was fairly clear that he was receiving nothing but custodial treatment. Furthermore, even the staff of the institution agreed that Donaldson was neither dangerous nor unable to care for himself. Apparently the only reason that Donaldson was confined was Superintendent O'Connor's bizarre policy that patients like Donaldson could be released only into the custody of their parents. Donaldson was nearly 50 years old and his parents were in their late 70s.

The Court of Appeals for the Fifth Circuit affirmed a jury verdict in the trial court awarding Donaldson $38,000 in damages. Both the trial and appellate courts held that Donaldson's "right to treatment" had been violated; it was in this case that the court of appeals issued its broad interpretation of the requirements of substantive due process paraphrased later in *Wyatt.* In the Supreme Court, however, that legal interpretation was rather severely narrowed.

Unlike the court of appeals, the Supreme Court declined to consider whether mental patients generally have a "right to treatment," arguing that the *Donaldson* case presented a much narrower question:

> There is no reason now to decide whether mentally ill persons dangerous to themselves or to others have a right to treatment upon compulsory confinement by the State, or whether the State may compulsorily confine a nondangerous, mentally ill individual for the purpose of treatment. As we view it, this case raises a single, relatively simple, but nonetheless important question concerning every man's constitutional right to liberty.
>
> . . . We need not decide whether, when, or by what procedures, a mentally ill person may by confined by the State on any of the grounds which, under contemporary statutes, are generally advanced to justify involuntary confinement of such a person—to prevent injury to the public, to ensure his own survival or safety, or to alleviate or cure his illness. . . . For the jury found that none of the above grounds for continued confinement was present in Donaldson's case.
>
> * * *
>
> A finding of "mental illness" alone cannot justify a State's locking a person up against his will and keeping him indefinitely in simple custodial confinement. Assuming that that term can be given a reasonably precise content and that the "mentally ill" can be identified with reasonable accuracy, there is still no constitutional basis for confining such persons involuntarily if they are dangerous to no one and can live safely in freedom.

Thus the Court held that substantive due process would be violated if Donaldson were confined without treatment; it declined to rule whether this narrowly defined "right to treatment" would be extended to other categories of people who are civilly confined or whether Donaldson's confinement would be constitutional if he had been treated. Perhaps the Court was relying on a tradition—not always followed—of deciding the case before it on the narrowest grounds; but the Court was also implying its reluctance to rule on a broad "right to treatment."

Thus even in the 1980s, it is still not clear whether people subject to civil commitment have a "right to treatment." The Supreme Court ruling in *Donaldson* was narrowly drawn. Several Fifth Circuit decisions have very clearly recognized a broadly defined "right to treatment," although the fact that the Supreme Court has specifically refused to uphold (or reverse) that view casts some doubt over the precedential value of those decisions. Most circuits have not addressed the "right to treatment" question at all.

Further indication of the current Supreme Court's attitude towards the judicial role in reviewing the confinement of people who are civilly committed can be drawn from its recent decisions regarding the confinement of the mentally retarded. In *Pennhurst State School v. Halderman*, 451 U.S. 1 (1982), both the institutional setting and the quality of the treatment received by patients were found to be so inadequate that the condition of the patients actually deteriorated as a result of their confinement. As a result of these factual findings, the Federal District Court for the Eastern District of Pennsylvania ruled that commitment of the mentally retarded to such an institution—presumably justified by the state's interest in their condition—was a violation of substantive due process, as well as a violation of the Eighth Amendment's prohibition on cruel and unusual punishment, recognizing what the court termed a constitutional "right to habilitation" for the mentally retarded. The district court also found that these conditions violated various state and federal statutory rights to adequate habilitation.

The Third Circuit Court of Appeals affirmed the lower court decision, but narrowed the legal basis for the "right to habilitation," holding only that confinement under such conditions violated the rights created under the federal Developmentally Disabled Assistance and Bill of Rights Act. The court of appeals chose not to rule on the broader constitutional issues. The Supreme Court, however, reversed the decision of the court of appeals. The Court argued that the federal statute was not intended to create any substantive rights for the retarded but that, in the eyes of the Court, the statute was intended to do "no more than express a congressional preference for certain kinds of treatment."

In form this decision did no more than interpret the meaning of a federal statute and remand the case for further consideration of the other issues which were technically not before the Court. But most observers read the decision as again signaling a reluctance of the Court to recognize any broadly defined rights for those who are civilly confined or to endorse judicial review of the quality of the conditions in state institutions.

A similar reluctance on the part of the Court has also been read into a more recent decision, again involving the Pennsylvania state institutions for the retarded. In *Youngberg v. Romeo,* 457 U.S. 307 (1983), the Court took a very narrow view of the rights of those who are civilly confined and the judicial role in their enforcement. Romeo, a severely retarded adult, claimed that he had not received adequate care, had been repeatedly injured by his own violence and that of other patients throughout his confinement, and had been frequently physically restrained (e.g., shackled to a bed) for long periods of time. Asking for civil damages, he filed suit under the same civil rights statute involved in the *Donaldson* litigation. Following a jury trial, the district court found for the defendant, but on appeal the circuit court ruled that the definition of Romeo's constitutional rights included in the district court's instructions to the jury had been too narrow. According to the Third Circuit, Romeo's constitutionally protected liberty included an interest in both his personal safety and his freedom of movement, and neither could be denied by the state even if he were civilly confined unless the state had an "over-riding, non-punitive state interest." The court further ruled that substantive due process required that Romeo be given "minimally adequate treatment" designed to treat his condition.

The Supreme Court affirmed the decision of the court of appeals, but did so only in the narrowest terms. The Court did agree that civilly confined people such as Romeo have constitutionally protected rights to personal safety and to the freedom of movement, but it redefined those rights and held that the court of appeals' definition of "over-riding, non-punitive interests" did not allow the states sufficient discretion. Rather, the Court held that the state needed only a reasonable basis for overriding Romeo's interest in personal safety or in freedom of movement. The Court also agreed that there is a constitutional "right to habilitation" but—somehow—argued that Romeo's particular case raised the "right to habilitation" only in terms of his personal freedom and personal safety, not the care and treatment he was receiving. Justice Rehnquist, writing for the majority of the Court, virtually ignored the issue of habilitation in terms of the overall conditions of the institution or the care given to Romeo.

[W]e agree that respondent is entitled to minimally adequate training. In this case, the minimally adequate training required by the Constitution is such training as may be reasonable in light of respondent's liberty interests in safety and freedom from unreasonable restraints. In determining what is "reasonable"—in this and in any case presenting a claim for training by a state—we emphasize that courts must show deference to the judgment exercised by a qualified professional. By so limiting judicial review of challenges to conditions in state institutions, interference by the federal judiciary with the internal operations of these institutions should be minimized. . . . For these reasons the decision, if made by a professional, is presumptively valid; liability may be imposed only when the decision by the professional is such a substantial departure from accepted professional judgment, practice, or standards as to demonstrate that the person responsible actually did not base the decision on such a judgment.

CONCLUSION

From reviewing the cases discussed in this chapter and, particularly the substantive due process cases, it is apparent that the Supreme Court's current mood towards the definition of the rights of people who are civilly committed and confined has become decidedly conservative. The Court has been reluctant to recognize broadly defined individual rights in this context, and even when providing for the enforcement of the elementary notions of due process, the Court in its most recent decisions has been careful to narrowly define the role of the judiciary in enforcing constitutional limitations on state discretion.

This conservative attitude was not reflected in *Jackson* and other cases decided in the early 1970s. And even today, some members of the Court and some lower courts have indicated a willingness to define the rights of those who are civilly committed much more broadly and to take a more active role in enforcing those rights.

Many important constitutional questions remain to be answered, e.g., neither the right to refuse treatment nor the right to receive treatment has been definitively addressed. The most important questions yet to be decided, however, may involve not the definition of substantive principles, but the further delineation of the proper judicial attitude that the courts should adopt in defining and enforcing those principles. If the courts apply the current Supreme Court's judicially conservative attitude in addressing future questions involving the constitutionality of civil commitment and confinement, then this attitude will be far more determinative of the real nature of the constitutional rights of people who are civilly committed than any substantive principle or individual case decision. Thus such rights as the "right to treatment," if and when it is recognized by the Supreme Court, will be narrowly and conservatively defined, so long as the current Court's attitude remains unchanged.

Aside from general notions of whether the courts should be conservative or liberal in defining their role in protecting individual constitutional rights, there is some basis for questioning why the Supreme Court and many other courts are so insistent on limiting their role in defining the state's power of civil commitment. As the material in the next chapter will demonstrate, the modern view of the proper role of the courts in protecting individual rights is to demand that the government, meaning the legislative branch and the executive branch in carrying out legislative directives, must be subjected to careful judicial review—what will be called "close scrutiny"—whenever important individual rights are affected by government activities. Yet while *Jackson* and some of the lower court "right to treatment" cases arguably carried out such a review, the most recent Supreme Court decisions have not. Indeed, at least in *Jones* and in the "right to habilitation" cases, the Court has implied that even where individual liberty is severely curtailed by civil commitment, the state is to be given virtually unfettered discretion in deciding who shall be civilly committed, by which procedures, and under what conditions. After reviewing the cases in the next chapter, it may be instructive to compare this attitude towards protecting individual liberty in civil commitment with the attitude of the Court towards protecting the privacy interest of people using contraceptives or women seeking (privately funded) abortions. There is clearly a difference between the judicial posture towards protection of the liberty interest at stake in civil commitment and that towards the privacy interest involved in these other cases, but the rationale for this different and more deferential attitude towards government discretion in civil commitment has never been fully developed in the case law. This too remains to be addressed by future decisions.

In reviewing the principles established by these cases, it is also worth noting that Justice Blackmun's observation in *Jackson* has not really been answered by subsequent decisions. The substantive limits on the power of the state to civilly commit and confine people have been more frequently litigated, as he apparently thought appropriate, but the result has hardly been a clearer definition of those limits. It is still not clear, for instance, what bases a state can claim for civil commitment. Can a state justify confinement of a nondangerous person merely because the individual would benefit from treatment? Can the state, without treatment, simply confine people who are mentally ill and dangerous? The nature and duration of civil confinement must at least bear a reasonable connection to the purpose for that commitment.

But what are valid state purposes and what types of confinement do they justify? The answers to these questions still await clarification and will eventually be answered, however reluctant the courts are to address them.

As a final observation on the material in this chapter, it should be reemphasized that these civil commitment cases are good examples of American legal process as well as illustrations of important principles of law. As with the other police power cases, articulating the limits on the state's power to civilly commit involves a definition of both the power of government over individual people and the powers of the branches of government with respect to one another. Nowhere can the practical problems of judicial intervention into executive and legislative discretion be better illustrated (with the possible exception of the attempts of the judiciary to enforce school desegregation). Not only do the practical realities of litigation weigh heavily against the enforcement of individual rights such as the "right to treatment," but the ability of the courts to require affirmative remedial steps is both theoretically and practically limited. (*See* further discussion in end notes to this chapter.) In any event, it is important to emphasize that legal rights, at least as defined in these materials, are those both defined by the law and enforceable through the legal system. What is enforceable depends on a number of determinants of legal decision making, not the least of which are the practical realities of litigation.

END NOTES

1. Since this chapter is intended to emphasize the diversity among the states in the scope and structure of civil commitment statutes, as well as the fact that the courts tolerate this diversity, researching a state's civil commitment law can be a good exercise—although one that can be considerably complicated if the search of the state's law includes not only the statute (as most recently amended) but also the state regulations and other administrative interpretations, and the case law that has interpreted the statutory framework.
2. The procedural due process issue is raised in this chapter in order to highlight the difference between "procedural" and "substantive" due process, and to illustrate the deferential attitude of the courts even when enforcing constitutional protections; however, the procedural due process cases could be examined in more depth and used to trace the same pattern illustrated by *Jackson* and the substantive due process cases discussed in the latter section of the chapter: the courts in the late 1960s showed an initial interest in rigorously protecting the constitutional rights of the civilly committed, but that enthusiasm was moderated in later years, particularly in the decisions of the Burger Court. *See, e.g.,* Vitek v. Jones, 445 U.S. 480 (1980); Parham v. J.R.,

442 U.S. 584 (1979); Addington v. Texas, 441 U.S. 418 (1979); In re Gault, 387 U.S. 1 (1967); Specht v. Patterson, 386 U.S. 605 (1967).

For an academic treatment of various issues arising out of civil commitment procedures and some interesting case studies, see D. WEXLER, MENTAL HEALTH LAW: MAJOR ISSUES (1981).

3. For a companion case to *Jackson* and *McNeil* raising slightly different issues but still reflecting the increased willingness of the Supreme Court—at least in the early 1970s—to examine the bases and resulting confinement of civil commitment, see Humphrey v. Cady, 405 U.S. 504 (1972).

4. The dissenting opinion in *Jones*, written by Justice Brennan with the concurrence of Justices Marshall and Blackmun, highlights very well the basic differences between the majority opinion in *Jones* and the more active posture taken by the Court in earlier decisions. Indeed, Justice Brennan's attack on Justice Powell's opinion goes beyond the usual tone of judicial criticism and stops just short of a personal attack. Conversely, a similar illustration of these differences can be found by comparing the narrowly drawn majority opinion in *Donaldson* with the strongly worded concurring opinion of Justice Burger—who seems almost obsessed in his opposition to the notion of a "right to treatment."

5. For the latest round in the on-going *Pennhurst* litigation, see Pennhurst v. Halderman, 104 S. Ct. 900 (1984).

6. For a good analysis and reference to other "right to treatment" cases, see Brandt, *Pennhurst, Romeo, and Rogers: The Burger Court and Mental Health Law Reform* , 4 J. LEGAL MED. 323 (1983). Mills v. Rogers, 457 U.S. 291 (1982), is a particularly good illustration of the reluctance of the Supreme Court, indeed the extreme reluctance, to look at the quality of treatment actually received. The lower court decision, Rogers v. Okin, 478 F. Supp. 1342 (D. Mass. 1979), *aff'd* , 634 F.2d 650 (1st Cir. 1980), raises—and fully examines—a number of issues, although the central focus of the case is on the right of patients to refuse psychiatric treatment. Ironically, the Supreme Court decision in the same litigation goes to the other extreme—clearly side-stepping the major issues and exhibiting the same sort of reluctance to examine the circumstances or conditions of confinement that has become characteristic of the Court in the Burger years.

7. It is important in analyzing all of these cases, but particularly the "right to treatment" cases as illustrated by the *Wyatt* litigation, to emphasize the practical problems and determinants of such litigation. Had discharged employees not been willing to fund a civil lawsuit, Ricky Wyatt's case, however meritorious, might never have been heard. More importantly, if it had not arisen at a time and under circumstances where a number of civil rights and professional groups were willing to underwrite the costs of the extended litigation, the case might have developed very differently (or have been settled more pragmatically), even if it had been pursued by the employees. Conversely, it is questionable whether the resources and interest drawn to the *Wyatt* litigation are always available. "Landmark lawsuits" have a certain attraction. Enforcement of the principles they establish on a state-by-state ba-

sis—an equally expensive proposition—may not have the same appeal.

It is also worth speculating about how the strategy of the lawsuit changes, depending on who sponsors the litigation. *Wyatt* was argued on behalf of the patient-plaintiffs, but it was funded by the employees initially and eventually by various groups largely concerned for the improvement of conditions in mental hospitals. Notably lacking, for instance, is any indication that the sponsors of the litigation would have been willing to urge the court to release the patients or award civil damages for any particular patient. In contrast, in *Donaldson*, the court was asked primarily to award Donaldson retroactive monetary damages (or had he still been confined, to release Donaldson), both of which are arguably much more easily enforceable judicial remedies. More importantly, it is worth considering whether the threat of release of patients or of civil damages has a greater impact on the defendants in a lawsuit, as opposed to the possibility that they will be ordered to provide a better treatment program, as the defendants were in *Wyatt*. In practical terms, a "right to treatment" enforced by the threat of civil damages must have a very different impact than the "right" recognized in *Wyatt*.

For a general discussion of the circumstances under which government officials can be sued for civil damages, see Note: *Civil Rights Suits Against State and Local Government Entities: Rights of Action, Immunities, and Federalism*, 53 S. CAL. L. REV. 945 (1980).

For some background on the circumstances and the results of the *Wyatt* litigation, see WYATT V. STICKNEY: RETROSPECT AND PROSPECT (L. Jones & R. Parlour eds. 1981).

4

The Right to Privacy and Governmental Control over Family Planning Decisions

The government's powers in matters involving health and health care are extensive. As described in earlier chapters, the state government has what are known as police powers, giving the state broad authority to act, inherent in the constitutional basis of the government. The federal government can also act in matters relating to the public's health, although its authority, in theory, is somewhat more prescribed. At the least, its authority must be based on one or more of the explicit provisions of the federal Constitution.

The relationship between the government and the individual in matters relating to health is not entirely one-sided. In chapter 2 a variety of situations were illustrated in which the state's powers to govern its citizens were held not to outweigh certain substantive individual rights. In chapter 3, using civil commitment as an example, other limitations on the government's exercise of power were discussed, specifically the procedural safeguards that the government is required to follow in civil commitment and the right of the individual to require that the government substantively justify the realities of civil confinement in terms that are at least reasonably related to the state purpose served by commitment.

In this chapter the focus will be on the development of another substantive individual right in the health care context, the right to privacy. Chapters 2 and 3 examined certain situations in which the legal system weighs a valid governmental purpose against recognized individual rights. At some point the individual's rights become so important that limitations are imposed on the government's exercise of power. This chapter will examine the right to privacy and how it has been interrelated with attempts by state and, more recently, the federal government to exercise authority over sexual conduct and family planning decisions. This should both illustrate the nature of the right to privacy and, more importantly, define more specifically the form and the nature of the process by which courts weigh state interests against those of individual people.

THE ORIGIN OF THE RIGHT TO PRIVACY

The concept of privacy is difficult to define. It involves at the least a notion of the individual's right to make certain personal decisions without outside interference. But whatever its exact definition, privacy probably has always been a cherished human value; certainly it has been in American society. And with the advent of a more complicated, institutionalized society, privacy has become even more important and essential to the maintenance of individual integrity. There were once areas and activities into which one who sought privacy could escape, but increasingly these outlets are becoming unavailable. In fact, many of our economic and social activities are direct threats to individual privacy, and this has created a series of conflicts often pitting the objectives of society (or one group within society) against the individual's objective of preserving privacy. It is in this type of societal conflict that the law often becomes one—but only one—means by which resolution is attempted.

It should be noted, however, that the importance of privacy has been recognized in the law in some but not all circumstances. The legal rights that define the relationship betweeen one individual and another often reflect a purpose of protecting privacy. The legal recognition of private property is a prime example. The law recognizes the right of the individual to control the possession and the use of certain tangible and intangible things—a house, a business, or even an idea. It recognizes this by prohibiting or requiring certain activities by others or imposing penalties on those who violate these mandates. The law of torts (*see infra* chapter 9) also recognizes and protects privacy in a variety of circumstances; the fact that one individual can sue another for personal assault or defamation is in part based on a notion of privacy. In some jurisdictions any "invasion of privacy" may be an actionable tort and a basis for civil liability.

On the other hand, the protection of individual privacy from governmental interference does not have such a long tradition in the law.

There is no explicit provision recognizing a right to privacy in the Constitution (although at least one state, California, has such a provision in its state constitution). Moreover, until the last decade or so, neither the state legislatures nor Congress had been moved to adopt statutory rights to privacy against government intrusion.

There are, of course, a number of federal constitutional provisions that, arguably, protect certain aspects of privacy. The First Amendment protects the freedom of association and the free exercise of religion from governmental interference; the Fourth Amendment prohibits governmental searches and seizures unless certain conditions exist; even the rarely remembered Third Amendment recognizes the importance of individual privacy by prohibiting the mandatory housing of soldiers in citizens' homes. However, it was not until 1965 that a general constitutional right to privacy protecting the individual from governmental interference was recognized. Before that time privacy was protected from governmental interference only under certain circumstances and in some indirect ways, but privacy had never been recognized as an individual right defining a general relationship between the people and the government. Consequently, the interpretation of the right to privacy and its applications are of recent origin and are still unfolding; but they also provide a good illustration of how modern courts define their role in protecting constitutionally established rights.

THE RIGHT TO PRIVACY: USE OF
CONTRACEPTIVES BY MARRIED PEOPLE

The landmark case that established for the first time an explicit constitutional right to privacy was *Griswold v. Connecticut*, 381 U.S. 479 (1965).

In 1961 the Planned Parenthood League of Connecticut opened a center in New Haven for the distribution of birth control information. After only nine days of operation, Griswold, the Executive Director of Planned Parenthood, as well as the medical director of the clinic were arrested. They were charged with giving information, instruction, and medical advice to married people for the purposes of contraception. In Connecticut at that time it was a crime to use contraceptives:

> Any person who uses any drug, medicinal article or instrument for the purpose of preventing conception shall be fined not less than fifty dollars or imprisoned not less than sixty days nor more than one year or be both fined and imprisoned.

Griswold and the medical director were tried for aiding and abetting this crime and found guilty. They appealed through the state court system to no avail and eventually to the Supreme Court, which accepted jurisdiction. The basic thrust of their appeal was that the law prohibiting the use of contraceptives was in violation of a constitutional right to privacy.

The members of the Supreme Court were rather divided as to the reasoning for their decision, but by a seven-two decision (two separate concurring opinions and two separate dissenting opinions were written in addition to the majority opinion), the Court reversed the criminal convictions and declared the Connecticut law unconstitutional as applied.

Justice William Douglas wrote the majority opinion. He cited a long list of constitutional rights that had been recognized and protected by the Court, despite the fact that these rights were not explicitly defined in the provisions of the Constitution. From these precedents he reasoned:

> The foregoing cases suggest that specific guarantees in the Bill of Rights have penumbras, formed by emanation from those guarantees that help give them life and substance. (citation omitted) Various guarantees create zones of privacy. The right of association contained in the penumbra of the First Amendment is one, as we have seen. The Third Amendment in its prohibition against the quartering of soldiers "in any house" in time of peace without the consent of the owner is another facet of that privacy. The Fourth Amendment explicitly affirms the "right of the people to be secure in their persons, houses, papers, and effects, against unreasonable searches and seizures." The Fifth Amendment in its Self-Incrimination Clause enables the citizen to create a zone of privacy which government may not force him to surrender to his detriment. The Ninth Amendment provides: "The enumeration in the Constitution, of certain rights, shall not be construed to deny or disparage others retained by the people."

> The Fourth and Fifth Amendments were described . . . as protections against all governmental invasions "of the sanctity of a man's home and the privacies of life." We recently referred . . . to the Fourth Amendment as creating a "right to privacy, no less important than any other right carefully and particularly reserved to the people."(citation omitted)

> We have had many controversies over these penumbral rights of "privacy and repose. . . ." (citation omitted) These cases bear witness that the right of privacy which presses for recognition here is a legitimate one.

> The present case, then, concerns a relationship lying within the zone of privacy created by several fundamental constitutional guarantees. And it concerns a law which, in forbidding the *use* of contraceptives

rather than regulating their manufacture or sale, seeks to achieve its goals by means having a maximum destructive impact upon that relationship. Such a law cannot stand in light of the familiar principle, so often applied by this Court, that a "governmental purpose to control or prevent activities constitutionally subject to state regulation may not be achieved by means which sweep unnecessarily broadly and thereby invade the area of protected freedoms." (citation omitted) Would we allow the police to search the sacred precincts of marital bedrooms for tell tale signs of the use of contraceptives? The very idea is repulsive to the notions of privacy surrounding the marriage relationship.

We deal with a right of privacy older than the Bill of Rights—older than our political parties, older than our school system. Marriage is a coming together for better or for worse, hopefully enduring, and intimate to the degree of being sacred. It is an association that promotes a way of life, not causes; a harmony in living, not political faiths; a bilateral loyalty, not commercial or social projects. Yet it is an association for as noble a purpose as any involved in prior decisions.

Justice Douglas's opinion was not unusual in its logic. He recognized that the proper role of the judiciary is not to interfere with the legislative process unless it is necessary to protect a constitutional right. In keeping with judicial traditions, the state legislature should be allowed wide discretion under its police powers to regulate most economic and social activities, particularly those that relate to health. In fact, the opinion specifically recognized the right of the state to regulate the use of contraceptives. However, where the exercise of authority by the state interferes too greatly with a constitutional right, "sweep[s] unnecessarily broadly," it infringes on that right, the exercise of power is beyond constitutional limits, and the courts must intervene.

The unusual nature of the opinion was that it created, or at least recognized for the first time, a new constitutional right. And not only did the *Griswold* case create a right to privacy with far-reaching implications, it also suggested the possibility that other rights might be found in the penumbral light of the specific guarantees of the Constitution. Although in many situations the Court has had to look to the implications of the explicit provisions of the Constitution in order to apply those provisions to a given set of circumstances, rarely has any case been so explicit—or so graphic—in finding that there are rights implied in the Constitution.

But having recognized for the first time a right to privacy, *Griswold* interpreted only one application of this right and gave only an outline of its nature. The majority opinion speaks generally of "zones of privacy" and specifically of one of these zones, sexual activity between married people. The opinion does not claim that the state cannot invade this zone of privacy in any way; it implies, at least, that the state could regulate the sale or manufacture of contraceptives; however, the state cannot directly prohibit the use of contraceptives since by doing so it interferes too greatly with the privacy of married people.

What was crucial to this case and to future applications of the right to privacy was the holding that where important constitutional rights such as the right to privacy are involved, the courts must actively question the justification for the exercise of state power and the method by which the state seeks to achieve that justification. And where that power "sweeps too broadly" or has a "maximum destructive impact," the courts must intervene and invalidate that legislation.

In *Griswold*, finding that such an individual right was interfered with, the Court examined the legislation and found no governmental interest that could not be achieved through less invasive means. It therefore invalidated the state legislation and the criminal prosecution of Griswold.

THE RIGHT TO PRIVACY: GIVING CONTRACEPTIVES TO SINGLE PEOPLE

The *Griswold* case had a nationwide impact and many state legislatures amended their state statutes to conform to the apparent dictates of the *Griswold* opinion. Among these states was Massachusetts.

Prior to the *Griswold* decision, among the "Crimes Against Chastity, Morality, Decency, and Good Order" defined in the Massachusetts criminal statutes was the following:

> [Anyone who] . . . sells, lends, gives away, exhibits, offers to sell, lend or give away . . . any drug, medicine, instrument, or article whatever for the prevention of conception or for causing unlawful abortion, or advertises the same, or writes, prints, or causes to be written or printed a card, circular, book, pamphlet, advertisement or notice of any kind stating when, where, how, of whom, or by what means such article can be purchased or obtained, or manufactures or makes any such article shall be punished by imprisonment in the state prison for not more than five years or in jail or the house of corrections for not more than two and one half years or by a fine of not less than one hundred nor more than one thousand dollars.

After the *Griswold* case that statute was amended by the state legislature to make an exception for contraceptives given to a married individual by a physician or a pharmacist with a prescription. In effect, contraceptives were to be treated as prescription drugs available only to married people.

A fair reading of the *Griswold* case immediately after its decision might have led to the conclusion that the Massachusetts law as amended might still be valid. Certainly Douglas' glittering praise of the marital relationship left a clear impression that it was sexual conduct within the association of marriage that was the zone of privacy protected by the Constitution. Moreover, there was the implication in the decision that the state could regulate contraception in some ways, including the use by unmarried people. But such an inference, however reasonable, was soon to be invalidated in *Eisenstadt v. Baird*, 405 U.S. 438 (1972).

William Baird's name has been associated with a number of social causes, and in the late 1960s he was renowned in Massachusetts for his crusades to free birth control from the strict legal restraints imposed in that state. He openly violated these laws and eventually forced his own prosecution in order to challenge their constitutionality.

Thomas Eisenstadt was also a man with a cause, but in his case the purpose was to further his own political career. As the elected sheriff of a county with a large Catholic population, it was only natural that he would be eager to prosecute Baird.

In May of 1967, Baird gave a lecture on birth control at Boston University. His presentation included exhibits and displays of contraceptive devices, and after his address he invited members of the audience to help themselves to available samples. Baird was approached by an unmarried woman, and he personally handed her a can of vaginal foam. At that point Sheriff Eisenstadt's conveniently placed police officers arrested Baird.

Baird was charged with both exhibiting contraceptives and giving contraceptives to an unmarried person in violation of the statute cited above. He was tried and convicted. He appealed through the state court system; the Massachusetts Supreme Judicial Court reversed the conviction for exhibiting contraceptives as violative of Baird's right to free speech secured by the First Amendment to the Constitution. The court upheld his conviction for the giving of contraceptives.

Baird filed a writ of habeas corpus in federal court. (This is one means of appealing a state court conviction on grounds that it violates the Constitution.) His appeal was dismissed in the federal district court, but in the federal circuit court of appeals Baird was successful, and the court ordered him released. Sheriff Eisenstadt then appealed to the Supreme Court.

As interpreted by Justice Brennan, writing for the majority, Baird's argument essentially challenged the constitutionality of the Massachusetts statute under the equal protection clause of the Constitution. (*See* chapter 5 for a more detailed analysis of equal protection.)

Examining the statute according to the principles of equal protection as then interpreted by the Court, Justice Brennan held that "the question for determination in this case is whether there is some ground of difference that rationally explains the different treatment accorded married and unmarried people under [the Massachusetts statute]." He then reasoned that if the purpose of the Massachusetts statute were to regulate dangerous health-related devices, one of Eisenstadt's claims, not only would the statute be based on the erroneous assumption that all contraceptive devices can be dangerous, but there would be the patent absurdity that only unmarried people are protected from the danger. The statute would therefore be unnecessarily broad and discriminatory.

If the purpose of the statute were to deter premarital sex, which the state also argued, then there would also be some inherent contradictions in the statute. First of all, it would be an attempt to deter premarital sex by punishing those who commit the act with pregnancy. In addition, the Court stated: "Aside from the scheme of values that assumption would attribute to the State, it is abundantly clear that the effect of the ban on the distribution of contraceptives to unmarried people has at best a marginal relation to the proffered objective."

The Court also pointed to the irony of a contraceptive law that proposed to regulate premarital sex, but apparently did not discourage extramarital sex. In addition, the Court noted that contraceptives were legal in Massachusetts as long as they were used for the prevention of, disease but not when they were used to prevent conception.

Finally, the Court pointed to perhaps the most ludicrous aspect of the statute. In Massachusetts fornication is only a misdemeanor punishable by a $30 dollar fine or 90 days in jail. If the purpose of the contraceptive law were to prohibit premarital sex, it is rather strange that aiding the crime is a serious felony while the crime itself is a misdemeanor.

The Court reasoned, therefore, that the real purpose of the statute was an attempt to prohibit contraception itself, a codification of the value that contraception is immoral; the only reason the statute was directed solely at premarital sexual relations is that the state was constitutionally forbidden after *Griswold* from extending this prohibition to married people. The question for the Court was, assuming this was the purpose of the statute, could the state prohibit the use of contraceptives by the unmarried as immoral?

The Court, somewhat surprisingly, declined to answer the question.

> We need not and do not, however, decide that important question in this case because, whatever the rights of the individual to access to contraceptives may be, the rights must be the same for the unmarried and the married alike.

If under *Griswold* the distribution of contraceptives to married persons cannot be prohibited, a ban on distribution to unmarried persons would be equally impermissible. It is true that in *Griswold* the right of privacy in question inhered in the marital relationship. Yet the marital couple is not an independent entity with a mind and heart of its own, but an association of two individuals each with a separate intellectual and emotional makeup. If the right of privacy means anything, it is the right of the *individual* married or single, to be free from unwarranted governmental intrusion into matters so fundamentally affecting a person as the decision whether to bear or beget a child. See *Stanley v. Georgia*, 394 U.S. 557 (1969). See also *Skinner v. Oklahoma*, 316 U.S. 535 (1942); *Jacobson v. Massachusetts*, 197 U.S. 11, 29 (1905).

On the other hand, if *Griswold* is no bar to a prohibition on the distribution of contraceptives, the State could not, consistently with the Equal Protection Clause, outlaw distribution to unmarried but not to married persons. In each case the evil, as perceived by the State, would be identical, and the underinclusion would be invidious.

Justice Brennan's equal protection analysis in *Baird* was rather convoluted and somewhat contradictory. He claimed he was only testing the state legislation to see if it had a rational basis, implying a limited judicial role. In fact, his examination of the statute and its relation to valid state purposes has to be viewed as much more demanding. Indeed, in terms that later would be adopted by the Court, Brennan clearly was "closely scrutinizing" the legislation (*see Roe v. Wade*, next section, and chapter 5). Nonetheless the decision, whatever its internal logic, in essence established two very important principles. First of all, it recognized that the right to privacy protected by the federal Constitution, however it is fully defined, at least includes the decisions of unmarried people concerning contraception and, perhaps, other sexual activities. Second, it clearly established that when the right to privacy is involved, the Court will be willing to examine the legislative discretion of the state closely and rather suspiciously, accepting the rationale of the state only when, in the Court's view, it actually serves a valid state purpose and does so with a minimal impact on individual privacy.

The Court was soon to be deciding other cases further clarifying both the substantive definition of the right to privacy and the role of the courts in its protection.

THE RIGHT TO PRIVACY:
THE 1973 ABORTION CASES

In the late 1960s and early 1970s in several parts of the country there were a number of legal attacks on state laws that attempted to prohibit or greatly restrict the availability of voluntary abortions. Some of these suits were successful; others were not. All were controversial. Finally in 1972 the issue found its way to the Supreme Court in the companion cases of *Roe v. Wade*, 410 U.S. 113 (1973), and *Doe v. Bolton*, 410 U.S. 179 (1973).

In *Roe v. Wade* a single woman suing under the assumed name of Jane Roe challenged the constitutionality of the Texas abortion statute which made procuring or attempting an abortion except for the purpose of saving the life of the mother a felony. Roe claimed that the statute infringed on her constitutional right to privacy, citing the analogous decisions in *Griswold* and *Eisenstadt* as support. The state defended its statute with the argument that the prohibition of all but "medically necessary" abortions was a valid exercise of the state's police powers in a matter relating to the public's health. Once again the Court was faced with the task of balancing the exercise of state authority against the allegation that it infringed on an individual constitutional right.

Much as it had in its earlier right to privacy decisions, the Court in *Roe* began its decision with an analysis of the extent of the state's authority and the purposes achieved by the statute. Justice Blackmun, writing for the majority, started with a long account of the legal controls that have been exercised over abortion decisions throughout history, beginning as early as the Persian, Greek, and Roman empires, tracing these controls through their development over the centuries in the English common law and comparing these controls to the legal restraints imposed in many states. In every case he found that abortions were much more freely available in other times and other societies than under American criminal abortion statutes of which the Texas law was typical. Blackmun then detailed the official opinions on abortion of the American Medical Association, the American Public Health Association, and the American Bar Association with their criticisms of the restrictive policies reflected in those criminal statutes.

Blackmun was not, of course, suggesting that the law of other societies or the opinions of professional associations have any direct precedential effect on interpretations of American law. He was, however, emphasizing the point that the restrictions placed on abortion in states such as Texas were neither traditional, based on long experience, nor above criticism. Furthermore, since the police powers of the state are defined as those powers traditionally considered inherent in government (*see* chapter 2), it is at least relevant to look at these other societies and, particularly, the English common law from which our legal system developed.

But more than anything else, Blackmun's long historical introduction was a tacit acknowledgment of the obvious emotional and political overtones of this case; with the extent of public attention drawn to this case, it is understandable that the opinion would go into elaborate and somewhat unnecessary detail to demonstrate that the decision was given very careful consideration by the Court.

Having placed the issue in its proper historical and political perspective, the opinion then turned to the Texas statute and the purposes that could be cited as supporting this exercise of power. Blackmun first found that there were two principal bases that could be cited as valid purposes for restricting abortion decisions: (1) protecting the mother from a dangerous risk to her health and (2) protecting prenatal life.

On the other hand, Blackmun found that the "zones of privacy" protected by the Constitution included the right of a woman to terminate her pregnancy and that, therefore, there was an important constitutional right at stake. Given these conflicting interests, both of which are important but neither of which is absolute, the Court proceeded with the following analysis:

> [T]he State does have an important and legitimate interest in preserving and protecting the health of the pregnant woman . . . [and] it has still another important and legitimate interest in protecting the potentiality of human life. These interests are separate and distinct. Each grows in substantiality as the woman approaches term and, at a point during pregnancy, each becomes "compelling."
>
> With respect to the State's important and legitimate interest in the health of the mother, the "compelling" point, in the light of present medical knowledge, is at approximately the end of the first trimester. This is so because of the now established medical fact . . . that until the end of the first trimester mortality in abortion may be less than mortality in normal childbirth. It follows that, from and after this point, a state may regulate the abortion procedure to the extent that the regulation reasonably relates to the preservation and protection of maternal health. Examples of permissible state regulation in this area are requirements as to the qualifications of the person who is to perform the abortion; as to the licensure of that person; as to the facility in which the procedure is to be performed, that is, whether it must be a hospital or may be a clinic or some other place of less-than-hospital status; as to the licensing of the facility; and the like.
>
> This means, on the other hand, that, for the period of pregnancy prior to this "compelling" point, the attending physician, in consultation with his patient, is free to determine, without regulation by the State, that, in his medical judgment the patient's pregnancy should be terminated. If that decision is reached, the judgment may be effectuated by an abortion free of interference by the State.

With respect to the State's important and legitimate interest in potential life, the "compelling" point is at viability. This is so because the fetus then presumably has the capability of meaningful life outside the mother's womb. State regulation protective of fetal life after viability thus has both logical and biological justifications. If the State is interested in protecting fetal life after viability, it may go so far as to proscribe abortion during that period, except when it is necessary to preserve the life or health of the mother.

This balancing of interests relies on two critical conclusions. The first is that the state's interest in protecting "life" must be a protection of individual people, not the unborn or the "potentiality" of a person. The state can have an interest in protecting property and other "non-person" interests, but in order to justify the infringement of an individual constitutional right as a protection of "life," as in this case the invasion of a woman's right to privacy, the state must justify its exercise of power as for the protection of a living person.

The second critical conclusion is that a fetus becomes a living person only after it becomes viable, i.e., capable of life outside of the mother's womb; based on the status of medical knowledge at that time, this was after approximately 24 to 28 weeks of pregnancy.

Based on these conclusions, the Court in *Roe* effectively developed guidelines for states to follow in regulating abortions. During the first trimester a state cannot justify regulation of a woman's right to terminate her pregnancy on any grounds (except to the extent that it regulates medical procedures generally). There is no viable fetus; there is no risk to her health; there are always some risks to any medical procedure, but in order to regulate this particular procedure, the state would have to have some grounds for regulating this procedure more strictly than it does other medical procedures. If anything, a first trimester abortion is safer than many surgical procedures and, according to the evidence presented to the Court, safer than the delivery of a baby.

After the first trimester of pregnancy, but before viability, the state can regulate abortion in some ways, but, again, only if the regulation is reasonably related to the protection of maternal health. Thus, as Blackmun suggests, although prohibiting abortion would be overly broad and not a reasonable attempt to protect the mother, regulating the facilities where the procedure is performed or setting the qualifications of whoever performs abortions might be reasonable and constitutionally acceptable.

However, in the third trimester, the state can regulate abortion and prohibit it altogether, since at that point the fetus becomes viable and, therefore, a life, and the protection of the life of an individual person is a compelling, if not a paramount, state purpose. The only exception listed by the Court is that a state may not proscribe abortion if it is necessary to preserve the life or the health of the mother.

In the companion case of *Doe v. Bolton* the Georgia criminal abortion statute was challenged by "Mary Doe." That law declared the performance of an abortion a crime unless performed by a physician and, "based upon his best clinical judgment," the abortion was "necessary" because of (1) the risk of permanent and serious injury to the mother, (2) the likelihood that the fetus if born would be physically or mentally defective, or (3) the fact that the pregnancy was a result of rape.

However, even with the consenting judgment of her physician, a woman was allowed a legal abortion under Georgia law only if a number of other conditions also were satisfied. These conditions included requirements that (1) two other physicians concur in writing with the first physician's judgment, based on independent medical examinations; (2) the abortion be performed in a hospital licensed by the state health department and accredited by the Joint Commission on Accreditation of Hospitals; and (3) the procedure be approved by a committee of no fewer than three members of the hospital's medical staff.

The decision in *Roe v. Wade* held that any statute that prohibits abortion in the first two trimesters of pregnancy is unconstitutional. Therefore the portion of the Georgia statute limiting legal abortions to those where the mother was endangered, the fetus defective, or the pregnancy a result of rape was invalid. The more difficult issue presented by *Doe* was whether the second portion of the Georgia statute requiring professional concurrence in the abortion and regulating the setting in which an abortion can take place was valid. In each of the previous right to privacy cases the Supreme Court had indicated that the state could exercise its power to regulate family planning decisions. Even where it interferes with individual privacy, regulation can be constitutional, as long as the regulation is reasonable and does not interfere too greatly with the constitutional right to privacy. In *Roe v. Wade* the Court had specifically upheld the right of the state to regulate abortion decisions and the conditions under which they could be performed, as long as the regulation was reasonably related to a legitimate state purpose such as the protection of maternal health.

That was exactly the issue before the Court in *Doe v. Bolton*. Were the conditions imposed on legal abortions in Georgia reasonably related to a legitimate state purpose? How far would the Court go in examining the exact nature of an attempt to regulate abortion decisions? The message that was delivered in the opinion was very clear: the right to privacy is important enough that the courts will look rather closely at any exercise of state power that infringes on a protected zone of privacy and will examine almost skeptically the state's underlying justification and the means by which it is carried out. In this case, the Court held that the conditions imposed by Georgia on abortion decisions were not reasonably related to any legitimate state purpose.

The requirements that abortions be performed only in hospitals that are licensed by the state and accredited by the JCAH were held invalid because there was no reasonable relationship between these requirements and the state's legitimate interest in protecting the health of the mother or regulating the quality of medical care. JCAH accreditation involves only a general evaluation of a hospital and not an evaluation of the hospital's capabilities to perform abortions. Therefore, there was no reason to restrict abortions to only JCAH hospitals when other forms of nonabortion hospital care are not similarly restricted. The Court also found no showing by the state that only licensed hospitals were suitable for abortions, when, to the contrary, there was a great deal of evidence presented throughout the case that abortions under some circumstances could easily and safely be performed in other health facilities.

With respect to the requirement of the concurring approval of a hospital committee prior to an abortion in Georgia, the Court found no reasonable basis for this condition either. The Court again held that the state had shown no reason for treating abortion differently from other medical or surgical decisions:

> We conclude that the interposition of the hospital abortion committee is unduly restrictive of the patient's rights and needs that, at this point, have already been medically delineated and substantiated by her personal physician. To ask more serves neither the hospital nor the State.

The Court then went on to the third condition imposed by the Georgia statute:

> There remains, however, the required confirmation by two Georgia-licensed physicians in addition to the recommendation of the pregnant woman's own consultant (making under the statute, a total of six physicians involved, including the three on the hospital's abortion committee). We conclude that this provision, too, must fall.
>
> The statute's emphasis, as has been repetitively noted, is on the attending physician's "best clinical judgment that an abortion is necessary." That should be sufficient. The reasons for the presence of the confirmation step in the statute are perhaps apparent, but they are insufficient to withstand constitutional challenge. Again, no other voluntary medical or surgical procedure for which Georgia requires confirmation by two other physicians has been cited to us. If a physician is licensed by the State, he is recognized by the State as capable of exercising acceptable clinical judgment. If he fails in this, professional censure and depri-

vation of his license are available remedies. Required acquiescence by co-practitioners has no rational connection with a patient's needs and unduly infringes on the physician's right to practice. The attending physician will know when a consultation is advisable—the doubtful situation, the need for assurance when the medical decision is a delicate one, and the like. Physicians have followed this routine historically and know its usefulness and benefits to all concerned. It is still true today that "[r]eliance must be placed upon the assurance given by his license, issued by an authority competent to judge in that respect, that he [the physician] possesses the requisite qualifications."

APPLICATION OF THE 1973 DECISIONS

Since *Roe* and *Doe*, the authority of the courts to closely scrutinize legislation prohibiting or limiting access to abortions has been consistently upheld by the Supreme Court. (The Court has, however, defined the courts' role more conservatively with regard to federal and state decisions not to provide funding for abortions; *see* chapter 5.) Only where this judicial examination finds that the state has a compelling interest has the Court allowed state legislation to interfere with the fundamental interest of privacy involved in abortion decisions. Understandably, few state efforts have survived such rigorous judicial examination.

This judicial protection of the right to privacy and autonomy in abortion decisions has hardly defused the underlying political controversy. Many states and some local communities have made considerable —and, in some cases, rather ingenious—efforts to fashion restrictive abortion legislation that attempts to steer just clear of the judicially imposed constraints on their authority. And critics, both in academia and in the halls of practical politics, have taken every opportunity to voice the opinion that the courts have "gone too far" into legislative prerogatives in their abortion decisions.

Nonetheless, the courts, led by a number of Supreme Court rulings, have consistently taken an aggressive posture in reviewing abortion-restrictive legislation. In *Planned Parenthood of Missouri v. Danforth*, 428 U.S. 52 (1976), for example, legislation was enacted following the 1973 abortion decisions that legalized abortions in that state as required by *Roe* and *Doe*, but imposed a long list of conditions on providers who performed them, including (1) the requirement that a woman must consent in writing to the abortion and certify that the consent is "informed and freely given and not the result of coercion," (2) the requirement that the consent of a parent be given for a woman under the age of 18, (3) the requirement of the written consent of the husband of any married woman, and (4) the prohibition of the use of saline amniocentesis after the first trimester of pregnancy.

Again with elaborate detail, the Supreme Court examined the underlying state purposes cited as justifying each of these conditions in light of the privacy interest that was affected. The Court held that the state could impose a condition requiring that the woman give written and informed consent. (There were no statutory requirements for informed consent for other surgical procedures in Missouri, but informed consent would have been required by the common law of that jurisdiction. *See* note at end of chapter 9.) In doing so, however, the Court noted that this requirement of consent had very little impact on the exercise of the woman's autonomy. But the Court struck down the requirements of parental and spousal consent. Spousal consent, according to the *Danforth* decision, would allow the state legislature to give the husband a unilateral veto, a power which the Constitution would not allow to the state itself. Whatever interest the state had in protecting the interests of the husband could not outweigh the privacy interest of the woman seeking the abortion. And while the Court recognized that the state also had an interest in protecting immature minors and in safeguarding the integrity of families, the Court ruled that such interests could not be carried out by a requirement of parental consent imposed on all women of a particular age: ". . . Any independent interest the parent may have in the termination of the minor daughter's pregnancy is no more weighty than the right of privacy of the competent minor mature enough to have become pregnant."

With regard to the proscription of saline amniocentesis as an abortion procedure after the first trimester, using logic similar to that followed in *Doe*, the Court held that the state did have a compelling interest in protecting maternal health, but that there was no reasonable connection between maternal health and a prohibition on the use of a procedure that was shown to be commonly used and, in terms of maternal mortality, even safer than carrying a child to term.

The Supreme Court's most recent pronouncements on the abortion issue still demonstrate the insistence by the Court that the fundamental right of privacy involved in abortion decisions requires that the judiciary jealously oversee legislative attempts to limit or prohibit the exercise of that right. *City of Akron v. Akron Center for Reproductive Health*, 462 U.S. 416 (1983), involved a municipal ordinance that (1) required all abortions after the first trimester to be performed in a hospital, (2) required the consent of a parent for a minor under the age of 15 or of a court having jurisdiction over the minor, (3) required a physician to explain to the patient the status of her pregnancy, the development of her fetus, the date of possible viability, the physical and emotional complications involved, and the alternatives to abortion (e.g., adoption), and (4) prohibited abortions until after a 24 hour waiting period following the woman's written consent.

Even acknowledging the critics of its earlier decisions, the Court, nonetheless, stayed its decade-long course. The hospital-only requirement was invalidated. The Court pointed to the general use of dilatation and evacuation procedures in nonhospital settings and found no showing by the state that the hospital-only requirement furthered any governmental interest in maternal health. The Court also struck down the parental consent rule:

> [A] State's interest in protecting immature minors will sustain a requirement of a consent substitute, either parental or judicial. . . . [H]owever . . . the State must provide an alternative procedure whereby a pregnant minor may demonstrate that she is sufficiently mature to make the abortion decision herself or that, despite her immaturity, an abortion would be in her best interests. (citation omitted) . . . [I]t is clear that Akron may not make a blanket determination that *all* minors under the age of 15 are too immature to make this decision or that an abortion never may be in the minor's best interests without parental approval.

(Akron had no existing judicial procedure for determining either maturity or a minor's best interests in such situations).

The Court also invalidated the requirement that the informed consent be provided by a physician and that the consent be followed by a 24-hour waiting period. Again, the Court closely scrutinized the purposes for requiring informed consent and for conditioning the circumstances under which it would be obtained and found that there was no compelling interest in imposing these requirements on abortion decisions if they were not imposed on other surgical procedures as well.

In one of the companion cases to *Akron*, *Planned Parenthood v. Ashcroft*, 462 U.S. 476 (1983), Missouri had revised its abortion legislation following the decisions in *Danforth*. The revised statute still attempted to limit the availability of abortions by requiring (1) that second trimester abortions be performed only in hospitals, (2) that pathology reports be prepared on every abortion, (3) that a second physician participate in any abortion after viability, and (4) that unemancipated minors under the age of 18 secure either parental consent or judicial consent.

As in *Akron*, the Court struck down Missouri's hospital-only requirement but it upheld the other conditions created by the Missouri legislation. Justice Powell, speaking for a Court that appeared to be somewhat more divided on these issues than it had been in other cases, held that with postviability abortions the state had a compelling interest in the life of the fetus which was served by the requirement of a second physician. The pathology report requirement was also upheld because it furthered the state's interest in maternal health and it required little more of abortion procedures than the state required of other surgical procedures. (Missouri required pathology reports for all surgical procedures in hospitals; the abortion requirement applied to clinic abortions as well as those in hospitals.)

As to the controversial consent provisions, the Court reaffirmed its position that the state could require parental consent for immature minors, but only where the minor had an opportunity to demonstrate that she was mature or, if immature, that the abortion would still be in her best interests. But unlike the ordinance *Akron*, which did not provide such an opportunity, the Court concluded that Missouri law gave this opportunity to all minors and therefore that a parental consent requirement for unemancipated minors under the age of 18 could be validly imposed.

In the third of the 1983 decisions, *Simpoulos v. Virginia*, 462 U.S. 506 (1983), the Court also outlined conditions that could be constitutionally imposed on abortion. Virginia law limits second trimester abortions to hospitals or clinics licensed by the state. The Court held, ostensibly reaffirming its decision in *Doe*, that the state's compelling interest in maternal health did allow reasonable regulation of the setting where abortions take place and that, unlike a hospital-only requirement, limiting abortions to hospitals or to certain clinics was within the constitutional limits on state legislative discretion.

IMPLICATIONS OF THE
RIGHT TO PRIVACY CASES

The general consistency of the Court's rulings in these cases over the last ten years should guide future interpretation of abortion-restrictive legislation into at least the next decade. Judicial attitudes do change, both collectively and individually, and as a consequence, legal principles and their applications can be changed as well. But this line of cases rather firmly establishes the legal principles that define the protection to be given to individual autonomy in abortion decisions and the Court's general view of the relationship between the state and the individual, principles that are likely to be upheld for some time to come.

Clearly any state government activity must be within the broadly defined police powers. As was shown in *Jacobson* and its progeny, at the least the state must show a reasonable relationship between what it purports to do and the health, safety, welfare, or, in some cases, morals of the public; and, as illustrated by the "right to treatment" cases, our notion of substantive due process, the constitutional requirement of fundamental fairness, requires that in any application of the police powers there must be a reasonable connection between the state's purpose and the means chosen to achieve that purpose.

The abortion cases demonstrate that in circumstances where the state in exercising its valid powers interferes with certain constitutionally protected individual rights, the role of the court goes beyond simply requiring that the state be within its police powers and that the exercise of that power be reasonable. When what the Court now calls "fundamental interests" are at stake, a court should take a more active posture and require that the state show that it has a "compelling interest," and it should closely scrutinize both the relationship between that state interest and the legislative means by which the state attempts to further it, and the impact on the fundamental interest.

In functional terms, close scrutiny effectively puts the burden on the state to convince the court that there is a reasonable connection between the state's purpose and the state's means; and it requires that where the state legislation "interferes too greatly," or "sweeps unnecessarily broadly," or can be carried out by "less drastic means," the court must invalidate that legislation.

But while the rhetorical expression of the proper standard for judicial review of legislation that interferes with fundamental rights is critical to an understanding of these cases, the rhetoric of close scrutiny states only the underlying issues that must be addressed and, in some ways, imposes a kind of superficial clarity that probably does not exist. In applying this rhetoric and in resolving the issues that these cases raise, legal doctrine is both complicated and controversial. At best, establishing the proper manner in which to express the legal issues that the courts must address only clarifies appropriate questions, not their answers.

What is at stake here is power, the power of the government over the individual, the power of the government as distributed among its institutional branches. The abortion cases delineate that power in a range of circumstances and do so with considerable consistency. But given the importance of the interests that are at stake, it should not be surprising that at best they only suggest the outcome of decisions, even those involving very similar circumstances, in the years that come.

In defining the scope of the police powers, in adjudging the reasonableness of the connection between the state's purpose and the means for achieving it, and, most particularly, in interpreting the courts' role as implied by the requirement of "close scrutiny," it is helpful to consider again the distinction between judicially liberal and judicially conservative philosophy. The willingness of some courts and of some judges to view the judicial role broadly, to review the validity of executive and legislative decisions rigorously, or to identify fundamental interests and, therefore, protect them from governmental interference, reflects as much individual judicial philosophy as the dictates of legal doctrine or legal tradition. What is regarded as a judicial liberal tends to take an expansive view of the court's role in making these determinations. Thus a judicial liberal is more likely to recognize that fundamental interests are at stake and, consequently, to subject state legislation to rather rigorous review. A judicial conservative, on the other hand, tends to view the proper definition of the judicial role more narrowly, in the sense that he or she is less likely to recognize that a given set of circumstances represents interference with a fundamental interest and is therefore more likely to defer to the discretion of the state or local legislatures.

This distinction between judicial philosophies, though critical to an understanding of judicial decision making, is far more complicated than simply a distinction between liberals and conservatives. Judges who tend to be liberal in defining individual fundamental interests may be more conservative in their attitudes when property or economic interests are at stake, as suggested in the analysis of the *Lochner* and *Jacobson* cases in chapter 2, and as will be considered again in chapter 6. Moreover, the liberal or conservative label tends to be an epithet more often than a self-declaration; few judges will admit openly to being either. More often they will claim to be merely following the dictates of their constitutionally prescribed role. And, of course, some judges are simply inconsistent in their judicial philosophies, or at least they appear to be so.

In the next chapter the power of the state over the individual and the power of the courts vis-à-vis the legislatures will be further examined, as will this distinction between liberal and conservative judicial attitudes and its influence on legal doctrine.

END NOTES

1. For a good "insider's view" of the process by which the Supreme Court justices, both individually and collectively, developed their opinions in the right to privacy cases, see B. WOODWARD & S. ARMSTRONG, THE BRETHREN: THE INSIDE STORY OF THE SUPREME COURT (1979).

2. There was a peripheral, but nonetheless important, standing question raised in the earlier contraceptive and abortion cases. In each of these cases, the individual subject to criminal prosecution was claiming to be protected from the state activity because of the right to privacy of other people, e.g., Baird was opposing his conviction on the basis of the right to privacy of single people using or receiving contraceptives. For a discussion of the standing issues, see Roe v. Wade, 410 U.S. 113, 123–29 (1973), Eisenstadt v. Baird, 405 U.S. 438, 443–46 (1972), Griswold v. Connecticut, 381 U.S. 479, 481 (1965).

3. *Roe v. Wade* and the cases that follow it rely heavily on the notion of viability and the conclusion that viability begins at approximately the end of the second trimester. Marking viability as the beginning of the point where the state's interest becomes "compelling" (as chapter 5 will demonstrate, the state has an interest prior to that point, but it is not "compelling") is itself an interesting legal distinction. But it is also worth considering what will happen as the technology to sustain a fetus outside of the womb becomes more sophisticated and the point of viability becomes increasingly earlier in pregnancy.

4. It is also worth noting that in both *Roe* and *Doe* the opinion makes reference to the "right" of a physician to practice. This dicta has not gone unnoticed by the medical profession. In fact, on repeated occasions both state and national medical associations have challenged various governmental restrictions on their practice or reimbursement, arguing that the abortion cases recognized a physician's right to practice as a fundamental interest. *See, e.g., North Carolina v. Califano, infra* chapter 6. *See also* Association of Am. Phys. & Surg. v. Weinberger, 395 F. Supp. 125 (N.D. Ill. 1975), *aff'd*, 423 U.S. 975 (1976). Not unexpectedly, no court has recognized a right to practice as a fundamental interest. *See also* end note 4 to chapter 5.

5. Clearly the issue that has given the Supreme Court the most trouble involves the requirement of parental consent for minors. In addition to the 1983 decisions summarized in this chapter, see Bellotti v. Baird, 443 U.S. 622 (1979). *See also* Planned Parenthood of Mo. v. Danforth, 428 U.S. 52, 72-75 (1976).

6. Even though the Court has been relatively consistent in the abortion cases over an extended period of time, it must also be noted that by 1983 there are some signs of a growing dissention on the Supreme Court with regard to the Court's attitude towards abortion legislation. The various concurring and dissenting opinions in *Ashcroft*, for instance, indicate that some members of the Court would sharply limit the role of the courts; yet others would exercise even greater control over state legislative discretion.

7. While the abortion cases are obviously important in their own right, they are included in these materials as an illustration of the "fundamental interest/close scrutiny" test of legislation. One way to understand the application of this test and how it distributes power among the branches of government is to consider how it might (or might not) be applied to similar but distinct areas of the law. An excellent example, and one which has not been clearly decided by the courts, is the criminal prosecution of homosexual conduct. Is there a fundamental interest at stake? If so, the courts would closely scrutinize the legislative purposes, demanding the state show it has a "compelling interest" and that the connection between the purpose and the criminal statute is at least reasonable. If not, the review of the legislation and its purposes would be less demanding. For examples of how these questions have been addressed, see Doe v. City of Richmond, 403 F. Supp. 1199 (E.D. Va. 1975), *aff'd*, 425 U.S. 901 (1976), *reh'g denied*, 425 U.S. 985 (1976); *cf.* State v. J.O., 69 N.J. 574, 355 A.2d 195 (1976).

It is also not clear whether the Court considers medical care decisions sufficiently "private" to warrant close scrutiny. *See* Rutherford v. United States, 442 U.S. 544 (1979).

8. In *Roe v. Wade* the Court said "if the state is interested in protecting fetal life after viability, it may go so far as to proscribe abortion during that period, except when it is necessary to preserve the life or health of the mother." This language apparently gives the state the option, "it may go so far . . .," although if it does exercise that option it must make exception for maternal health or life. 410 U.S. at 163–64.

It is hard to imagine a state making the choice *not* to proscribe postviability abortions (and presumably such abortions might be subject to prosecution as homicide). Most states do proscribe such abortions, although they make exception for circumstances where the life or health of the mother is at stake, as explicitly approved by the *Roe* opinion; but some states also make exception where the pregnancy is a result of rape or incest, or where the fetus is deformed. Are such exceptions constitutional? Perhaps such statutes raise some of the same issues discussed in the cases above, but in a somewhat novel fashion, i.e., is there a fundamental interest at stake once the fetus becomes viable, and if so, can the state interest in prohibiting the birth of certain kinds of children be sufficiently compelling to outweigh that interest?

5

Social Welfare in the United States: The Rise and Fall of Judicially-created Entitlements

The last several chapters have focused on the relationship between the government and the individual, first to define the general nature of the police powers of the state, and then to analyze how those powers must be balanced against certain procedural and substantive rights of the individual. This chapter will once again examine the relationship between the government—in this case both state and federal government —and the individual, but with the primary purpose of defining the discretion of government in determining the scope and nature of social welfare programs. In particular, this chapter will examine the discretion of government to establish limits or conditions for social welfare programs and the constraints on that discretion imposed by the constitutional requirement of equal protection. Once again, it will be necessary both to define the relationship between the government and the individual and, in doing so, to define the division of power between the judicial and the legislative branches of government.

THE DEVELOPMENT OF SOCIAL WELFARE PROGRAMS IN THE UNITED STATES

At the turn of the century, welfare benefits—meaning cash benefits or in-kind services—were available to the poor only under the most restrictive circumstances. Although the state or local government in virtually all jurisdictions provided a general relief program for the poor, assistance was generally available only to the totally destitute. In some

jurisdictions, assistance was limited to those who were born in the jurisdiction. And while in a few states cash benefits were provided, in most
jurisdictions assistance took the form of the poor farm or orphanage.
Some state and local governments provided clinics, hospitals, or programs for medical care or other social services; others did not. The
poor might find medical care through the charity wards or clinics of
hospitals, but by and large the poor with medical needs or lacking the
means for support had to rely on the traditions of private charity or go
to the "almshouse" or "county farm," or simply go without. Welfare,
to the extent that it existed, was regarded politically as a matter of state
or local prerogative. Welfare benefits were something that government
could choose to provide, but no one could demand or expect.

Nor was there much in the way of social insurance in the early
part of the twentieth century. As the Depression would soon demonstrate, the American economic system had done little to insure continued income for the unemployed or subsistence for the aged or retired
worker. The availability of medical care to the general public, as medicine became more effective and therefore more expensive, was also inadequate—even if somewhat less politically visible. Insurance for medical expenses or retirement or disability benefits would not become
widely available until after World War II.

These nineteenth century traditions changed abruptly with the
New Deal politics of Franklin Roosevelt. Roosevelt led Congress to enact a variety of public work and economic development projects and to
invest vast amounts of federal revenues in programs intended to stimulate the economy, and he underwrote the effects of his policies by establishing a number of what were described as "social security" programs. (Political conservatives would argue that Roosevelt broke with
constitutional as well as political traditions. But the newly created roles
for the federal government would survive constitutional challenge, as
will be explained in chapter 6.)

The original Social Security Act established a number of related
programs and created a statutory structure that would be the basic
framework for federal social welfare programs for the next 50 years.
Principally, it established two social welfare "tracks": the social insurance programs, Social Security and unemployment insurance; and the
welfare programs.

The unemployment program was a state-administered program of
cash assistance for a limited period of time for unemployed former
workers, paid for by a federal trust fund fueled by a tax on employers
and employees. Social Security was a federally administered program of
cash benefits to retired former workers, and, later, their dependents
and survivors (Old Age, Survivors, and Dependents Insurance,

OASDI), also financed by a federal trust fund supported through employer and employee contributions. Both of these programs were billed politically as social insurance—distributing benefits paid for by the people who eventually received them.

The federal welfare programs established by the Social Security Act, on the other hand, were federally-supported (through general revenues), state-administered programs of cash assistance to the "deserving poor." The federal legislation gave each state the option (and the incentive of 50-80 percent federal funds) to provide cash benefits to the poor who were aged (Old Age Assistance, OAA), blind (Aid to the Blind, AB), or dependent children (Aid to Dependent Children, ADC). These categorical distinctions, with only slight modifications, and the distinctions between welfare for the poor and social insurance for workers, would become permanent features of the American social welfare framework.

Between 1935 and 1965 the basic structure of these programs remained largely intact, although the programs were gradually extended. In the 1950s Social Security eligibility was expanded to include benefits for disabled former workers, and welfare eligibility was extended to require states with welfare programs to include aid to the (totally) disabled poor (ATD), and to (some) adults in families with dependent children (AFDC). And, gradually, the welfare programs were expanded to include some assistance for medical care, first in the form of allowance for medical expenses in the determination of available income, and later by providing vendor payments directly to medical care providers. The structure of the federal unemployment program was unchanged, although the benefit period was occasionally extended, particularly during times of economic recession, and eventually federal general revenues were used to supplement the trust fund.

In 1960, Congress further modified the scope of this "safety net" by enacting the Kerr-Mills program, allowing states to provide medical assistance for the aged poor, including those on welfare and also those with slightly higher incomes but with high medical expenses, a forerunner of the "medically needy" concept that would be developed later under Medicaid.

The first major structural expansion in the Roosevelt-initiated social welfare programs came with the enactment of the Social Security Amendments of 1965 and the establishment of Medicare and Medicaid. Following several flirtations with proposals for nationalizing health insurance, Congress by the 1960s had become seriously interested in the notion of a federal health insurance program for the aged. The resulting politics were both intriguing and sobering. (The American Medical Association's heavy-handed opposition to federal involvement in health insurance would be a major force in shaping Medicare, but at a cost to its public image which it has never fully recovered.) And the eventual legislative product was somewhat unexpected. Medicare, ostensibly extending medical benefits to people over 65 who were eligible for Social Security, was enacted, as had been expected for several years. But at the same time, Congress enacted Medicaid, a program with a much shorter legislative and political history, extending medical benefits to the poor, principally those who were eligible for welfare (the categorically needy), but also allowing states the option to provide medical benefits to the aged, the blind, the disabled, or families with dependent children with income or resources exceeding welfare limits (the medically needy).

The 1972 amendments to the Social Security Act also substantially restructured federal social welfare programs. Medicare benefits were extended to include disabled people who had been recipients of Social Security benefits for longer than two years. Medicare coverage was also extended to people with end-stage renal disease (ESRD). And three of the four welfare programs (OAA, AB, and ATD) were "federalized" into a single Supplemental Security Income program (SSI); following 1972, cash benefits for these three categories of "welfare" recipients would be provided and administered by the federal government. Only AFDC remained as a state-administered welfare cash assistance program. (But since the higher SSI income levels set by federal law effectively expanded the number of people on welfare in many states, the federal amendments allowed states to limit their Medicaid eligibility for the SSI population, permitting states to use the preexisting ATD, AB, and OAA eligibility standards for determining Medicaid eligibility, and creating in those states an eligibility structure for Medicaid and welfare that defies any but the most convoluted explanation.)

By the 1980s, social welfare in the United States would still closely follow two tracks. Social Security is still billed as a federal insurance program for disabled or retired former workers, their dependents, and their survivors; Medicare eligibility (other than for ESRD services) extends to some disabled former workers, and virtually everyone over 65. The states, with the help of federal funds, administer the basic welfare programs: AFDC and Medicaid. The states also administer the unemployment program, but unemployment retains its identity as an insurance program for former workers. SSI stands out as the hybrid, a welfare program principally financed and administered by the federal government.

Viewed together with various state and local welfare programs, social services programs, food stamps and other nutritional programs sponsored by the federal government, and other governmental retirement programs (e.g., programs for veterans or railroad workers), American social welfare is a complicated patchwork, the structure of which can only be explained with reference to its political and social history, and the adequacy of which has become a major political controversy.

CONSTITUTIONAL RESTRICTIONS ON LEGISLATIVE DISCRETION: THE EVOLUTION OF THE "JUDICIAL ENTITLEMENT"

By both design and intent, this patchwork of social welfare programs is both inadequate and inequitable. Many people are denied public assistance not because of their relative need but due to the categorical requirements and other characteristic restrictions on eligibility for federally sponsored social welfare programs. In addition, in interpreting program requirements, many states and, particularly under the Reagan administration, the federal government have frequently developed unusually restrictive definitions of such terms as "disability," and "families with dependent children" (many states, for instance, insist that only single parent families are "dependent"), restrictive methods for calculating available resources or income, and other means for narrowing eligibility for these programs or limiting the benefits that are made available. Even for people who are eligible, cash assistance or other benefits are often quite limited, particularly in the state-administered programs.

Some of these restrictions can be justified as legitimate attempts to allocate state and federal funds to the most needy or to devise administratively workable eligibility and service conditions. Others are more obviously the result of an exclusive concern for cost cutting, or, in some cases, philosophical or political prejudice. (Some of these latter restrictions, as will be illustrated later in this chapter, even work to the economic disadvantage of the government.) The fact that AFDC assistance levels have always been uniformly and considerably lower than assistance levels for the blind, the disabled, and the aged, can only be explained by prevailing attitudes toward "welfare mothers" and the greater political sympathy towards those considered to be more "deserving" welfare recipients.

It must be recognized that social welfare programs are expensive and that it is virtually impossible to devise any "means tested" benefits program that can successfully define levels of need without making at least some imperfect distinctions. But the inadequacy and the inequity of American social welfare are created by political choice as much as by economic or administrative necessity.

In the earlier part of this century, these inequities may have drawn relatively less attention. As noted earlier, welfare was regarded politically as a privilege; and in the judicial decisions involving a review of social welfare programs, it is fairly clear that social welfare was regarded as a legal privilege as well. But in the 1960s, challenges to some of these inequities raised a number of controversial legal questions, particularly questions which essentially asked the courts to determine whether the individual rights secured by the federal Constitution impose constraints on government discretion in shaping and conditioning social welfare programs.

In one of the first important decisions regarding the substantive powers of the state to limit welfare eligibility, *Shapiro v. Thompson*, 394 U.S. 618 (1969), the Supreme Court suggested that the judicial role in these controversies might well be an active one.

Thompson was an unwed mother with one child and pregnant with her second. She moved from Massachusetts to Connecticut to live with her mother. Connecticut denied her application for AFDC on the ground that under state law she had to be a resident for a period of one year prior to her eligibility. (Note this was not a residency requirement, but a durational residency requirement; residency requirements have been generally upheld.) Thompson argued that such a condition on welfare eligibility was the kind of governmental discrimination prohibited by the equal protection clause of the Fourteenth Amendment. The Supreme Court agreed.

In reviewing the state law, the Court first held that certain purposes that the state might be achieving by this law were impermissible. In particular, the Court ruled that discouraging immigration of new state residents was an impermissible state purpose since the right of all citizens to travel freely between the states is a constitutionally protected right: "If a law has 'no other purpose . . . than to chill the assertion of constitutional rights by penalizing those who choose to exercise them, then it [is] patently unconstitutional'."

Nor could the state validly impose a durational residency requirement for the purpose of favoring "old residents" over "new residents." Such a distinction was also constitutionally impermissible—"an invidious discrimination"—even if at the same time it achieved other legitimate state purposes:

> We recognize that a State has a valid interest in preserving the fiscal integrity of its programs. It may legitimately attempt to limit its expenditures, whether for public assistance, public education, or any other program. But a State may not accomplish such a purpose by invidious distinctions between classes of its citizens. It could not, for example, reduce

expenditures for education by barring indigent children from its schools. Similarly, in the cases before us, appellants must do more than show that denying welfare benefits to new residents saves money. The saving of welfare costs cannot justify an otherwise invidious classification.

Following a similar analysis, the Court then went on to consider several other purposes which the state claimed should justify the distinction between Thompson and other state residents. The Court found that the state could validly claim an interest in easing the administration of welfare programs (e,g., durational residency requirements are arguably one way to prevent fraud), just as it could claim that such conditions encourage potential recipients to find work. Nonetheless, since the means adopted to achieve these purposes penalized the exercise of a constitutional right, the mere showing of a valid state interest was insufficient; to satisfy equal protection, the state must show in such cases that it has a "compelling interest" to justify the classification.

Read broadly, the *Shapiro* decision created a major role for the courts in shaping the contours of social welfare programs. Indeed, following the apparent direction of the Court, many lower courts immediately after *Shapiro* took an equally critical look at a variety of state and federal welfare eligibility and benefit restrictions, leading some authorities to argue that in the future the entitlement to welfare benefits would be determined as much by judicial decision as by legislative policy. (For a similar line of cases involving the judicial recognition of a constitutional right to a pretermination hearing and other procedural due process safeguards, see the cases cited at the end of this chapter.)

While such an argument proved to be overstated, to some extent the Court in the late 1960s and early 1970s was, in fact, expanding the scope of judicial power under the equal protection clause. Traditionally, the Fourteenth Amendment's mandate that "no state shall deny to its citizens the equal protection of the laws" (applied as well to the federal government by the interpretation of the Fifth Amendment) had been interpreted only to prohibit "invidious discrimination," language which suggested that a classification or distinction was invalid only if it had an impermissible purpose (such as racial discrimination or the denial of a constitutional right) or had no purpose whatsoever.

In *Shapiro* and the cases that followed it, the interpretation given equal protection was an expanded variation on these traditional equal protection principles. Using language similar to that evolving at the same time to express the authority of the courts to protect substantive constitutional rights, the Court in these cases essentially established what modern courts call the "two-tier" test of equal protection. Under the "two-tier" test, when a legislative (or executive) classification is challenged as a violation of equal protection, a court must first consider whether the classification either affects a constitutionally protected "fundamental interest" (or, as was articulated in later cases, creates a "suspect" classification). If so, then the role of the court is to "closely scrutinize" the purposes of the state and the means for achieving those purposes, and only where the classification serves a "compelling interest" is the classification held to be constitutional (the "first-tier" test). But where no "fundamental interest" (or "suspect" classification) is involved, the court must find only that the state's classification is rationally related to a legitimate state purpose (the "second-tier" test). Thus the "two-tier" test, as developed in *Shapiro* and the cases that followed, by allowing the courts to invalidate government classifications even when there was a valid (but not compelling) state interest, effectively expanded equal protection beyond the traditional prohibition of "invidious discrimination," classifications that were impermissible or that had no purpose whatsoever.

The *Shapiro* decision, while not adopting this "two-tier" rhetoric verbatim, was clearly submitting the Connecticut statute to close scrutiny. And in doing so, the Court was at least suggesting that other social welfare classifications might be viewed as affecting the exercise of a fundamental interest and, therefore, might be subject to close scrutiny as was the durational residency requirement in *Shapiro*. And if under close scrutiny the state's interests in preserving the fiscal integrity of the program, or in easing its administration, or the other reasons cited by Connecticut were not enough to justify a social welfare classification, then many other existing social welfare classifications might also be invalidated by judicial review under the equal protection clause.

But ironically, the "two-tier" test as applied to social welfare programs in the Supreme Court decisions that followed *Shapiro* would not have the effect of expanding the judicial role in shaping the extent of social welfare programs as some authorities had feared (and others had hoped). To the contrary, rather than require close scrutiny of government social welfare classifications, the Supreme Court in the cases that followed *Shapiro* indicated that most social welfare classifications should be held only to the "second tier" of the "two-tier" test and should be upheld so long as they are rationally related to a valid state purpose.

In *Dandridge v. Williams*, 397 U.S. 471 (1970), the Court had little trouble in upholding a Maryland statute which imposed a maximum ceiling on the level of AFDC cash benefits; the Maryland law increased cash benefits as family size increased, but by diminishing amounts, and only up to a maximum of $250 per month. Dandridge claimed that such a classification effectively discriminated against large families and therefore violated the constitutional mandate of the equal protection clause. Virtually ignoring *Shapiro*, the Court held that the state could justify such a restriction on benefits on at least four different bases: this restriction encourages recipients to find employment, encourages family planning, maintains parity between welfare recipients and the working poor ($250 per month was roughly equivalent to minimum wage), and attempts to allocate state funds to those in the most need. Moreover, in evaluating these purposes, the Court required only that the state meet the "second tier" of the "two-tier" test of equal protection, i.e., it required only that the state classification be rationally related to a legitimate state interest:

> We need not explore all the reasons that the State advances in justi-fication of the regulation. It is enough that a solid foundation for the reg-ulation can be found in the State's legitimate interest in encouraging em-ployment and in avoiding discrimination between welfare families and the families of the working poor. The Equal Protection Clause does not require that a State must choose between attacking every aspect of a problem or not attacking the problem at all. (citations omitted) It is enough that the State's action be rationally based and free from invidious discrimination. The regulation before us meets that test.

Through the remainder of the 1970s and into the 1980s the ra-tional basis test of *Dandridge*, and not the close scrutiny of *Shapiro*, was repeatedly cited as the judicial role that should be adopted in evaluat-ing most social welfare classifications, as well as virtually all other legis-lative or executive classifications that involved the expenditure of pub-lic funds. For example, in *San Antonio School District v. Rodriguez*, 411 U.S. 1 (1972), the Court followed the same logic as that adopted in *Dandridge* in holding that Texas could maintain a public school financ-ing system that had resulted in "poor" districts receiving substantially less revenues than "nonpoor" districts. Essentially, the state system was held only to a rational basis test, rejecting the arguments that public education involved a fundamental interest or that governmental dis-tinctions that created de facto discrimination against the poor were sus-pect classifications.

The only major exception to the rule that social welfare classifica-tions would be subjected only to a rational basis test came in *Memorial Hospital v. Maricopa County*, 415 U.S. 250 (1974), where the Court re-jected an Arizona state law that conditioned eligibility for state-funded medical care on a one year residency requirement. Narrowly reaffirm-ing the *Shapiro* decision, the Court held that since a fundamental inter-est (again the constitutionally protected right to travel) was affected by the state condition imposed on the medical benefits program, the stat-ute should be closely scrutinized, and the state's interest in the fiscal in-

tegrity of the program and in administrative convenience were not sufficiently compelling to justify the interference with the exercise of a
fundamental right; therefore, the statute violated the requirement of
equal protection.

THE "TWO-TIER" TEST OF EQUAL PROTECTION AND GOVERNMENT FUNDING FOR ABORTIONS

Ironically, the acid test for the Court's adherence to the interpretation
of equal protection that evolved during the 1970s arose in the Court's
consideration of several cases involving first state, then federal, attempts to deny funding for abortions.

Following the decisions in *Roe v. Wade* and *Doe v. Bolton*, many
states, under political pressure from the "Right to Life" movement,
amended their Medicaid programs to limit funding for abortions. Prior
to that, as required by federal law, states had offered a range of services
including family planning services to eligible Medicaid beneficiaries.
However, the federal law gave states considerable discretion in interpreting the scope and limits on the services covered within the outlines
of the federal requirements. A number of states redefined their interpretation of the federal mandate to limit Medicaid-funded abortions to
those which were "medically necessary," or to create other conditions
intended to eliminate most nontherapeutic abortions.

In two companion cases decided in 1977, *Beal v. Doe*, 432 U.S.
438 (1977), and *Maher v. Roe*, 432 U.S. 464 (1977), the Court upheld
the constitutionality of state-imposed restrictions on Medicaid funding
for abortions. Justice Powell, writing for the majority in *Maher v. Roe*,
outlined the requirements of equal protection and the application of
those principles to abortion funding limitations:

> The basic framework of analysis of such a claim is well settled:
>
>> "We must decide, first, whether [state legislation] operates to the
>> disadvantage of some suspect class or impinges upon a fundamental
>> right explicitly or implicitly protected by the Constitution, thereby
>> requiring strict judicial scrutiny. . . . If not, the [legislative] scheme
>> must still be examined to determine whether it rationally furthers
>> some legitimate, articulated state purpose and therefore does not
>> constitute an invidious discrimination . . . ." *San Antonio School Dist.
>> v. Rodriguez.* . . .
>
> * * *
>
> This case involves no discrimination against a suspect class. An indi-
> gent woman desiring an abortion does not come within the limited cate-
> gory of disadvantaged classes so recognized by our cases. Nor does the

fact that the impact of the regulation falls upon those who cannot pay lead to a different conclusion. In a sense, every denial of welfare to an indigent creates a classification as compared to nonindigents who are able to pay for the desired goods or services. But this Court has never held that financial need alone identifies a suspect class for purposes of equal protection analysis (citation to *Rodriguez* and *Dandridge*). Accordingly, the central question in this case is whether the regulation "impinges upon a fundamental right explicitly or implicitly protected by the Constitution." The District Court read our decisions in *Roe v. Wade* . . . and the subsequent cases applying it, as establishing a fundamental right to abortion and therefore concluded that nothing less than a compelling state interest would justify Connecticut's different treatment of abortion and childbirth. We think the District Court misconceived the nature and scope of the fundamental right recognized in *Roe*.

* * *

. . . *Roe* did not declare an "unqualified constitutional right to an abortion," as the District Court seemed to think. Rather, the right protects the woman from unduly burdensome interference with her freedom to decide whether to terminate her pregnancy. It implies no limitation on the authority of a State to make a value judgment favoring childbirth over abortion, and to implement that judgment by the allocation of public funds.

The Connecticut regulation before us is different in kind from the laws invalidated in our previous abortion decisions. The Connecticut regulation places no obstacles—absolute or otherwise—in the pregnant woman's path to an abortion. An indigent woman who desires an abortion suffers no disadvantage as a consequence of Connecticut's decision to fund childbirth; she continues as before to be dependent on private sources for the services she desires. The state may have made childbirth a more attractive alternative, thereby influencing the woman's decision, but it has imposed no restriction on access to abortions that was not already there.

Having found that the statute neither created a suspect class nor affected a fundamental interest, Justice Powell went on to review the Connecticut abortion limitation under the less rigorous rational basis test and concluded that the law did rationally further the state's "strong and legitimate interest in encouraging normal childbirth."

Not all of the Court's members agreed with the majority's decision or its interpretation of equal protection. In a strongly worded dissent to *Beal v. Doe*, three justices argued that limitations on abortion funding do impact on a woman's fundamental right to privacy, and that the Court, if it had subjected the statute to close scrutiny, should have found that the state law served no compelling state interest. In a separate dissenting opinion, Justice Marshall made an even more fundamental criticism of the opinion of Justice Powell:

The Court's insensitivity to the human dimension of these decisions is particularly obvious in its cursory discussion of appellee's equal protection claims in *Maher v. Roe*. That case points up once again the need for this Court to repudiate its outdated and intellectually disingenuous "two-tier" equal protection analysis. (citations omitted) As I have suggested before, this model's two fixed modes of analysis, strict scrutiny and mere rationality, simply do not describe the inquiry that the Court has undertaken—or should undertake—in equal protection cases. . . .

. . . [A]n equal protection analysis far more in keeping with the actions rather than the words of the Court (citations omitted) carefully weighs three factors—"the importance of the governmental benefits denied, the character of the class, and the asserted state interests. . . ."

The various justices' opinion in *Beal* and *Maher* stake out both the modern view of equal protection as applied to social welfare programs and the criticism of that interpretation in this context. They also illustrate the implications of these conflicting views for the balance of power between the courts and the legislatures. The majority of the Supreme Court is insistent that equal protection analysis requires an application of the "two-tier test," an analysis which when first suggested in *Shapiro* implied that the courts might take a very broad role in reviewing at least some of the conditions and limitations that could be imposed on social welfare programs. But the majority is equally insistent that the "two-tier" test as applied to most welfare eligibility or benefit limitations—or to virtually any other governmental spending program—requires only that a state show that the limitation involved is rationally related to a valid state purpose. In almost all situations, spending programs do not involve either a fundamental interest or a suspect class; therefore close judicial scrutiny is generally not required. And since such interests as saving state funds, easing the administration of the program, or encouraging welfare recipients to work have all been viewed as valid state purposes, then obviously virtually any welfare limitation will meet the "second tier" of the "two-tier" test. Furthermore, the modern interpretation of equal protection goes beyond these pragmatic considerations to include an even more expansive notion of permissible government purposes. Part of the significance of *Beal* and *Maher* was that the Court in these decisions went so far as to accept as valid and rational a state interest in encouraging childbirth— an interest which will likely have a heavier burden on the fiscal integrity of welfare programs than funding abortions. Encouraging welfare recipients to have "normal childbirth" may be attractive to a state for political reasons, but it will certainly be costly in both the long and the short run to its welfare budget. Nonetheless, for purposes of equal protection analysis, it is a legitimate state purpose according to the majority view.

The three-justice dissent in *Beal* did not attack the logic of the "two-tier" test directly but criticized what they viewed as a mechanical application of that test, an application of the test which allowed a finding that the constitutional interest in privacy is not affected by denying funding for abortions—and therefore a finding that no fundamental interest was involved. The dissenting judges would clearly have demanded a showing of a "compelling state interest" in *Beal* and *Maher*. It is not even clear whether the dissenting judges would have allowed the state's interest in encouraging "normal childbirth" to satify the "rational basis" test. Thus the dissent would much more narrowly define government discretion under either "tier" of the "two-tier" test.

But most importantly, over and above the disagreement between the majority and the dissenters involving the specific outcome of these cases, the split on the Court involved a fundamental difference—however it is phrased—between a judicial view that social welfare programs are largely a matter of legislative discretion, perhaps even absolute discretion, and a judicial view that would be willing to recognize judicially enforced limits on legislative prerogatives, at least in some circumstances. After *Shapiro*, it appeared that at least where constitutional rights were involved, the Court would be asked to review social welfare classifications in some depth. If the majority's view of equal protection is that *not* funding does not involve or affect fundamental rights, then the majority view is that state social welfare classifications need only be rational in almost any circumstance. Simply put, according to that view, the "two-tier" test has virtually only "one tier" for social welfare programs, and that "tier" is easily satisfied. Indeed, the majority view as most recently expressed almost implies that *Shapiro* and *Maricopa County* are no longer to be upheld. (*But see* note at end of chapter.) The dissent would be much more willing to limit legislative discretion at least in cases where fundamental rights are at stake, including some situations where the impact on that fundamental right is created by a decision not to fund its exercise.

Justice Marshall's separate dissent (he concurred with two other justices in the dissent described above) carried this latter point to its logical conclusion. He argued that if the "two-tier" analysis of equal protection would result in such a cursory review of all social welfare classifications, even where important constitutional rights might be involved, then he would reinterpret the equal protection argument, even if that reinterpretation would give the courts very broad power over legislative classifications. Justice Marshall would limit legislative discretion in shaping social welfare programs—or, as his critics would argue, expand judicial power—whenever after balancing all relevant factors the individual's interest outweighed that of the government.

But whatever the merits of these dissenting arguments, at least a majority of the Supreme Court has retained a fixed hold on both the letter and the substance of the "two-tier" test of equal protection, and has severely limited the role of the courts in applying that test to social welfare programs.

This view of equal protection was affirmed again in 1980. During the late 1970s, conservative political forces and the increasingly well-organized "Right to Life" movement forced Congress to amend repeatedly the appropriations for the Department of Health, Education, and Welfare (later to be renamed the Department of Health and Human Services) to prohibit the use of federal funds, including funding for the Medicaid program, for any abortion except under very narrowly defined circumstances. Under restrictions adopted in the so-called Hyde Amendment and applicable in 1977–78, abortion funding was prohibited unless the life of the mother would be endangered if the fetus were carried to term, or unless the woman's pregnancy was a result of rape or incest. Thus some abortions necessary to protect the health (but not the life) of the woman could not be funded under Medicaid or any other federal programs.

A variety of lawsuits attempting to enjoin the Hyde Amendment were filed, eventually resulting in the Supreme Court decision in *Harris v. McRae*, 448 U.S. 297 (1980).

The Hyde Amendment raised new legal issues for the Court since the previous abortion funding decisions in *Beal* and *Maher* had involved state prohibitions on nontherapeutic abortions; unlike the 1977 Supreme Court decisions, *McRae* involved a federal prohibition on both nontherapeutic and some therapeutic abortions. Moreover, in *McRae* the restrictions on funding for abortions were attacked by a wider range of constitutional arguments. In addition to the argument that the Hyde Amendment violated the requirement of equal protection, the federal law was also challenged as a direct violation of (1) the constitutional right to privacy, (2) the prohibition under the establishment clause of the First Amendment against any "law respecting an establishment of religion," and (3) the freedom of religion protected by the free exercise clause of the First Amendment. In essence, plaintiffs in *McRae* tried to make a more explicit attack on the political sentiment behind the congressional enactment of the Hyde Amendment.

Nonetheless, the Supreme Court was unmoved by any of the plaintiffs' arguments and decided the case in much the same manner as it had in its earlier abortion funding decisions. In addressing the right to privacy argument, Justice Stewart (generally regarded as a swing vote between the judicial conservatives and the judicial liberals on the Court) reviewed the prior decisions of the Court in *Roe v. Wade*, the cases that followed *Roe*, and *Maher* and *Beal*, the abortion funding cases. Stewart argued that the federal law involved issues virtually identical to those of *Beal* and *Maher*, but distinguishable from *Roe*.

> The Hyde Amendment, like the Connecticut welfare regulation at issue in *Maher*, places no governmental obstacle in the path of a woman who chooses to terminate her pregnancy, but rather, by means of unequal subsidization of abortion and other medical services, encourages alternative activity deemed in the public interest. The present case does differ factually from *Maher* insofar as that case involved a failure to fund nontherapeutic abortions, whereas the Hyde Amendment withholds funding of certain medically necessary abortions. Accordingly, the appellees argue that because the Hyde Amendment affects a significant interest not present or asserted in *Maher*—the interest of a woman in protecting her health during pregnancy—and because that interest lies at the core of the personal constitutional freedom recognized in *Wade*, the present case is constitutionally different from *Maher*. . . .

> * * *

> But, regardless of whether the freedom of a woman to choose to terminate her pregnancy for health reasons lies at the core or periphery of the due process liberty recognized in *Wade*, it simply does not follow that a woman's freedom of choice carries with it a constitutional entitlement to the financial resources to avail herself to the full range of protected choices. The reason why was explained in *Maher*. . . .

In essence, the majority of the Court was once again holding that the constitutionally protected interest in privacy is not affected by a governmental decision not to fund the exercise of that interest, to be distinguished from a government attempt to prohibit or regulate the exercise of that interest.

Justice Stewart also dismissed the arguments that the Hyde Amendment either constituted an establishment of religion or an interference with the free exercise of religion. As for the establishment argument, the Court ruled that "if the government has a secular legislative purpose, if its principal or primary effect neither advances nor inhibits religion, and if it does not foster an excessive governmental entanglement in religion," then it does not violate the First Amendment, even if the purpose of the government action coincides with a religion-based objective. With regard to the free exercise of religion argument, the Court—rather strangely—ruled that none of the original plaintiffs to the lawsuit had shown that their personal religious beliefs were affected by the Hyde Amendment and therefore held that they lacked standing to raise the free exercise argument.

With regard to the equal protection argument, Stewart returned to the majority view of the "two-tier" test of equal protection. Finding that no fundamental interest was involved, since the right to privacy was not affected, and that no suspect classification was created by the legislative restriction, the Court upheld the Hyde Amendment as "rationally related to a legitimate governmental objective."

It follows that the Hyde Amendment, by encouraging childbirth except in the most urgent circumstances is rationally related to the legitimate governmental objective of protecting potential life. By subsidizing the medical expenses of indigent women who carry their pregnancies to term while not subsidizing the comparable expenses of women who undergo abortions (except those whose lives are threatened), Congress has established incentives that make childbirth a more attractive alternative than abortion for persons eligible for Medicaid. These incentives bear a direct relationship to the legitimate congressional interest in protecting potential life. Nor is it irrational that Congress has authorized federal reimbursement for medically necessary services generally, but not for certain medically necessary abortions. Abortion is inherently different from other medical procedures, because no other procedure involves the purposeful termination of a potential life.

After conducting an extensive evidentiary hearing into issues surrounding the public funding of abortions, the District Court concluded that "[t]he interests of . . . the federal government . . . in the fetus and in preserving it are not sufficient, weighed in the balance with the woman's threatened health, to justify withdrawing medical assistance unless the woman consents . . . to carry the fetus to term." 491 F. Supp., at 737. In making an independent appraisal of the competing interests involved here, the District Court went beyond the judicial function. Such decisions are entrusted under the Constitution to Congress, not the courts. It is the role of the courts only to ensure that congressional decisions comport with the Constitution.

Where, as here, the Congress has neither invaded a substantive constitutional right or freedom, nor enacted legislation that purposefully operates to the detriment of a suspect class, the only requirement of equal protection is that congressional action be rationally related to a legitimate governmental interest. The Hyde Amendment satisfies that standard. It is not the mission of this Court or any other to decide whether the balance of competing interests reflected in the Hyde Amendment is wise social policy. If that were our mission, not every Justice who has subscribed to the judgment of the Court today would have done so. But we cannot, in the name of the Constitution, overturn duly enacted statutes simply "because they may be unwise, improvident, or out of harmony with a particular school of thought." (citations omitted) Rather, "where an issue involves policy choices as sensitive as those implicated [here] . . . the appropriate forum for their resolution in a democracy is the legislature."

GOVERNMENTAL DISCRETION AND LIMITS ON SOCIAL WELFARE PROGRAMS IN THE 1980S

By the 1980s, the majority view of the requirement of the equal protection clause is quite clear, at least as it applies to limitations and conditions on social welfare programs. For at least a decade the Supreme Court has consistently reduced the requirement that government not "deny to any person within its jurisdiction the equal protection of the law" to a fixed series of rhetorical questions. In reviewing the constitutionality of government action challenged under the equal protection clause, the courts first look at the government action and ask whether it creates a suspect classification or creates a classification that affects a fundamental interest. If so, the courts closely scrutinize the purposes of the government and the means chosen to achieve those purposes and demand that the government show a compelling interest that justifies the classification created. Understandably, there is virtually no way in which a decision *not* to provide funding can be characterized as compelling, and thus no social welfare condition or requirement would survive such close scrutiny. But if there is no suspect classification or fundamental interest affected, as is almost always the case, then the courts require only that the classification be rationally related to a valid government purpose; and given the purposes that are recognized as valid reasons for making social welfare classifications, virtually any welfare condition or requirement will survive this rational basis test.

Both in form and in substance this analysis of the requirements of equal protection is parallel to that which evolved out of the judicial interpretation of substantive due process and the judicial review of legislation which interferes with individual rights such as the right to privacy as discussed in chapter 4. Indeed, the legal principles underlying the two lines of cases are in large part identical; there are only a few real differences between the cases discussed in this chapter and those in chapter 4. The legislative actions challenged in these cases were affirmative decisions to fund certain people or activities but exclude others, as opposed to decisions to prohibit or restrict any activity directly. The challenges to the funding decisions examined in this chapter questioned the relative equity of government actions, whereas the challenges to the restrictions on abortion or other family planning activities in chapter 4 questioned the absolute equity of certain government actions. That is to say, *Roe v. Wade* and the other cases in chapter 4 asked whether under the due process clause and the substantive protections of the Constitution the government had the power to prohibit or regulate abortions or other activities involving sexual conduct. The abortion funding cases and the other welfare cases discussed in this chapter ask whether under the equal protection clause the government, given that it chooses to fund some activities, can choose not to fund others. Equal protection analysis essentially raises questions of discrimination. Due process and substantive constitutional rights raise questions of fairness. But both lines of cases involve the same basic issues: What is the extent of the authority of the government over the individual? And what is the extent of the authority of the courts over the discretion of the other branches of government? As indicated in chapter 4, these are the fundamental questions regarding the power of the government. It should hardly be surprising that the modern view of government power and its distribution should lead to at least some parallels between these two lines of cases, since both raise these same basic questions, albeit in somewhat different ways.

The cases in this chapter demonstrate that the substantive authority of the state or federal legislatures, at least with regard to social welfare programs, is virtually unfettered by judicial constraints. Whether analyzed using the traditional language of invidious discrimination, prohibiting discrimination that had no valid purpose, or under the "second tier" of the "two-tier" test, equal protection places only the widest of limits on legislative discretion to condition or restrict the availability of social welfare benefits. *Dandridge* and other welfare cases make it clear that except where the exercise of constitutional rights are directly affected (*see* note at end of this chapter for one example) the state need only show a rational relationship to an interest in saving state funds, or facilitating the efficient administration of the state's programs, or achieving objectives such as the encouragement of welfare recipients to seek employment. The abortion funding cases make it clear that the definition of valid government purposes even extends to state interests as abstract as an interest in "promoting normal childbirth" or the federal interest in the life of an unborn fetus. Taken together these cases suggest that the only limit on government discretion would be where a social welfare classification is intended, and only intended, to deny the exercise of a constitutional right.

Beyond the specific holdings of these cases lies the broader principle, perhaps best reflected in Justice Stewart's opinion in *McRae*. Stewart's opinion confirms beyond doubt that the prevailing judicial attitude towards the constitutionality of social welfare programs is essentially conservative. The role of the courts is to be strictly confined to protecting individual rights as established in the Constitution; the definition of individual rights recognized by the Constitution is to be narrowly construed as well. Thus even where a court is sympathetic to the merits of the arguments by the individual denied social welfare assistance, as Justice Stewart hints that he is in *McRae*, the Court must defer to legislative discretion as long as the exercise of that discretion stays within these conservatively drawn constitutional constraints. Such judicial philosophy, Stewart argues, derives from a concern for the constitutional integrity of the legal system and should not be interpreted as an endorsement of the particular policy under consideration.

This prevailing judicial attitude towards the constitutional limits on government discretion with regard to social welfare programs may be cast in its best light by articulating more explicitly what Stewart's opinion only implies. Surely Stewart would admonish the critics of the *McRae* opinion to direct their criticism to the legislative body that enacted the Hyde Amendment as much as to the judicial body that refused to overturn that enactment. In fact, the general thrust of the Court's decision in *McRae* and the other cases discussed in this chapter is certainly intended to deflect the controversies over abortion funding and other social welfare limitations from the courts to the political arenas of the state and federal legislatures where, at least to a majority of the current Supreme Court, these controversies appropriately belong.

Another way to evaluate this judicial philosophy is to compare the principles in the cases involved in this chapter with the cases in the next chapter, which examine the relationship between the government and providers of health care. Those cases raise the same fundamental questions of government power, but do so under circumstances where political or philosophical sympathies for those that are subjected to government authority may be quite different than they are for those affected by social welfare classifications or by the exercise of state police powers over individual conduct.

END NOTES

1. For additional background on the American welfare "patchwork" and its historical development, see R. STEVENS & R. STEVENS, WELFARE MEDICINE IN AMERICA (1974); F. PIVEN & R. CLOWARD, POOR PEOPLE'S MOVEMENTS (1977). For discussion of other social welfare programs (with particular emphasis on health programs), see K. DAVIS & C. SCHOEN, HEALTH AND THE WAR ON POVERTY (1978).

   For a history of the development of the Medicaid program, see Wing, *The Impact of Reagan-Era Politics on the Federal Medicaid Program*, 33 CATH. U.L. REV. (1984). For an overview of the Medicare program, see *Financing Medicare: Explorations in Controlling Costs and Raising Revenues*, 62 MILBANK MEM. FUND Q. / HEALTH AND SOCIETY 143 (1984).
2. For an example of the expansive view of "entitlements" that might have been created by judicial decision—a view later rejected by the courts—see Reich, *The New Property*, 73 YALE L.J. 733 (1964).

3. While the cases discussed in this chapter largely concern substantive conditions that can be placed on social welfare programs, it would also be worth exploring a parallel line of cases that have examined the procedural rights that must be afforded social welfare recipients. At about the same time it decided *Dandridge*, the Supreme Court in Goldberg v. Kelly, 397 U.S. 254 (1970), held that AFDC recipients were entitled to pretermination evidentiary hearings prior to the termination of their cash benefits, arguing that it would be a violation of procedural due process to deny recipients such important benefits without sufficient procedural safeguards against invalid or erroneous decisions. *Goldberg* even suggested that the "brutal need" of welfare recipients for their benefits was sufficiently important to require hearings prior to the termination of any important social welfare benefit. In a subsequent decision, however, the Supreme Court narrowed the *Goldberg* holding, finding that in some cases an administrative review of the decision to terminate benefits might satisfy due process requirements. *See* Matthews v. Eldridge, 424 U.S. 319 (1976). Also, in O'Bannon v. Town Court Nursing Center, 447 U.S. 773 (1980), the Supreme Court held that patients have no constitutionally protected interest in receiving Medicaid-financed care in a particular nursing home and, therefore, refused to require a pretermination hearing for patients prior to the decertification of the nursing home in which they were being treated. The courts have been less clear, however, as to whether nursing homes or other providers are entitled to pretermination hearings or other procedural safeguards prior to decertification. *See, e.g.,* Case v. Weinberger, 523 F.2d 602 (2d Cir. 1975); Washington Nursing Center v. Quern, 442 F. Supp. 23 (S.D. Ill. 1977).

4. It is also possible to examine many of the same issues discussed in this chapter from the point of view of participating providers in Medicaid and Medicare. In many ways, providers are the "secondary beneficiaries" of these programs and, consequently, are also substantially affected by government decisions to limit or condition benefits or otherwise curtail government efforts under these programs. This has become increasingly true as federal and state cost containment efforts have turned to exclusions of certain costs, caps on inflation, industrywide averaging, and other cost-limiting reimbursement schemes.

Providers, and particularly their industry organizations, have been very aggressive in their opposition to cost-containment efforts, both politically and through the courts, frequently raising the same type of constitutional questions regarding limits on legislative and executive discretion discussed in this chapter. But despite their many efforts, providers have been remarkably unsuccessful in the courts; at least in terms of the constitutional limits on government discretion, provider challenges to government limits or conditions on reimbursement have virtually never been successful. In terms of substantive due process, the courts have uniformly held that government needs only a reasonable basis for excluding costs or otherwise limiting reimbursement, suggesting that any rationally implemented policy (including saving government funds) could justify the limitation of reimbursement. *See, e.g.*, Germantown Hosp. v. Heckler, 738 F.2d 631 (3d Cir. 1984). Nor is a denial of reimbursement regarded as a "taking of property." *See, e.g.*, Saint Mary of Nazareth Hosp. Center v. Department of HHS, 698 F.2d 1337 (7th Cir. 1983). Similarly, the courts have been unresponsive to the argument that distinctions or classifications between providers violate the requirements of equal protection. In Saint Francis Hosp. Center v. Heckler, 714 F.2d 872 (7th Cir. 1983), for example, the court of appeals upheld HHS's disallowance of return of equity for nonprofit hospitals on both statutory and equal protection grounds —applying a "rational basis" test, since the reimbursement decision involved neither a fundamental interest nor a suspect class.

The gist of these cases may be that there is virtually no limit on legislative or executive discretion (if exercised within its statutory authority) to limit or condition reimbursement so long as Medicaid and Medicare are voluntary programs. For a detailed discussion of the discretion allowed under "voluntary" spending programs, see Wing & Silton, *Constitutional Authority for Extending Federal Control Over the Delivery of Health Care*, 57 N.C.L. REV. 1423, 1439–60 (1979).

5. While the explanation of the "two-tier" test of equal protection in this chapter continues to be descriptive of the modern analysis of the requirements of the Fourteenth Amendment, there is at least one line of cases that has proven to be an exception to the general definition of the "two-tier" test. In several decisions, the Supreme Court has declined to rule that classifications based on sex are "suspect;" yet the Court has also been reluctant to allow sex-based classifications to be reviewed under a rationality test. Instead, sex discrimination has been reviewed under what might be regarded as a "third tier" of equal protection. *See* Mississippi Univ. for Women v. Hogan, 458 U.S. 718, 726 (1982).

Parenthetically, one of the likely effects of an Equal Rights Amendment would be to require a close scrutiny test for all sex-based classifications.

6. It can be instructive to apply the "two-tier" test of equal protection to situations involving racial classifications. Since race is clearly a suspect classification, any racial classification is subject to close scrutiny. But while it is unlikely that most forms of race discrimination could be justified by a compelling state interest, it is conceivable—at least where the racial classification is for the purpose of promoting racial equality. *See, e.g.*, Bakke v. Regents of Univ. of Cal., 438 U.S. 265 (1978).

7. If the abortion funding cases are to be taken in their broadest sense, it would appear that not funding an activity is not affecting or interfering with that activity; thus both decisions not to fund and decisions to condition funding an activity should be subject only to the "second tier" of equal protection analysis. Since saving money or promoting such goals as "normal childbirth" are acceptable justifications, "not funding" decisions will always be upheld. But does this mean that *Shapiro* and *Maricopa County* are effectively overruled? Both cases essentially involved decisions not to fund. In *Harris v.*

McRae —in a footnote—the Court attempted to explain that these cases are still good law, only distinguishable from most cases involving decisions not to fund. "A substantial constitutional question would arise if Congress had attempted to withhold all Medicaid benefits from an otherwise eligible candidate simply because that candidate had exercised her constitutionally protected freedom to terminate her pregnancy by abortion." Apparently, the government can choose not to fund an activity, but it cannot deny benefits to someone who exercises a constitutionally protected interest such as the right to travel or the right to privacy. Thus it would appear that the Hyde Amendment could not be amended to deny welfare or other benefits to any woman who has an abortion, or to people who travel across state borders, or to anyone who exercises a constitutionally protected right.

6

Government Regulation of Health Facilities

The previous four chapters have examined various legal principles that define the relationship between the government and individual people in matters relating to health and health care. This chapter will cover a distinct but related set of legal principles, principles that concern the relationship between the government and providers of health care. Specifically, it will examine the various state and federal government programs that have attempted to regulate health facilities, the constitutional bases for these programs, and some of the more important and more recent legal controversies that have arisen out of these efforts. As will become clear, the principles that define the relationship between the government and providers of health care involve many of the same concepts that were discussed in earlier chapters. These principles will also address the same basic issues of government power: the extent of the constitutional authority of the state and federal government and the extent of the authority of the courts in reviewing the exercise of discretion by the other branches of government. But as will also become clear, the rights of providers, although derived from the same legal principles as those of the individual, are defined and applied somewhat differently and, consequently, the constitutional authority of government to regulate health providers—and particularly health facilities—is analytically distinct from the authority of the government over the individual discussed in earlier chapters.

THE HISTORY OF GOVERNMENT REGULATION
OF HEALTH FACILITIES

Given the importance of institutional providers in delivering health care in this country, it should not be surprising to find that government, both state and federal, has attempted a wide variety of programs intended to control the quality, distribution, and, in some cases, the costs of American health facilities. If anything is surprising, it is that government regulation of health facilities is really a phenomenon of rather recent origins. While some state programs existed as early as the 1920s, most state—and all federal—regulatory programs postdate World War II and virtually all of the serious attempts to exercise direct control over health facilities have been initiated in the last 20 years. It must also be recognized that even these more recent "command and control" type regulatory efforts have been subjected to considerable political constraints. Thus government authority exercised to its fullest extent has rarely been tested in this context, and, consequently, the legal constraints on that authority have never been completely settled.

Most states have maintained hospital licensing programs at least since the late 1940s when the establishment of a state program of hospital licensing became a prerequisite for the receipt of federal Hill-Burton funds. All states now require that hospitals, nursing homes, and some other facilities be licensed, although the scope of licensing laws and the requirements they impose vary considerably from state to state.

Licensing statutes represent mandatory government control. They impose standards of quality that must be met by facilities to receive and retain a license to operate. Traditionally, however, these standards were directed towards the condition of the facility itself (for example specifying standards for equipment or for the structural integrity of buildings) and rarely imposed requirements that affected staffing patterns, admission practices, or the quality of the services delivered. As such, licensing has been generally regarded as setting minimum standards for safe facilities, not normative standards for the delivery of care. More critically, even where state licensing standards have been specifically directed to the quality of the services available at the institution (and even though the state's authority to enforce such standards is clearly constitutional), state programs have rarely been structured or administered in such a way as to permit any but the most cursory review of most health facilities.

In the 1950s a coalition of the American Medical Association, the American Hospital Association, and the American College of Physicians and Surgeons created the Joint Commission on the Accreditation of Hospitals (JCAH). The founders of the JCAH claimed that their purpose was to supplement state licensing programs with a private and voluntary program of self-evaluation. More sanguine authorities have interpreted the formation of JCAH as a politically motivated attempt to preempt any further government efforts to regulate the quality of hospitals. But whatever the original motivation, the result has been the development by the JCAH of quality standards for hospitals and of an accreditation process that has been generally regarded as more rigorous and thorough than state licensing programs. And while JCAH accreditation has always been nongovernmental and legally voluntary— no institution is required to be accredited—most hospitals have viewed accreditation as practically necessary, adding to the significance of accreditation to the quality regulation of hospitals.

With the enactment of Medicare in 1965, however, the role of JCAH in regulating the quality of hospitals became even more important. In order to participate in Medicare, institutional providers were required under the federal legislation to be certified, meaning that they must be licensed under state law, meet various requirements specifically defined in the federal statute, and meet additional standards of quality to be developed by DHEW. Institutional providers also had to be certified to participate in Medicaid, but the original federal statute allowed each state to develop its own standards for Medicaid certification. (By 1980, however, the certification requirements for institutional providers under both programs had been merged so that the certification standards for Medicare and Medicaid are now virtually identical.)

The original Medicare statute allowed DHEW full discretion to develop standards for nursing homes—a process that itself led to considerable controversy that has only been partially resolved by the 1980s. (*See* note at end of this chapter.) For hospitals, however, the federal statute authorized DHEW to "set such other requirements . . . necessary in the interests of health and safety . . . except that such other standards may not be higher than the comparable requirements prescribed by the JCAH. . . ." DHEW interpreted this language to allow the agency to adopt the JCAH accreditation standards as certification standards and to certify any facility that had JCAH accreditation without any additional review. In 1972, however, the Medicare statute was amended to clarify the authority of DHEW to make independent judgments and to develop additional standards for certification. Nonetheless, Medicare (and Medicaid) hospital certification still depends heavily on JCAH accreditation.

More recently, the JCAH has developed accreditation standards for nursing homes, as have some nursing home groups, but certification of nursing homes for Medicare and Medicaid remains predominantly a matter of compliance with federal and state requirements.

In addition to programs for licensing, accreditation, and certification, health facilities have also been subject to various utilization review requirements, principally those requirements imposed by their participation in Medicaid and Medicare. As the concern for the cost of Medicaid- and Medicare-funded services grew, even in the early years of the programs, the federal government developed a variety of utilization review requirements for institutional providers, largely involving in-house administrative audits. In 1972, Congress mandated more elaborate utilization controls over institutional providers participating in Medicaid and Medicare and authorized the creation of Professional Standards Review Organizations (PSROs), which would eventually review the quality of services rendered by all Medicaid and Medicare providers.

The original PSRO legislation envisioned an ambitious effort to police both the cost and the quality of services. Had it been fully implemented, local PSROs organized by physicians would have developed standards for necessity and appropriateness of care and overseen the review, both concurrently and retroactively, of virtually all services rendered to Medicaid and Medicare recipients in an inpatient setting. In implementation, however, the PSRO program has had only a partial resemblance to its original design. In the early years of the program, political resistance from provider groups—and infighting among them —inhibited the organizational development of both the local PSROs and the state level organizations that were to coordinate their efforts. By 1980, the PSROs had been established in most of the country, but the ambitious work program of PSROs—concurrent review of all inpatient Medicare and Medicaid admissions, retroactive medical care evaluations of these services, development of provider profiles—had been pared by both practical and budgetary considerations. While some areas boasted of remarkable successes, others were still courting the cooperation of local providers. Nationwide, only a very small percentage of Medicaid and Medicare services were subject to any kind of PSRO oversight. Moreover, in most areas, the actual reviews were delegated to the institutions themselves.

By the time President Reagan took office in 1981, political support for maintaining the PSRO program had waned considerably. The new administration urged Congress to discontinue the program on both budgetary and ideological grounds. Somewhat typically of federal health politics in the early 1980s, Congress refused to repeal the program altogether, as concern for the costs of government-sponsored medical care continued to be a dominant preoccupation, but the program was recast to reflect the influence of conservative politics, and federal PSRO funding was substantially curtailed. In 1981, DHHS was mandated to study the performance of existing PSROs and authorized to terminate up to 30 percent of the existing organizations. Most importantly, in 1982 the statutory authorization for the program was substantially reworked. The new legislation allows DHHS to contract with "Peer Review Organizations" (PROs) to perform some of the same type of utilization review activities conducted by PSROs. (State agencies are allowed but not required to contract with the new PROs for utilization review of Medicaid services).

If the law is implemented as originally written, all hospitals must contract with a PRO by October 1984 or lose eligibility for participation in Medicare. Contracts for establishing a PRO program in each region of the country are to be made by DHHS on a competitive bidding basis, allowing previous PSROs, other physician-sponsored organizations, and "physician access" organizations (i.e., organizations that can show they have physicians available to conduct reviews) as potential bidders; after October 1984, other organizations such as insurance companies will be eligible for PRO contracts.

By the end of 1984, the politics of PROs had taken on a decidedly schizophrenic character. Conservatives in Congress and within the administration were still dubious about the necessity of government-mandated peer review and struggling to limit federal funding for the new program. But the first round of PRO regulations issued by HHS outlined an ambitious work program for the fully developed PRO organizations, although primarily for inpatient hospital services. (The revised statute authorizes PRO review of services in other institutional settings and of services by individual providers as well.) Reflecting the concern for the effectiveness of PRO review, the regulations outline detailed performance criteria for PRO contracts, indicating that PROs will be evaluated in terms of their measurable impact on such indicators as admission and readmission rates, rates for certain types of procedures, and other measures relating to both cost and quality. Given the history of government-required utilization review programs, however, it is impossible to predict whether these newly designed peer review organizations will actually be required to carry out all of the responsibilities outlined in the initial regulations, or for that matter, if and when they will become fully operational.

GOVERNMENT PLANNING PROGRAMS

Although government-required utilization review holds out the potential for direct and substantial government influence over the delivery of health services, clearly the most serious attempts to directly influ-

ence institutional health care providers have involved the various programs to coerce or require the planned distribution of health care resources.

The earliest programs for joint planning efforts among providers
were largely local and voluntary. In the 1930s and 1940s, private voluntary agencies were established in several major cities to encourage hospitals to cooperate in their capital development efforts.

The first government-sponsored programs were established following World War II when Congress enacted the Hill-Burton program,
ostensibly to respond to what was perceived as a shortage of hospital
facilities in many areas of the country. Hill-Burton authorized federal
funds for each state to survey the need and to develop state plans for
the development of hospital facilities. It also provided matching funds
and loans for public or nonprofit facilities to assist in construction projects to meet the needs identified in the state Hill-Burton plan. Funded
projects had to comply with a number of requirements outlined in the
federal law, including the requirements that they provide a reasonable
amount of uncompensated care and a community service. (*See* note at
end of chapter.)

In later years the program was expanded to authorize the funding
of nursing homes and other health facilities and, in 1964, the modernization of existing facilities as well as new construction.

As a construction financing program, Hill-Burton was remarkably
successful. It has been estimated that in the first 20 years of the program over half of the hospitals in the country received Hill-Burton
assistance; and, at least until 1970, it was a major source of capital for
the hospital industry. Yet its success highlights its shortcomings. The
great bulk of Hill-Burton funds were channeled into projects for new
inpatient hospital beds; the need for ambulatory facilities, for example,
was largely overlooked. Moreover, Hill-Burton agencies could only encourage necessary modernization and construction. They had no authority to curb unnecessary projects. As a consequence, in most parts of
the country, Hill-Burton was viewed more as a hospital funding program than as a planning program. Indeed, Hill-Burton, particularly in
its latter years, has been described by some critics as a "pork barrel"
program, contributing as much to the oversupply of hospital beds as to
the rationalization or planned distribution of necessary health facilities.

In the 1960s, a number of additional federal efforts were made to
encourage health planning and a more rational distribution of health
care resources, most notably through the enactment of the Regional
Medical Program (RMP) in 1965 and the Comprehensive Health Planning Program (CHP) in 1966.

In theory, the regional agencies financed through the RMP were to encourage the coordination of research and the distribution of information from the medical schools and other research institutions to medical practitioners, with particular emphasis on the "killer diseases": cancer, heart disease, and stroke. To do so, RMP invested over one billion dollars during the first ten years of the program, both to fund the local RMP agencies and the individual projects that they developed: targeted research, training programs, data exchange, and direct patient care on a demonstration basis. Yet in retrospect, RMP made little visible progress towards the coordinated effort that was the original objective of the program. Even more so than Hill-Burton, RMP became viewed primarily as a spending program, responding primarily to medical politics and local concerns.

The CHP legislation established for the first time a national network of state and local health planning agencies. The federal legislation provided funds to state governments to maintain a state health planning agency and a consumer-dominated advisory council and to develop a statewide plan for the distribution of health resources. It also provided funds to locally based nonprofit agencies to develop comparable plans for their local areas. Functionally, these agencies were to encourage voluntary compliance with these plans and to establish a grand "Partnership for Health" between government, providers, and consumers, although the federal legislation mandated that this be done without interference with "existing patterns of private professional practice of medicine."

Understandably, the reality of CHP fell somewhat short of these ambitions. The state and local agencies proved to be unable to overcome either the political or the technical barriers to the establishment of the comprehensive health planning network envisioned in the original legislation. Chronically understaffed, heavily dependent on private sources for a share of their funding, and with no regulatory authority to require compliance with their planning efforts, CHP agencies provided the testing grounds for various health planning activities but had little demonstrable impact on the actual distribution of health care resources.

While Hill-Burton and these other federal efforts were essentially funding voluntary planning programs and, in some cases, encouraging the compliance with their directives, many states in the late 1960s and early 1970s were turning to more direct regulation of the health care industry, principally through the enactment of certificate of need legislation.

A certificate of need program authorizes a state agency to regulate the construction or expansion of institutional health facilities. State

programs vary considerably in their administrative structure, procedures for decision making, and methods for appeal and review, as well
as in their relationship to various other state and local health planning
activities. All states cover hospital and nursing home construction;
some include outpatient and other facilities (and, since 1974, virtually
all states meet the certificate of need program requirements necessary
for participation in the federal health planning program described below). Certain specified categories of projects or capital expenditures
above a minimum dollar cost are subject to review to determine the
"necessity" of the project, by comparison with either various criteria or
a developed state plan. In a few states, the closing or reduction of services is also subject to certificate of need review.

If a proposal is found to be "unnecessary," in most states the project cannot be licensed. It is worth noting, however, that few states actually police compliance with certificate of need decisions. Thus while
it is unlikely that a facility would openly defy a decision denying a certificate of need, it is frequently alleged that conditions or assurances attached to certificate of need approval are later violated. In such circumstances, states have little practical remedy to require compliance. It
is also worth noting that after nearly two decades of experience there is
substantial doubt as to the ability of state certificate of need programs
to have any real impact on the distribution of health facilities or to affect health care resources otherwise, although the explanation for this
failure is the subject of considerable debate.

In 1972, Congress also adopted the certificate of need concept,
and gave health planning agencies a potential source of regulatory authority. A new section 1122 was added to the Social Security Act, giving each state the option of contracting with DHEW to review the capital expenditures of Medicaid, Medicare, and Maternal and Child
Health program providers. These decisions would be made, presumably, as part of existing health planning or certificate of need programs. Based on such review—and independent of any action taken
under state law—DHEW can disallow a proportion of federal reimbursement under these programs for health facilities that make unnecessary capital expenditures or that are out of compliance with existing
state health plans.

THE NATIONAL HEALTH PLANNING AND
RESOURCES DEVELOPMENT ACT OF 1974

Thus by the 1970s a welter of federal, state, and local agencies shared in
the frustrating task of planning and, in some cases, regulating the dis-

tribution of health care resources. The National Health Planning and Resources Development Act of 1974 attempted to coordinate and bring additional national direction to these somewhat disjointed efforts. Under the 1974 legislation, CHP, RMP, and Hill-Burton were effectively superseded by a single federal program intended to combine and redirect previous development, planning, and regulatory activities.

As had been the pattern of previous federal efforts, the bulk of the planning activities funded under the new legislation was to be performed at the state and local level. Nonetheless, the 1974 legislation attempted to create a more active role for the federal government. DHEW—assisted by a national advisory council—was mandated to exercise unprecedented levels of control over both the state and the local planning agencies funded. (For example, the federal statute outlined in considerable detail the supervision by DHEW over day-to-day activities of both the local and state agencies.) DHEW was also mandated to develop national health planning guidelines for the supply, distribution, and organization of health resources and services according to a series of statutory objectives—the first federally established national health planning standards. All state and local planning and other activities had to be consistent with these objectives and guidelines. While participation in the new program was voluntary for each state, states that failed to comply with these and other requirements of the act were subject to losing federal funds under this and some other federal programs.

At the state level, the 1974 legislation required essentially a reorganization of all preexisting and federal planning programs. Principally, the state had to authorize a single state health planning agency to carry out various health planning and resource development activities outlined by the federal legislation. The state also had to authorize an advisory committee, the State Health Coordinating Council (SHCC) according to complicated membership requirements still reflecting the "Partnership For Health" notion. A majority were to be consumers (a portion of whom were to be nominated by the local health systems agencies) and at least one-third were to be direct providers of medical care. The SHCC's primary responsibility was to advise the state agency in carrying out its various activities and in the development of the state plans required by the federal law.

The state agency was required under the federal law, in addition to various supervisory functions over local health systems agencies (HSAs) (1) to implement and carry out a certificate of need program in accordance with requirements in the statute, (2) to serve as the state agency for purposes of the federal "Section 1122" certificate of need program described above, (3) to develop a statewide plan for the distribution of all health care resources within the state, and (4) to prepare a state medical facilities plan setting priorities for the allocation of health resource development funds. These latter funds were ostensibly a redirection of the Hill-Burton and RMP programs providing grants, loans, and interest subsidies for a variety of projects (e.g., conversion of existing facilities to new health services or upgrading substandard facilities).

At the local level, the 1974 legislation also redirected previous activities, authorizing DHEW to create (with advice from each state) local health planning areas and funding local HSAs. Preexisting CHP agencies, as well as other nonprofit or local government agencies, were allowed to compete for HSA designation. The governing bodies of the designated HSAs, as with their CHP predecessors, were to be composed of a majority of consumers, "broadly representative" of the region's providers, and in compliance with other conditions specified in the federal statute. As orginally conceived, these local HSAs were to be responsible for a broad range of planning activities including:

— various surveys of the health status of area residents, the utilization of health services, and existing health care resources

— the development of a "health systems plan," a long-range projection of the distribution of health care resources, and an "annual implementation plan," outlining the short term priorities to be funded each year (the legislation authorized the annual appropriation to each HSA of an area health service development fund for such projects)

— the review and approval of applications for federal funding under various federal health programs, and the review and comment on all other applications

— recommendations to the state agency on applications for health facility development funds and, most importantly, certificate of need applications based on the HSA's plans

— review and recommendations on the necessity of all existing health services in their area (although the federal legislation did not require that there be any regulatory efforts to implement these decisions)

The implementation of the 1974 legislation proved to be the high water mark for federal control over the distribution of health care resources. By 1980, all states were at least attempting to carry out the various health planning activities required by the federal law, sharing these responsibilities—with varying degrees of success—with a network of local HSAs covering virtually the entire nation. And despite the reluctance of some states to do so under federal mandate, virtually all states established certificate of need programs subjecting hospitals and most other institutional providers to direct public control over their capital expenditures and major service expansion decisions.

A few states have carried this regulatory strategy even further. As early as the late 1960s, several states had experimented with mandatory rate setting for hospitals and other institutional providers, first for public reimbursement programs and, by the late 1970s, for all payers. By the 1980s the number of states attempting some form of rate setting program was indicative of the odd politics of the decade. At a time when the Reagan administration was adopting a more conservative cost containment posture, preaching the importance of deregulation and the advantages of competition, an increasing number of states turned towards the direct regulation of all rates and charges by hospitals and other institutional providers in a manner not unlike the regulation of public utilities and other "quasi-public" institutions. Whether these states will, as they implement these programs, actually exercise substantial control over institutional rates and, ultimately, health care costs has yet to be answered. Both technical and political barriers to effective rate setting are considerable, and recent history would indicate that efforts to do so are likely to be frustrating.

POLITICAL CONSTRAINTS ON GOVERNMENT CONTROL OF HEALTH FACILITIES

Viewed summarily, the various state and federal programs for regulating the quality and distribution of health facilities discussed in the last two sections might appear to establish an extensive and complicated network of government control over American health facilities, as providers have often argued. But as noted in the introduction to this chapter, until relatively recently, few of these programs have actually exercised direct or substantial control over the autonomy of institutional providers, particularly with regard to the services that they provide. Even where programs have been empowered to flex real regulatory muscle, both the scope of these programs and their administration have been subject to the considerable political constraints created by provider opposition and by prevailing public attitudes towards "big government" regulation.

In fact, as many authorities have pointed out before, the political acceptability of health facility regulation has never been complete; as mentioned earlier, political attitudes in recent years have been nearly schizophrenic in character. Even during a time when the cost of institu-

tional health care is increasingly the focus of blame for the skyrocket-
ing cost of health care generally, and when both state and federal government are plagued with notions of "something must be done," at
neither level of government has there been sufficient political consensus to formulate any consistent or lasting public policy. At each critical
juncture, either the political opposition of provider interests or the easily aroused American distrust of governmental solutions has sufficiently
diluted political support for regulatory efforts. Even the efforts to reorient federal policy towards "competition" and "deregulation" by the
Reagan administration have been only partially successful, due in large
part to these same political constraints.

Perhaps the most telling chapter in the history of health facility
regulation was written by the consideration and eventual rejection of
President Carter's proposal for a federal hospital cost containment program. Originally billed as an interim "holding action" pending the enactment of his national health insurance proposal (which never mater-
ialized), Carter eventually focused his health care cost containment
strategy on the enactment of a federal limit on revenues to be collected
by virtually all hospitals. As it worked through Congress, the original
proposal evolved into two basic alternatives from which many varia-
tions emerged: a comprehensive program fixing a ceiling on the annual
rate of increase (originally 9 percent) for all revenues from all sources,
and a more modest proposal setting only the annual revenue increases
from Medicaid and Medicare. But in whatever form, and despite serious and prolonged debate, the concept of hospital cost containment
was eventually rejected by Congress. Following an impressive show of
force by the hospital industry, both the 95th and 96th Congresses rejected Carter's efforts. The only visible product of their deliberations
was a formal promise by the hospital industry to wage a "voluntary effort" to control hospital costs—an effort that would prove to be little
more than a public relations campaign.

Equally telling of the politics of health facility regulation was the
fate of the 1974 health planning legislation. Apparently the original
legislation represented only a temporary consensus; almost as soon as
the legislation was enacted, Congress began to retreat from the original
design of the program. Funds for the state level resource development
fund that was to reorient the Hill-Burton program have never been appropriated; nor have there been appropriations for area health service
development projects at the local level. Even appropriations for the
administration of the state and local agencies have become increasingly
controversial. By the end of the 1970s, continuation of the authorization for the program became a subject of intense debate, particularly
with regard to the federal specifications for the scope and structure of

the states' certificate of need programs and for other state level regulatory activities. (At one point the House of Representatives passed a nonbinding resolution calling for Secretary of DHEW Joseph Califano to resign for issuing national health planning guidelines that were too strict.) At the same time, some efforts were made to strengthen the control over health facilities; e.g., state and local HSAs were required to consider compliance with the "charity care" requirements of Hill-Burton facilities in making health planning decisions. Other federal program changes are less easily characterized; e.g., the 1979 amendments to the federal law required health planning agencies to give greater consideration to the encouragement of "competition" in their planning and regulatory decisions.

By 1980, and with the election of President Reagan, Congress was even more disenchanted with health planning programs or, at least, federal control over their direction. While Congress rejected Reagan's proposal to repeal federal health planning programs altogether, it severely modified the structure of the program, taking authority away from local HSAs and allowing states more discretion in structuring their programs; most importantly, Congress drastically limited the funding of the program. Indeed, by 1982, Congress, unable to reauthorize the program, merely extend the program on a continuing resolution—at nearly one-half the funding level appropriated in 1980. In 1983 and 1984 Congress again was able to extend the program only via a continuing funding resolution, leaving the program's viability in further doubt.

CONSTITUTIONAL CONSTRAINTS ON
GOVERNMENT CONTROL OF HEALTH FACILITIES

These political constraints on health facility regulation not only have implications for current and future public policy, they also have effectively preempted the development of the law as it applies to these types of government programs. Since the extent of government regulation has been checked so often by political constraints, only rarely have the constitutional limits on government authority actually been tested. Even with a history of enforcement of state certificate of need programs that extends back over two decades, surprisingly few certificate of need controversies have developed into legal battles raising the constitutionality of these programs. For that matter, the fact that there have been few legal battles can only be interpreted as evidence that there have been few controverted decisions—and it certainly supports the general observation that these programs have been something less than a success. Moreover, of those legal battles that have been fought, most have concerned statutory or administrative issues; frequently certificate of need litigation appears to have been more a dilatory tactic, or an attempt to induce political compromise, than an attempt to force judicial interpretation of basic constitutional principles.

PSROs have spawned still fewer legal controversies, again a commentary on their impact on provider behavior. Licensing and certification programs have led to even fewer legal challenges to the underlying authority of government, probably for the same reason.

On the other hand, it is inevitable that such constitutional challenges will be litigated, particularly if public policy moves in the direction of greater government control over health facilities. The "all payer" rate setting programs that have been initiated in some states, if rigorously administered, will have a considerable impact on the prices charged by health facilities to both private and public payers and consequently will generate legal challenge. And while the Reagan administration has eschewed any interest in further federal control over health care delivery and originally sought to withdraw federal involvement in such activities as health planning programs, the possibility of continued and perhaps more stringent federal regulatory control will be a permanent item on the congressional agenda, regardless of the prevailing ideology in the White House. Thus the constitutionality of such proposals as hospital cost containment will be periodically subject to debate, even if not enacted.

An intriguing primer on these issues, and some, although not definitive, guidance as to the manner in which they might be judicially decided can be found in a series of decisions involving the planning programs of one state, North Carolina.

Following the lead of many other states, and before there were federal incentives to do so, North Carolina enacted its first certificate of need law in 1971. Two years earlier the state legislature had empaneled a legislative commission to study the problem of inflating health care costs. Among the final recommendations of the commission was the establishment of a state certificate of need program. The 1971 statute extended certificate of need controls to all new construction, construction of additional bed capacity, or conversion of existing beds to new licensing categories.

Aston Park Hospital was a 50-bed hospital serving Asheville, North Carolina and the surrounding rural area. There were seven other hospitals in the multicounty area served by Aston Park. Three of these hospitals were in Asheville. The state certificate of need agency found that there were 978 beds in the area (641 of which were in Asheville) and projected that only 94 additional beds were needed to provide adequate hospital care for the area. Another Asheville hospital had been granted permission under a "grandfather clause" in the 1971 legislation to build 90 beds. Therefore Aston Park's application to build a new facility with a bed capacity of 200 was denied.

Aston Park appealed the agency's decision through the state courts, and in *In the Matter of Certificate of Need for Aston Park Hospital, Inc.*, 282 N.C. 542, 193 S.E.2d 729 (1973), the North Carolina Supreme Court invalidated the certificate of need legislation based on several provisions of the state constitution.

Principally, the court ruled that the certificate of need legislation violated the "Law of Land" clause of the state's constitution, essentially parallel to the due process requirement of the federal Constitution. The court analyzed the police powers of the state as applied by this legislation in light of the state "due process" requirement:

> Obviously, the police power extends to reasonable regulation of hospitals, both as to their construction and as to their operation. However, the fact that the business of a hospital is per se related to the public health does not mean that every regulation of its activities falls within the scope of the police power. (citations omitted) "If a statute is to be sustained as a legitimate exercise of the police power, it must have a rational, real or substantial relation to the public health, morals, order, or safety, or the general welfare. . . . [T]he power to regulate a business or occupation does not necessarily include the power to exclude persons from engaging in it. When this field has been reached, the police power is severely curtailed. . . ."
>
> We find no reasonable relation between the denial of the right of a person, association, or corporation to construct and operate on his or its own property, with his or its own funds, an adequately staffed and equipped hospital and the promotion of the public health. Consequently, we hold that [the statute] is a deprivation of liberty without due process of law, in violation of . . . the Constitution of North Carolina insofar as it denies Aston Park the right to construct and operate its proposed hospital except upon the issuance to it of a certificate of need.

While the North Carolina Supreme Court was not following the same rhetoric, clearly the court was "closely scrutinizing" the state's legislation—much in the way that modern courts have applied the notion of substantive due process when fundamental constitutional rights are involved. The requirement that the state's exercise of the police power be reasonably related to a valid state purpose was interpreted by the court in very narrow terms. While the court would have apparently accepted "reasonable regulation" such as licensing, it would not interpret the police powers to include the prohibition altogether of a hospital's expansion. The court would neither defer to the state legislature's judgment concerning the reasonableness of this form of regulation, nor accept any of the justifications cited by the state as sufficiently "compelling." The state had argued that the shortage of personnel to staff hospitals and the oversupply of beds in the area would result in inefficient delivery of services and excess costs. Such state interests, the court held, do not justify a denial of the hospital's economic interest in building a new facility. Indeed, it was fairly clear that the North Carolina court would not accept any government justification for imposing prohibitory controls on private enterprises entering the market.

In contrast, virtually every other jurisdiction that has considered the constitutionality of state certificate of need programs under the due process requirement of the federal Constitution or under comparable requirements of state constitutions has been far less protective of the interests of providers. In all other jurisdictions that have addressed the issue, the courts have been more willing to defer to the decision by their state legislatures that this type of government control is appropriately related to the public health or welfare. In this regard, the North Carolina opinion in *Aston Park* and its protection of the economic interests of health facilities has been frequently compared to the nineteenth century judicial attitude towards substantive due process applied in such cases as *Lochner v. New York* and eventually rejected by most modern courts. Thus, for example, in New York, the first state to adopt a certificate of need program, the state's supreme court upheld the constitutionality of the program in an opinion that framed the issue in traditional police power terms: in regulating economic activities, the legislature should be given great discretion so long as there is a reasonable basis for the activity.

> The legislation resulted from an exhaustive study by a joint legislative committee (citation omitted). Therefrom it appears that the uncontrolled construction of unnecessary or substandard hospital and nursing home beds may be one of the causes of the spiraling costs of medical care. Thus, it is unnecessary to rely on the presumption that the Legislature has investigated and found facts necessary to support the legislation. (citation omitted) "'Where the questions of what the facts establish is a fairly debatable one, we accept and carry into effect the opinion of the Legislature. . . .' Nor may courts substitute their judgment for the Legislature so long as there can be discovered 'any state of facts either known or which could reasonably be assumed' to afford support for the legislative decision to act."
>
> It is now recognized that the operation of the so-called nursing homes bears a reasonable relation to the health, safety and welfare of a community and is subject to licensing and regulation as a valid exercise of the police power (citation omitted). The proliferation of such homes be-

yond the needs of a geographical area with spiraling costs to the users thereof bears a similar reasonable relation to the welfare of the community and may not be found to be an invalid exercise of the police power.

Using slightly different language, and giving somewhat greater weight to the property interest of the providers subject to certificate of need review, the Supreme Court of Alabama upheld the state certificate of need program. It held that so long as there is a "legitimate bona fide relationship between a permissible public purpose" and the legislation and the balance struck between the public interest and the individual rights affected is "reasonable and fair," the legislation is constitutional.

Ironically, the decision of the North Carolina Supreme Court in *Aston Park* set the stage for an important test of federal authority with regard to health planning programs. Immediately following the *Aston Park* decision, Congress enacted the 1974 health planning legislation which required, among other things, that states establish certificate of need programs in order to qualify for funding under the act and under various other federal programs. Essentially, North Carolina was required to enact a program that had been declared unconstitutional by its own supreme court or lose what was estimated to be nearly $50 million a year in federal funds. In response, North Carolina, along with several provider organizations, filed suit in federal court claiming that the federal law was unconstitutional. Essentially, North Carolina questioned whether the federal "conditional spending authority" could be used to coerce the state into either violating or amending its own state constitution; such a federal law, it argued, would interfere with the sovereignty of the state as protected by the Tenth Amendment and other provisions of the federal Constitution. The provider groups argued that the federal law "seeks to convert private facilities into public facilities subject to federal regulation and interferes with the physician-patient relationship," contending that interference with such interests protected by the Constitution is prohibited.

In *North Carolina ex rel. Morrow v. Califano*, 445 F. Supp. 532 (E.D.N.C. 1977), *aff'd mem.*, 435 U.S. 962 (1978), a three judge district court upheld the federal law despite these constitutional challenges.

Reviewing previous interpretations of the broad powers of the federal government to tax and spend for the general welfare, the court found that this authority clearly includes spending for health and health-related activities and also includes the authority to condition the receipt of funds. Conditional spending could be limited only if the condition served no legitimate national purpose or if the condition were not voluntary but legally coercive, i.e., where compliance was required by threat of sanction other than withdrawal of funding.

Applying these principles to North Carolina's argument, the *Califano* court held:

> The plaintiff argues that however valid such power may be generally, this power of the federal government to attach conditions to grants to the States is not an unlimited one and may not be stretched to validate "coercive conditions." What it urges is the necessary consequence of the requirement of a State certificate of need law. . . . [The Supreme Court in previous decisions] declared as a general rule, that when the condition attached by Congress to an appropriation grant available to the states relates to a "legitimately national" purpose, inducement or temptation to conform does not go beyond the bounds of the federal government's legitimate spending power in any constitutional sense.
>
> * * *
>
> . . . It is unfortunate that its Constitution, as presently phrased and interpreted, might prevent compliance by North Carolina, with the federally established condition. Simply because one State, by some oddity of its Constitution may be prohibited from compliance is not sufficient ground, though, to invalidate a condition which is legitimately related to a national interest. . . .
>
> It must be remembered that this Act is not compulsory on the State. Unlike the legislation faulted in *State of Maryland v. Environmental Protection Ag., supra,* 530 F.2d 215, it does not impose a mandatory requirement to enact legislation on the State; it gives to the states an *option* to enact such legislation and, in order to induce that enactment, offers financial assistance. Such legislation conforms to the pattern generally of federal grants to the states and is not "coercive" in the constitutional sense.
>
> * * *
>
> We find equally unpersuasive that this Act, with its certificate of need condition, threatens "the integrity of a recognized state government" and the "Republican form of government" and is therefore violative of the Guaranty Clause of the Constitution, Article IV, Section 4, or the Tenth Amendment. As we have already observed, the statutory condition on which the plaintiff directs its attack is not mandatory but is to be adopted or not at the option of the State and its burden on the State, if it should operate to terminate the plaintiff's right to participate under the federal health assistance programs, would not be coercive.

With respect to the providers' constitutional claims, the court dismissed their arguments without elaboration, holding simply that they found no basis in the Constitution for such claims.

Thus it would appear that Congress can constitutionally condition federal funds to achieve virtually any national purpose including regulating health and health-related activities. Moreover, it is clear from

Califano and other judicial decisions that the definition of "national purpose" is to be left primarily to the discretion of Congress; indeed, at least in the last 50 years, the courts have never invalidated a federal spending program for exceeding constitutional limits; nor have they invalidated a condition imposed as part of a spending program. No court, for example, has ever invalidated a condition or regulatory program imposed on providers participating in Medicaid or Medicare. (*See* note on reimbursement limits at the end of chapter 5). Nor have they invalidated any condition imposed on states participating in Medicaid or other health funding program. Apparently so long as participation is literally voluntary, the coercive effect of economic incentives to participation will not affect the constitutionality of federal regulation achieved through conditional spending. And while modern courts have shown some concern for the impact of federal authority on state sovereignty (*see* note at end of this chapter), it appears that a requirement that a state maintain a health facility regulation program or lose federal funding does not exceed constitutional limits, so long as the state's participation is viewed as voluntary.

In this regard, the definition of the scope of the conditional spending authority in this context is little different from the definition of the authority of the federal government to impose limits or conditions on spending for social welfare, education, or other programs as discussed in chapter 5. Paralleling the analysis of the due process and equal protection arguments in such cases as *Harris v. McRae,* the *Califano* court was essentially saying that the congressional discretion to spend for health regulation programs is to be given virtually unlimited latitude by the courts, and that constitutionally protected interests, even the interests of the state in its sovereignty, are not sufficiently affected or violated by this type of conditional spending program. Thus such programs are not subject to any greater judicial review than to insure that the condition relates to a legitimate national purpose. The virtual dismissal of the providers' arguments in *Califano* that the federal health planning legislation violates the constitutional rights of health facilities or interferes with the physician-patient interest also parallels the logic of *McRae.* Just as the federal government is virtually unlimited in its discretion not to fund an activity, the federal government may have equally broad discretion to encourage state regulatory activities by conditional spending. The providers' interest, however, if it is protected by the state or federal constitutions, can always be raised in a challenge to the state activity itself; nothing in the *Califano* case, for instance, affected the ruling of the North Carolina Supreme Court that the state's certificate of need program was unconstitutional. The *Califano* decision essentially ruled that the congressional funding of certifi-

cate of need was constitutional, as was the refusal to fund health planning or other related activities in states that did not have certificate of
need programs.

The principles illustrated by the *Aston Park* and *Califano* cases
leave open several issues for speculation. First of all, while *Califano* appears to make a distinction between voluntary and coercive, it does not
definitely address the possibility that a state's choice of participation
may be legally voluntary but, practically speaking, required or coerced.
For example, if a state were required to have a certificate of need program or lose all federal health funds, it is unlikely that any state would
have a real choice but to comply. Would this be sufficient interference
with state sovereignty? Or, if the federal government were to national-
ize health financing, would Congress be given unlimited discretion to
condition that program and its effect on either state government or
private providers—so long as participation were legally voluntary?

It is also worth speculating about the extent of federal authority
to regulate health facilities or to require states to do so, under the interstate commerce authority. Thus far, Congress has been reluctant to
rely on the power created by the interstate commerce clause of the federal Constitution as the basis for health or health-related programs.
Virtually all federal health planning and regulatory programs have
been achieved through conditional spending. Yet this is largely a result
of political constraints, not constitutional limit. Modern courts have interpreted the federal power to regulate interstate commerce quite
broadly. Indeed, at least since the 1930s, the Supreme Court has consistently interpreted that authority to give Congress virtually unlimited
discretion to "adopt any reasonable means it considers appropriate" to
regulate private economic activities so long as they can be characterized as either affecting or moving through interstate commerce.

And while none of the programs discussed earlier in this chapter
have been enacted as an exercise of the commerce authority, the federal labor laws and the federal antitrust laws—both directed at activities to the extent that they are engaged in interstate commerce—have
been interpreted to apply to hospitals, nursing homes, and virtually all
health care providers. Federal occupational health and safety programs
and the various federal environmental protection programs have also
imposed direct regulatory controls, both on state governments and on
private individuals and institutions, again exercising the federal power
over interstate commerce. (Carter's hospital cost containment program
in its more ambitious forms also would have required justification as a
regulation of interstate commerce.)

Clearly Congress under its authority to regulate interstate commerce could institute federal planning or regulatory controls over

health care providers, and in doing so would likely be given by the courts broadly defined discretion, probably discretion at least as broad as the courts—except the *Aston Park* court—give the states in exercising the state's police powers. (For a reference to judicial interpretations of the interstate commerce authority and the standard for judicial review, see note at end of chapter.)

The only possible constitutional check on federal authority to regulate interstate commerce recognized in recent years has been where that authority was seen as interfering too greatly with state sovereignty. It was in the context of federal minimum wage laws—extending to all employers "engaged in interstate commerce"—as applied to state-administered mental institutions that the Supreme Court in 1976 raised the possibility that congressional discretion may be checked, even where legitimately within the enumerated powers of the federal government, where it affects state sovereignty too greatly. (For a more recent decision modifying that 1976 case, see note at end of chapter.)

Thus it is possible to envision Congress enacting a broadly defined hospital cost containment program or requiring mandatory rate setting for all health care providers as a legitimate exercise of the federal power to regulate interstate commerce. But it is at least conceivable that if these programs were to include regulation of state-administered programs, or to interfere with other traditional state health activities, the resulting impact on state sovereignty might prompt some courts to limit federal authority to carry out these programs.

But while these possibilities raise intriguing questions, the political constraints on such possible exercises of federal authority have effectively mooted any necessity to pursue them further. Congress, as mentioned above and as reflected by the history of health planning and regulatory programs chronicled at the beginning of this chapter, has always been reluctant to directly regulate health care delivery; the historic pattern has been to encourage or "coerce" state government to administer and develop regulatory programs. And under the politics of the Reagan administration, that political tendency has been even more pronounced. Thus the limits on federal authority, from a constitutional perspective, are unlikely to be tested, at least in the near future.

On the other hand, there is at least a likelihood that the near future will provide a testing of state constitutional authority. At least in some states, certificate of need programs are being continued, even as the federal mandate to maintain them is being pared away. Assuming that they are effectively and rigorously administered, at some point they are likely to engage the type of legal controversy which will include among other legal objections further attempts to constitutionally restrain legislative and executive discretion under such programs. For that matter, North Carolina re-enacted its certificate of need program in 1977—somewhat ironically, given its claims before the *Califano* court—and continues to review the necessity of various health facility projects. At least in North Carolina, and possibly elsewhere, the underlying constitutionality of certificate of need programs will be further litigated.

Similarly, if more states continue to follow the lead of those that have already adopted rate setting programs, eventually they will spawn the type of legal controversy that will test the limits of state authority in that context as well. Even if the state's authority to regulate providers continues to be broadly defined by most courts, certainly mandatory rate setting, rates based on industrywide averaging, fixed lids on annual budget increases, or other "real dollar" regulatory controls will be sufficiently controversial to provoke providers to challenge the state's authority, even if such challenges are unlikely to be successful.

CONCLUSION

If the few cases that have already been contested before the courts are an indication of the manner in which future courts will view the constitutionality of state and federal health facility regulation, then the relevant constitutional principles that outline the limits on government authority in this context are rather clear. Both Congress under its enumerated powers and the state legislatures under their police powers have extensive authority to maintain or require health planning programs, certificate of need controls, quality standards, or limits on rates or prices, subject only to the broadest of judicially imposed constraints. Indeed, the definition of government authority in this context differs little from the principles enunciated in earlier chapters, both with regard to the broad definition of the powers of government in matters relating to health and health care, and in the delineation of how that power is divided among the branches of government. The constitutional limits imposed on government authority to regulate health care providers and the government authority to regulate individual conduct as discussed in earlier chapters appears to differ mainly in that most courts do not view the regulation of health care providers—at least the programs that have been implemented to date—as affecting or having an impact on any fundamentally protected constitutional right. Thus legislative prerogatives are given the broadest of definition, and the oversight role of the courts is rather minimal. As a result, considerable, almost unchecked, power is allowed to the state and federal legislatures. The scope and nature of the government role in formulating health policy are left primarily to the machinations of the legislative process and the political influences that affect that process, and are not greatly affected by constitutional principles.

This does not preclude entirely, however, the judicial role in determining the direction of state and federal health policies. As the next chapters will demonstrate, the courts have a role in interpreting legislative mandates entirely apart from their role in determining the constitutionality of that legislation.

END NOTES

1. For additional background on licensing, accreditation, and certification, as well as an overview of health facility planning and regulatory programs, see sources cited in Wing & Craige, *Health Care Regulation: Dilemma of a Partially Developed Public Policy*, 57 N.C.L. REV. 1165 (1979). For reference to the development of licensing and certification standards for nursing homes, see Butler, *Assuring the Quality of Care and Life in Nursing Homes: The Dilemma of Enforcement*, 57 N.C.L. REV. 1317 (1979). For reference to the most recent nursing home certification standards, see 42 C.F.R. §§ 442.12–442.13 (1983). (Note that the introductory explanation to the original issuance of these regulations discusses some of the political constraints involved. 45 Fed. Reg. 22936 (1980).)

2. Many of the same issues discussed in this chapter involving government authority and the legal and political constraints on that authority could also be demonstrated by a review of health personnel regulation. In fact, the earliest example of state government regulation of health care delivery involved physician licensing programs, initiated in some states early in the nineteenth century. For a review of the history of government regulation of physicians and other health care personnel, see F. GRAD & N. MARTI, PHYSICIANS' LICENSURE AND DISCIPLINE: THE LEGAL AND PROFESSIONAL REGULATION OF MEDICAL PRACTICE (1979).

   It is clear that with regard to licensing and other personnel regulation, the primary restraint on the authority of legislatures to adopt regulatory measures and on administrative and executive discretion in carrying out these programs involves the political clout of providers—not the constraints of the state and federal constitutions.

   It is also worth noting that the terms "certification," "accreditation," "registration," and "licensing" are not used consistently from state to state and vary somewhat from the usage of those terms in the context of health facility regulation.

3. For a description of the Hill-Burton program, the "charity care" requirements, and their enforcement, see Wing, *The Community Service Obligation of Hill-Burton Health Facilities*, 23 B.C.L. REV. 577 (1982).

4. While providing the testing ground for health planning activities, and the battle grounds for almost constant skirmishes between the state and fed-

eral government, provider interests, and, on occasion, representatives of consumers, certificate of need programs have never been regarded as particularly successful, regardless of the yardstick used to measure success. For a critical discussion and a summary of the literature, see C. HAVIGHURST, DEREGULATING THE HEALTH CARE INDUSTRY 53–76 (1982). For a more sympathetic description, see Weiner, *Participatory Procedure and Political Support for Hospital Cost Containment Programs: Limits on Open Administrative Process*, 57 N.C.L. REV. 1197 (1979).

5. As the text indicates, all courts that have considered the constitutionality of certificate of need programs, except for the North Carolina Supreme Court in its *Aston Park* decision, have upheld the state's substantive authority to enact such legislation; but the issue has been actually contested in surprisingly few jurisdictions. Goodin v. State *ex. rel.* Okla. Welfare Comm'n, 436 F. Supp. 583 (W.D. Okla. 1977); Mount Royal Towers, Inc. v. Alabama Bd. of Health, 388 So.2d 1209 (Ala. 1980); Merry Heart Nursing and Convalescent Home v. Dougherty, 131 N.J. Super. 412, 330 A.2d 370 (1974); Attoma v. State Dep't of Social Welfare, 26 A.D.2d 12, 270 N.Y.S.2d 167 (1966).

   Mount Royal Towers is a particularly good case since it reviews the history of economic regulation at both the state and federal levels from the nineteenth century to date; it also distinguishes between various tests of "rationality" and "reasonableness."

   For a classic definition of the broad scope given states in regulating economic activities, see Nebbia v. New York, 291 U.S. 502 (1934) (regulation of milk prices); Williamson v. Lee Optical of Okla., 348 U.S. 483 (1955) (regulation of opticians' services).

6. In addition to the *Califano* decision, the constitutionality of conditional spending was also reviewed and upheld in litigation challenging the PSRO legislation and other utilization review requirements imposed on providers participating in Medicaid and Medicare. *See* Association of Am. Phys. & Surg. v. Mathews, 395 F. Supp. 125 (N.D. Ill. 1975), *aff'd*, 423 U.S. 975 (1975).

7. For more extensive discussion of federal power under the conditional spending or interstate commerce authority, including an analysis of the limits imposed by the judicial concern for state sovereignty, see Wing & Silton, *Constitutional Authority for Extending Federal Control Over the Delivery of Health Care*, 57 N.C.L. REV. 1423 (1979).

8. While somewhat parenthetical, the state sovereignty issue may deserve separate examination. In National League of Cities v. Usery, 426 U.S. 833 (1976), a sharply divided Supreme Court held that the federal fair labor standards law could not be applied to require the payment of minimum wages to employees of state and local government. (The case involved the challenge to the subminimum wages paid by states to inmates of state mental institutions.) This was the first time in at least three decades that the Supreme Court had shown an interest in protecting state sovereignty. A similar concern for limiting the constitutional authority of the federal gov-

ernment over state government was evidenced one year later in Environmental Protection Ag. v. Brown, 431 U.S. 99 (1977). Nonetheless, a later decision of the Supreme Court—equally sharp in its division among the justices—cast doubt on the original implications of *National League of Cities.* *See* EEOC v. Wyoming, 460 U.S. 226 (1983).

9. Another possible constitutional issue that has been effectively mooted by political constraints involves the extent of state (or federal) government authority to close or decertify existing health facilities. While it would involve an application of the same principles discussed in this chapter, it is likely that at least some courts would view such an unprecedented regulatory measure as either involving an existing property interest to the extent requiring closer judicial scrutiny or a "taking" of property requiring compensation. For a discussion see Kopit, *Hospital Decertification: Legitimate Regulation or a Taking of Private Property?*, 1978 UTAH L. REV. 179.

10. The revised North Carolina certificate of need program—which, thus far, has not been successfully challenged—is codified at N.C. GEN. STAT. §§ 131E-175 to -199 (Supp. 1983). In 1982, it was amended to impose a moratorium on the construction of all nursing home beds in the state. *See* Act of Oct. 10, 1981, ch. 1127, § 31, 1981 N.C. Sess. Laws 1622, 1645.

11. While the political influence wielded by providers can discourage legislatures from pursuing regulatory strategies, it can also lead to the promotion of certain types of regulatory schemes, namely those that limit market entry and competition rather than promote quality, as conservative theorists have frequently argued. For example, in North Carolina (and many other states) dental hygienists can work only under the direct supervision of a dentist; this is arguably an attempt to regulate the quality of hygienists' services but more likely an attempt to protect the "turf" of the dental profession. Such legislation was upheld as constitutional in Delancy v. Garren, No. 82-339-CIV-5 (E.D.N.C. Aug. 1982), (*aff'd* without published opinion by the Fourth Circuit in 1983).

12. As indicated in the text, state "all payer" rate setting programs appear to be the "new game in town;" for reference on their history and recent developments, see Esposito, Hupfer, Mason & Rogler, *Abstracts of State Legislated Hospital Cost-Containment Programs*, HEALTH CARE FIN. REV., Dec. 1982, at 129, 143; Worthington, Tyson & Chin, *Prospective Reimbursement in Maryland*, TOPICS IN HEALTH CARE FIN., Fall 1979, at 59.

For a review of their constitutionality, see Massachusetts General Hosp. v. Weiner, 569 F.2d 1156 (lst Cir. 1978); *In re* Monmouth Medical Center Rate Appeal, 185 N.J. Super. 20, 447 A.2d 192 (1982).

7

The Scope of Discretion of Administrative Agencies in Matters Affecting Health and Health Care Delivery

Previous chapters have considered governmental authority in the broadest sense, examining the extent of state and federal government authority and the constitutional limits that can in some circumstances check or proscribe the exercise of that power. But as suggested in the conclusion to chapter 6, the definition of the constitutional parameters within which state and federal legislatures, executive agencies or officials, and the courts share governmental authority establishes only one important set of legal rights or principles relevant to an understanding of government authority in matters affecting health and health care. In addition to questions concerning the constitutionality of a legislated program or mandate, significant and controversial questions can often be raised concerning the nature and terms of the legislation, and, particularly, the extent of governmental authority that is vested in the agencies or officials given the responsibility for administering the legislation.

In the most simplistic terms, the answers to such questions derive largely from statutory interpretation. Quite literally, assuming that the legislature has acted constitutionally, defining the scope and nature of the administrative discretion of an agency is a matter of determining what the agency has been empowered to do by the legislature that created the agency or its authority. Thus the rule-making authority of an administrative agency, i.e., its authority to issue regulations and, in some cases, other interpretations of law, is determined primarily by examining the statutory language of the agency's legislation. Similarly, the agency's adjudicatory functions, its authority to provide—or with-draw—funding; to apply standards for health, safety, or environmental protection; to make decisions regarding the distribution of health care resources; or any other adjudicatory activity are determined in the same manner: by examining the language of the authorization statute that created the agency or its programs and the authority that is dele-gated to the agency by that legislation. The same principle applies to the procedures that are to be followed in carrying out these various re-sponsibilities. An agency must follow those procedures outlined in the agency's authorization statute or, where procedures have not been specified in the legislation, follow the terms of the administrative pro-cedures act of that particular jurisdiction. An administrative proce-dures act is simply a statute that defines the procedures to be followed by agencies unless other procedures are specified in the authorization legislation for each agency.

While this principle of statutory definition of authority can be ab-stractly presented as simple and straightforward, its application to spe-cific agencies is complicated by a number of factors. First, as outlined in chapter 1, the executive branch of government, particularly in recent years, includes an extensive array of programs and agencies that can be viewed generically in only the vaguest terms. In fact, today the state and federal executive hierarchies include an endless variety of agen-cies, ranging from traditional hierarchial structures, to the quasi-autonomous commissions and boards of the "fourth branch" agencies, to the complicated networks of private and public agencies that are typ-ified by health planning programs. Moreover, Congress, as well as the state legislatures, has created increasing and increasingly complicated governmental responsibilities for these administrative agencies; simply describing, let alone understanding, the workings of any one of them can be a difficult undertaking.

Second, as might be expected, the interpretation of statutory pro-visions is not always a simple or straightforward task. The results of leg-islative process are sometimes fairly clear, but just as often rather vague and sometimes intentionally so. As the material that follows will dem-onstrate, interpreting the language of a statute and delineating the au-thority explicitly or implicitly created by that language can be difficult and frustrating, as well as controversial.

Finally, and most critically, the components of the executive branch of state and federal government are probably best viewed not as a network of agencies or programs but as a series of decision-making processes, each carried out by various individual and institutional deci-sion makers. That is to say, a rule-making or adjudicatory decision of an administrative agency invariably involves not a single decision by a single official or agency, but a series of such decisions.

Rule-making or adjudicatory decisions often begin with an investigation or hearing by an agency's staff, initiated in some cases by the agency or in other cases on the application of a member of the public. Generally there is a preliminary decision made within the agency, but typically a board or commission, or even the head of the agency, will be empowered to review the initial decision and even disregard it altogether. In some agencies, there are several levels of decision and review. These decisions, in turn, may be subject to appeal to an administrative appellate board within or independent of the agency; and generally an administrative decision can be appealed through the courts (or even to a specially created judicial body). The final decision of an agency, therefore, can be, and often is, the result of a protracted decision-making process by a series of decision makers. Consequently, the authority of the agency can be fully understood only with reference to the entire process and to the individual decisions at each level within that process.

The difficulty this creates for understanding the scope and nature of the authority of a particular administrative agency can be fully appreciated only with reference to a specific agency and specific decisions by that agency. The authority of local welfare departments, for example, to make individual Medicaid eligibility determinations (an example of an adjudicatory decision) involves, in most states, an initial decision by an eligibility worker. That decision can be appealed to a supervisor within the local welfare office who is empowered to make an independent determination of eligibility. But the supervisor's decision can also be appealed, and the local agency will hold an administrative hearing, usually before an official of the agency or possibly before an administrative law judge. Even that decision is subject to several levels of appeal within the state Medicaid agency and eventually to the courts. To fully understand the nature of the agency's authority and its discretion to allow or deny Medicaid eligibility under a particular set of circumstances, it would be necessary to sort out each of the decisions at each level of the process and the scope of discretion allowed to each decision maker. The principle for doing so would be rather simple, at least on its face: both the substantive authority of each decision maker and the procedures that must be followed would be determined primarily by reference to the state and federal statutes that authorize the Medicaid program as well as the regulations and other agency-made interpretations of those statutes.

Other agencies might follow quite different procedures in making adjudicatory type decisions, even decisions that are quite similar to Medicaid eligibility decisions. As the material later in the chapter will demonstrate, the authority of administrative agencies can be distributed by the legislature through the executive branch and through the courts in a wide variety of ways. In this regard, the civil commitment procedures examined in chapter 3 for purposes of illustrating the requirements of procedural due process could also be viewed as alternative examples of how administrative authority can be distributed between the agents of the executive branch (i.e., law enforcement officials and various state or local mental health professionals) and the courts. Holding aside constitutional considerations, the scope and nature of the authority to civilly commit is determined primarily by the provisions of the civil commitment statute of each particular jurisdiction.

These same notions can also be illustrated by reference to the rule-making authority of such administrative agencies as certificate of need agencies, the Federal Trade Commission, the boards that issue medical or other health professional licenses, or any others of the wide variety of health-related administrative agencies. From agency to agency, and from jurisdiction to jurisdiction, the authority to issue regulations is carried out through a process that involves a series of decision makers both within and without the agency. Thus rule making, like adjudicatory decisions, does not involve a single decision but a lengthy and complicated decision-making process. And while the procedures generally followed by state and federal agencies in issuing regulations tend to be more uniform than the various adjudicatory decision-making processes, there is still a considerable amount of variation from agency to agency. Nonetheless, the basic principle defining the power of an agency to issue regulations, the distribution of that power among various decision makers, and the procedures to be followed during the decision-making process remain the same. The substantive and procedural rule-making authority of an administrative agency is determined primarily by interpreting the scope of the authority created by the agency's legislation.

It should be obvious that the role of the courts in defining the authority of administrative agencies is critical. As illustrated above, the courts are generally given at least some direct role in reviewing the merits of administrative decisions. Typically, the agency's authorizing legislation will give some court the discretion to overturn an adminstrative decision if it is "arbitrary or capricious," or if it lacks "substantial evidence," as will be examined in more detail in the next section. The scope of judicial review of the merits of the decision can be defined— by the statute—rather broadly or very narrowly and, in a few cases, the agency's statute will specifically preclude any judicial review of the agency's decisions altogether. (*See* discussion in note at end of chapter.)

Whatever the role of the courts in reviewing the merits of the specific decision itself, the courts also retain their role in adjudicating the constitutionality of the agency's statute. Thus, anyone opposed to an agency's decision can claim that the authorizing legislation and, therefore, the decision made under that authority are unconstitutional, and the courts will exercise their traditional role in interpreting the constitutionality of legislation, in addition to whatever role they play in reviewing the merits of administrative decisions.

But the courts in their role as "interpreters of law" are primarily responsible for interpreting statutes as well. Thus the various questions that have been posed above regarding the substantive and procedural authority of administrative agencies are issues that are ultimately decided before the courts. A statute could be interpreted to delegate considerable discretion to a particular agency, and may even be interpreted to preclude judicial review of that decision; but it is the role of the courts to make these interpretations of the kind of decisions that can be made, the discretion of the various decision makers in the decision-making process, and the procedures that must be followed, including, somewhat ironically, the definition of their own role in reviewing decisions.

In this regard, the material in this chapter parallels the issues addressed in previous chapters. The principal concern here is the definition of governmental power; in the present context, the power of agencies of the executive branch. In order to understand this power, it is necessary to define the extent of the authority of various government agencies over private individuals or institutions. But to do so, it is also necessary to define the manner in which that power is distributed among the branches of government and, particularly, the manner in which the authority of the executive is checked or proscribed by the courts. The significant difference between the material in this chapter and that discussed in earlier chapters is that the definition of the scope and nature of government authority, and the delineation of the roles of the various branches of government in exercising that authority, is basically defined by statutory provision. In previous chapters, similar issues were defined primarily by reference to constitutional principles.

The remainder of this chapter will examine in considerable detail two rule-making decisions by a federal agency and the process by which they were made and reviewed, to provide an example of administrative decision making and illustrate how an agency's substantive and procedural authority is largely determined by statutory interpretation. Particular emphasis in these illustrations will be on the roles the courts played both in interpreting the statutory authority of the agency and in reviewing the substantive merits of each decision.

THE RULE-MAKING DISCRETION
OF THE OCCUPATIONAL SAFETY
AND HEALTH ADMINISTRATION:
THE BENZENE REGULATIONS

The Occupational Safety and Health Act of 1970 represented a major departure from previous governmental policy with regard to the mandatory regulation of health and safety in the workplace; never before had such direct and extensive control over private employers been attempted, and to the extent that government had previously regulated the work place, it had been largely the efforts of individual states. But in 1970, Congress, finding that "[P]ersonal injuries and illnesses arising out of work situations impose a substantial burden upon . . . interstate commerce," enacted legislation authorizing a wide-ranging list of research, educational, and, most critically, regulatory activities to be carried out by various federal agencies or, under the supervision of federal agencies, by each state. Central to the legislative scheme was the creation of the Occupational Safety and Health Administration (OSHA) within the Department of Labor, which was empowered by the new federal law to establish standards for health and safety for virtually all public and private workplaces. (For a full description of the legislation and the complicated network of state and federal agencies responsible for carrying it out, see sources cited in note at end of chapter.)

Specifically, two provisions of the 1970 statute gave the agency extensive regulatory powers: section 3(8) of the legislation gave OSHA (or to be technically correct, the Secretary of Labor on the recommendation of the assistant secretary in charge of OSHA) broad, ongoing regulatory authority to enact standards which require "conditions, or the adoption or use of one or more practices, means, methods, operations, or processes, reasonably necessary or appropriate to provide safe or healthful employment or places of employment." Furthermore, section 6(b)(5) of the legislation further prescribed the rule-making authority for the agency in issuing standards regulating toxic or other harmful materials:

> [The agency must] set the standard which most adequately assures, *to the extent feasible, on the basis of the best available evidence, that no employee will suffer material impairment of health or functional capacity* even if such employee has regular exposure to the hazard dealt with by such standard for the period of his working life. Development of standards under this subsection shall be based upon research, demonstrations, experiments, and such other information as may be appropriate. In addition to the attainment of the highest degree of health and safety protection for the employee, other considerations shall be the latest available scientific data

in the field, the feasibility of the standards, and experience gained under this and other health and safety laws. Whenever practicable, the standard promulgated shall be expressed in terms of objective criteria and of the performance desired. [emphasis added]

The procedures that OSHA was required to follow in issuing permanent regulations were also defined in the 1970 legislation. Before issuing regulations, OSHA may first request that a national advisory board be empaneled to consider the proposed regulations and make recommendations (within a fixed period of time but a maximum of 270 days). OSHA must then publish a regulation in proposed form in the *Federal Register* and allow anyone to submit written data or comments within 30 days or to request a public hearing on the proposed regulations. Such hearing must be held by OSHA within 60 days. (Typically, OSHA rule-making hearings are before an administrative law judge who compiles a transcript and record but does not exercise any independent decision-making role.) Following publication or a public hearing, OSHA then has 60 days to publish the final regulations. OSHA must consider the evidence it receives, but the agency is empowered to make an independent judgment in issuing final regulations according to the standard outlined in the legislation.

Final regulations are effective immediately on publication, although OSHA can delay the effective date or issue a variance or exception to individual employers under certain circumstances. Final regulations may be appealed to the federal circuit court of appeals. According to the OSHA statute, the court is required to review the basis for the decision but uphold the findings of the agency if supported by "substantial evidence" in the record considered as a whole. "Substantial evidence," as generally interpreted in this (and other) contexts, allows the court to review the administrative records but requires the court to uphold the findings so long as there is "such relevant evidence as a reasonable mind might accept as adequate to support a conclusion." (*See* discussion below.)

The 1970 legislation allows that in certain prescribed circumstances OSHA may issue emergency regulations. If the agency makes a finding that there is "grave danger" to an employee, a regulation can be issued without prior notice and it takes effect immediately on its first publication in the *Federal Register*; following such publication, however, the agency then has six months to issue permanent regulations as outlined above. The 1970 legislation also allowed that during the first two years following the enactment of the legislation OSHA could adopt and enforce without prior notice or public hearing "consensus standards" —standards that had been previously recognized by a federal agency or by a list of nationally recognized bodies.

Needless to say, the implementation of OSHA's rule-making authority under this legislation has been controversial, just as the legislation itself was only enacted in the face of considerable political resistance. Indeed, immediately following the enactment of the legislation, employer representatives brought a variety of constitutional challenges to the authority of Congress to enact such legislation, although these lawsuits were largely unsuccessful. (*See* discussion in notes at end of chapter.) But in addition to these constitutional challenges, the administrative decisions of OSHA interpreting the scope of its own authority and imposing health and safety standards on various workplaces have also generated considerable political and legal protest—and will likely continue to do so.

Two OSHA rule-making decisions in particular, involving the standards for benzene exposure in petroleum-related industries and for exposure to cotton dust in textiles manufacturing, represented important tests of the extent of OSHA's authority created by Congress in the 1970 legislation. They also provide good illustrations of how rule-making decisions are made and the constraints that can be imposed on administrative discretion by the courts.

In 1971, OSHA adopted as a "consensus standard" a standard limiting benzene exposure to 10 parts per million averaged over an eight-hour period with a ceiling concentration of 25 parts per million for a ten-minute period or a maximum peak concentration of 50 parts per million. This "consensus standard" was applicable to rubber manufacturers, petrochemical industries, and other petroleum-related workplaces. This standard had been previously adopted by several private industrial organizations, based largely on the nonmalignant toxic side effects of benzene. In 1974, however, the National Institute for Occupational Safety and Health (NIOSH), the research arm of OSHA, recommended further studies of the hazards of benzene based on the possible link between benzene exposure and leukemia. In 1976, based on additional research, NIOSH reported to OSHA that there was "conclusive proof" that benzene exposure increased the risk of leukemia and, consequently, formally recommended that OSHA issue standards setting occupational benzene exposure levels as low as possible. Significantly, none of the studies relied on by NIOSH in its recommendations considered the risks of benzene at levels below 10 parts per million.

Following further research—and a change of presidential administrations—NIOSH in 1977 again formally recommended that the agency issue regulations lowering the existing "consensus standard."

These recommendations were, of course, only the public face of a policy debate among the White House, the Secretary of Labor, and the staff of OSHA and NIOSH, one critical, albeit generally unrecorded, portion of the administrative decision-making process. Eventually, the decision was made to issue emergency regulations reducing the eight-hour benzene limit from 10 parts per million to 1, reducing the ten-minute exposure limit from 25 parts per million to 5, and eliminating altogether the 50 parts per million maximum allowance. The new standards would have gone into effect on their publication in May 1977; however, employer representatives were able to convince a federal district court to temporarily enjoin the emergency regulations, arguing that OSHA had exceeded its statutory authority. OSHA appealed the temporary injunction to the Fifth Circuit Court of Appeals, but when the appellate court refused to lift the injunction, OHSA abandoned its efforts to litigate its authority to issue emergency benzene standards. Instead, OSHA issued the same standards as proposals for permanent regulations according to the statutory procedures. Following publication in the *Federal Register* and receipt of written comments, the agency held public hearings in July 1977.

In their final form, OSHA modified the proposed regulations but basically adopted the original benzene exposure limits. Employers subject to the new standards (gas stations, for example, were exempted from the regulations) were required to monitor exposures to benzene, provide medical examinations whenever the airborne exposure exceeds .5 parts per million, and to institute whatever engineering controls are necessary to keep exposures below 1 part per million averaged over an eight-hour day or 5 parts per million for any 15-minute period. (Somewhat stricter standards were imposed for exposure to liquid benzene.)

In the extensive summary of the evidentiary record (184 pages) that accompanied the issuance of the final regulations, OSHA acknowledged the estimates by industry representatives that implementing such standards would be expensive, especially to some employers. OSHA estimated that the capital investment required to develop the necessary engineering controls could be over $260 million in the first year, in addition to $200 million for testing and training, and recurring annual costs of over $30 million. More importantly, of the 35,000 employees who would be affected by these controls, over two-thirds were in the rubber industry, where the compliance costs were estimated to be extremely low (less than $1500 per person). On the other hand, the petroleum refining industry would be required to spend over $25 million for only 300 workers at risk—a cost of over $80,000 per employee. The petrochemical industry claimed that it would be required to incur costs of over $20 million for fewer than 600 employees.

Most critically, in terms of litigation that was to follow, OSHA's summary of its administrative record indicated that it had not produced or received any direct empirical proof that exposures to benzene below 10 parts per million led to increased risk of cancer. The agency cited considerable data showing that there was increased risk of cancer, as well as other health risks, at exposure levels above the preexisting 10 parts per million standard. And the agency concluded from this record that there was no known safe level of exposure. (Industry representatives had argued that an extrapolated dose-response curve based on available studies of exposures above the 10 parts per million would show that exposures below 10 parts per million might be considered a safe risk, but OSHA rejected the industry's supporting evidence as inconclusive.)

Instead, OSHA, relying on its standard policy for carcinogens, concluded that in the absence of definitive proof of a safe level for a known carcinogen it must be assumed that any exposure level above zero presents some increased risk of cancer. The statutory authority of the agency under section 6(b)(5), according to OSHA's interpretation, was to set standards at the level demonstrated to be safe or at the lowest feasible level. The agency, therefore, concluded that it could set benzene standards at the lowest level technically and economically feasible for the affected industries, meaning a level which could be achieved without forcing any industry out of business.

Industry representatives appealed the issuance of the final benzene regulations, following the procedures outlined in the OSHA legislation, to the Court of Appeals for the Fifth Circuit. The industry argued that OSHA's new standards were not supported by "substantial evidence" in the record considered as a whole, the statutory standard of review for the merits of the decision by the court of appeals. The industry also argued that OSHA had misinterpreted its own statute, failing to read the "feasibility" language of section 6(b)(5) in light of the "reasonably necessary" language of section 3(8). Read together, the industry argued, the OSHA statute requires that the agency must not only find that there will be a benefit from the new regulations and that the standard will be technically and economically feasible, but that the proposed benefits will outweigh the projected costs of the new standard.

The court of appeals essentially agreed with the industry's reading of the statute and the argument that OSHA had exceeded the authority created by its authorization legislation. The court found that sections 3(8) and 6(b)(5) read together did require the agency to do a cost-benefit analysis of the new standards and that the agency had failed to do so. Moreover, the court found that one critical element of that analysis—the finding that the new standards would result in benefits to workers—was not supported by "substantial evidence" in the record taken as a whole.

OSHA's assumption that the standard is likely to result in benefits is not unsupported. The divided opinion in the scientific community over the existence or not of safe threshold levels of exposure to carcinogens provides substantial evidence which would support the finding that exposure to benzene at the present level of 10 ppm poses some leukemia risk. The general agreement in the scientific community that exposure to carcinogens at low levels is safer than exposures at higher levels permits the further factual deduction that reducing the permissible exposure limit from 10 ppm to 1 ppm will result in some benefit. This finding and deduction, however, does not yield the conclusion that measurable benefits will result, and OSHA is unable to point to any studies or projections supporting such a finding. As we noted in *Aqua Slide*, mere rationality is not equivalent to substantial evidence that conditions required by standards are reasonably necessary. 569 F.2d at 841. The lack of substantial evidence of discernable benefits is highlighted when one considers that OSHA is unable to point to any empirical evidence documenting a leukemia risk at 10 ppm even though that has been the permissible exposure limit since 1971. OSHA's assertion that benefits from reducing the permissible exposure limit from 10 ppm to 1 ppm are likely to be appreciable, an assumption based only on inferences drawn from studies involving much higher exposure levels rather than on studies involving these levels or sound statistical projections from the high-level studies, does not satisfy the reasonably necessary requirement limiting OSHA's action.

Clearly the Fifth Circuit Court of Appeals' interpretation of the authority of OSHA as created by the 1970 legislation and of the role of the courts in reviewing the exercise of that authority would greatly restrict the agency's discretion to set standards limiting exposure to such substances as benzene. While the court followed the traditional judicial interpretation of the term "substantial evidence," indicating that the courts should defer to agency discretion so long as there is some reasonable basis for the agency's findings in the administrative record, the court would not allow the agency to rely solely on the kind of policy judgment that OSHA had made about exposure to carcinogens in making a finding of benefit.

This does not mean that OSHA must wait until deaths occur as a result of exposure at levels below 10 ppm before it may validly promulgate a standard reducing the permissible exposure limit. *See Florida Peach Growers Association, Inc. v. United States Department of Labor*, 489 F.2d 120, 132 (5th Cir. 1974). Nevertheless, OSHA must have some factual basis for an estimate of expected benefits before it can determine that a one-half billion dollar standard is reasonably necessary. For example, when studies of the effects of human exposure to benzene at higher concentration levels in the past are sufficient to enable a dose-response curve to be charted that can reasonably be projected to the lower exposure levels, or when studies of the effects of animal exposure to benzene are sufficient to make projections of the risks involved with exposure at low levels, then OSHA will be able to make rough but educated estimates of the extent of benefits expected from reducing the permissible exposure level from 10 ppm to 1 ppm. Until such estimates are possible, OSHA does not have sufficient information to determine that a standard such as the one under review which it can only say might protect some worker from a leukemia risk is reasonably necessary.

The court of appeals' reading of the statute would have the agency record show "some factual basis" for estimating a measurable benefit, presumably empirically derived evidence or expert testimony. It also would require that the agency do a cost-benefit analysis comparing the costs of the engineering controls and other means for eliminating the exposure with the estimated benefit. A policy minimizing the risk from a known carcinogen until a safe level can be determined is not sufficient by itself to support an agency finding of a benefit; nor would the court's reading of the statute allow the agency to issue a standard without weighing the proposed benefits of the standard against the projected costs so as to show that the standard is both "feasible" and "reasonably necessary."

OSHA and several employee groups appealed the decision of the court of appeals to the Supreme Court, arguing that the Fifth Circuit court had misinterpreted the requirements of "substantial evidence" of a benefit and, by requiring a cost-benefit analysis of the standard, the requirements of sections 3(8) and 6(b)(5). The Supreme Court in *Industrial Union Dept. v. American Petrol. Inst.*, 448 U.S. 607 (1979), affirmed the decision of the court of appeals, but only by addressing the issue of whether the agency had found "substantial evidence" of a proposed benefit; it declined to address the cost-benefit question.

Looking to the language used throughout the 1970 legislation, the overall structure of that legislation, and its legislative history, the Court concluded that the agency was empowered to eliminate only significant risks of existing harms—meaning risks that could be supported by what the Court regarded as "substantial evidence." Without such a finding, the agency cannot claim that there would be a benefit from the proposed standards; and since there had not been a finding of a benefit, the Supreme Court, unlike the court of appeals, found no reason in this case to address the potentially more broad-reaching issue of cost-benefit analysis.

§ 3(8) . . . of the Act requires the Secretary, before issuing any standard, to determine that it is reasonably necessary and appropriate to remedy a significant risk of material health impairment. Only after the Secretary has made the threshold determination that such a risk exists with respect to a toxic substance, would it be necessary to decide whether § 6(b)(5) requires him to select the most protective standard he can consistent with economic and technological feasibility, or whether, as respondents argue, the benefits of the regulation must be commensurate with the costs of its implementation. Because the Secretary did not make the required threshold finding in these cases, we have no occasion to determine whether costs must be weighed against benefits in an appropriate case.

The Supreme Court also made some important disclaimers regarding the scope of its opinion and the issues that it did address. The Court acknowledged that the OSHA statute required only that the agency rely on the "best available evidence." And while clearly interpreting this language to require empirical evidence to support a finding of a measurable benefit, as had the court of appeals, the Court declined to elaborate on the nature of empirical evidence that would be sufficient to satisfy the statutory "substantial evidence" standard. The Court merely reiterated the traditional judicial interpretation of "substantial evidence," noting that such a standard is generally intended to allow the agency broad discretion in interpreting the weight of available evidence and to limit the judicial role to assuring the reasonableness of that discretion. Thus, in the Court's view, the decision to invalidate the issuance of permanent standards for benzene was based not on a weighing of the available evidence by the courts or a review of the reasonableness of the agency's judgment, but on a judicial determination that the agency had no evidence upon which to make the necessary finding, as required by the statute.

> In this case the record makes it perfectly clear that the Secretary relied squarely on a special policy for carcinogens that imposed the burden on industry of proving the existence of a safe level of exposure, thereby avoiding the Secretary's threshold responsibility of establishing the need for more stringent standards. In so interpreting his statutory authority, the Secretary exceeded his power.

Thus, the Supreme Court avoided ruling, at least for the moment, on the question of whether the statute requires OSHA to employ a cost-benefit analysis of its standards. But this issue, and questions requiring further delineation of the requirements of "substantial evidence," were soon to return to the Court in litigation involving OSHA standards for cotton dust.

THE RULE-MAKING AUTHORITY OF THE OCCUPATIONAL SAFETY AND HEALTH ADMINISTRATION: THE COTTON DUST REGULATIONS

In the deliberations over the original OSHA legislation, Congress had evidenced particular concern for occupational exposure to cotton dust and the various health risks associated with cotton dust, particularly byssinosis or brown lung disease. In apparent response, OSHA adopted as a "consensus standard" immediately following the enactment of the 1970 legislation a maximum exposure limit of 1,000 micrograms per cubic meter over an eight-hour day applicable to all cotton preparation and manufacturing. In 1974, NIOSH submitted a report to OSHA recommending that occupational exposure to cotton dust be more strictly limited, establishing a permissible exposure limit at the lowest feasible limit less than 200 micrograms per cubic meter of respirable dust. Shortly thereafter, OSHA published in the *Federal Register* an advance notice of proposed rule making based on these recommendations. Formal proposals for regulations were published in December 1976.

As it had with the benzene standards, OSHA received voluminous comments from scientists, labor unions, industry representatives, and cotton growers. Following the period for public comment, OSHA held 14 days of public hearings in three different cities. The transcripts from these hearings together with the written comments and other exhibits produced or received by the agency created an administrative record for the rule-making procedure of over 100,000 pages.

From this massive record, OSHA distilled its final regulations published, together with 60 pages of explanation, in the *Federal Register* in June 1978. In final form, the regulations outlined a short term–long term strategy that had been originally proposed in the NIOSH report. Employers would be required to establish over a four-year period engineering controls and practices to meet permissible exposure limits of respirable cotton dust of 200 micrograms per cubic meter for yarn manufacturing, 750 micrograms per cubic meter for slashing and weaving operations in the cotton industry, and 500 micrograms per cubic meter for all other processes in the cotton industry and for all nontextile, cotton-related industries.

In the meantime, employers were required to monitor cotton dust exposures, provide medical examinations to all employees, and immediately provide respirators to all employees subject to exposures above the compliance standards. Employees unable to wear respirators were to be transferred to other jobs without loss of pay or other employment benefits. During the four-year period, individual employers were also allowed to establish that compliance with the maximum exposure limits would be infeasible. Variances would be allowed for these employers, but their employees would have to be provided with respirators following the four-year period.

The issuance of the final cotton dust regulations was appealed to the Court of Appeals for the District of Columbia (this time by both industry representatives claiming that the standards were too strict and by employee groups claiming that they were too lenient). The industry objections to the standards in this case, unlike those in the benzene case, did not directly question the sufficiency of the finding that cotton dust exposure above the maximum levels would create a risk of brown lung or other health risks; primarily the industry challenged the overall strategy adopted by the agency and particularly the economic and technological feasibility of adopting engineering controls to achieve the standards adopted by OSHA. The industry argued that such controls were too expensive and, in some cases, technologically infeasible, especially since similar results could be achieved by simply requiring exposed employees to wear respirators or by transferring employees who develop the initial symptoms of brown lung disease to other jobs. As in the benzene case, the employer representatives urged the court to interpret the OSHA legislation to require the agency to do a cost-benefit analysis of the new standards.

Despite these industry arguments, the court of appeals upheld the cotton dust standards in all major respects. First, the court rejected the requirement of cost-benefit analysis that had been urged by the industry and adopted in the Fifth Circuit. (The benzene case was then pending before the Supreme Court.) According to the District of Columbia Court of Appeals, sections 3(8) and 6(b)(5) allow OSHA to establish the most stringent standards necessary to eliminate a significant health risk, bounded only by the requirement that the standard be technologically and economically feasible for the industry. The court read the OSHA legislation to require a finding of a benefit to workers, and a finding that the standard is economically and technologically feasible, but not a further finding that the proposed benefits would outweigh the estimated costs.

The Court of Appeals for the District of Columbia also rejected the argument that the agency lacked "substantial evidence" for its findings. The court reviewed the agency's administrative record—a record that it labeled "massive"—and concluded that OSHA had ample and, in this case, empirical evidence for each of its findings of the economic and technological feasibility of the new standards.

Thus, in *American Textile Manufacturers v. Donovan*, 452 U.S. 490 (1981), the Supreme Court was once again asked to address the questions that had been raised, but only partially settled, in the benzene case two years earlier. Does the rule-making authority created by sections 3(8) and 6(b)(5) require a cost-benefit analysis of proposed occupational health standards? What is the extent of the discretion vested in agency officials in making findings regarding benefits or regarding the economic or technological feasibility of proposed standards? And once again, the Court was faced with two very different interpretations of the agency's rule-making authority. OSHA—together with various employee groups—claimed that the 1970 legislation gives the agency the authority to promulgate any standard that eliminates or reduces a significant risk to the extent that the agency finds that the standard is economically or technologically feasible for the industry. This is the interpretation of the OSHA statute adopted by the District of Columbia Court of Appeals. The industry representatives, however, claimed that an OSHA standard must address a significant health risk and be shown to have benefits that will outweigh the resultant costs, the interpretation originally adopted by the Fifth Circuit in the benzene case.

To resolve the question of cost-benefit analysis, the Court once again examined the "to the extent feasible" language of section 6(b)(5) and the "practical and necessary" language of section 3(8), in light of the structure and legislative history of the legislation. (For further discussion of statutory interpretation, see note at end of chapter.) Ultimately it concluded that cost-benefit analysis is not required by the OSHA legislation:

> Taken alone, the phrase "reasonably necessary or appropriate" might be construed to contemplate some balancing of the costs and benefits of a standard. Petitioners urge that, so construed, § 3(8) engrafts a cost-benefit analysis requirement on the issuance of § 6(b)(5) standards, even if § 6(b)(5) itself does not authorize such analysis. We need not decide whether § 3(8), standing alone, would contemplate some form of cost-benefit analysis. For even if it does, Congress specifically chose in § 6(b)(5) to impose separate and additional requirements for issuance of a subcategory of occupational safety and health standards dealing with toxic materials and harmful physical agents; it required that those standards be issued to prevent material impairment of health to the extent feasible. Congress could reasonably have concluded that health standards should be subject to different criteria than safety standards because of the special problems presented in regulating them.
>
> * * *
>
> The legislative history of the Act, while concededly not crystal clear, provides general support for respondents' interpretation of the Act. The congressional reports and debates certainly confirm that Congress meant "feasible" and nothing else in using that term. Congress was

concerned that the Act might be thought to require achievement of absolute safety, an impossible standard, and therefore insisted that health and safety goals be capable of economic and technological accomplishment. Perhaps most telling is the absence of any indication whatsoever that Congress intended OSHA to conduct its own cost-benefit analysis before promulgating a toxic material or harmful physical agent standard. The legislative history demonstrates conclusively that Congress was fully aware that the Act would impose real and substantial costs of compliance on industry, and believed that such costs were part of the cost of doing business.

Having finally settled the issue of cost-benefit analysis, the Court then turned to the issue of the discretion of the agency—and the discretion of the courts—in making findings based on the evidentiary record. The Court first addressed the definition of "substantial evidence," primarily in terms of the role of the courts of appeals in determining whether the agency had satisfied the "substantial evidence" standard and the role of the Supreme Court in reviewing the decisions of the courts of appeals.

> [W]e have defined substantial evidence as "such relevant evidence as a reasonable mind might accept as adequate to support a conclusion". . . . The reviewing court must take into account contradictory evidence in the record . . . but "the possibility of drawing two inconsistent conclusions from the evidence does not prevent an administrative agency's finding from being supported by substantial evidence." (citations omitted) Since the Act places responsibility for determining substantial evidence questions in the courts of appeals, we apply the familiar rule that "[t]his court will intervene only in what ought to be the rare instance when the [substantial evidence] standard appears to have been misapprehended or grossly misapplied by the court below." (citations omitted) Therefore, our inquiry is not to determine whether we, in the first instance, would find OSHA's findings supported by substantial evidence. Instead we turn to OSHA's findings and the record upon which they were based to decide whether the Court of Appeals "misapprehended or grossly misapplied" the substantial evidence test.

The implications of this interpretation of the requirements of "substantial evidence" can be fully appreciated only with reference to several of OSHA's specific findings and the review given those decisions by both levels of appellate courts.

One of the industry's primary objections to the cotton dust standards was the requirement that the maximum exposure limits be achieved by engineering controls rather than by monitoring exposures to cotton dust and by transferring employees who develop initial brown lung symptoms or by requiring such employees to wear respirators.

The industry had strongly argued to the court of appeals that the agency had neither given sufficient consideration to this less expensive alternative nor provided adequate reasons for rejecting it. The court of appeals, however, dismissed this argument (and the Supreme Court upheld the court of appeals) and found that the agency had satisfied the "substantial evidence" standard:

> First, OSHA gave serious attention to the medical studies conducted by the textile industry and proffered to support the industry's alternative. These studies purport to show that medical surveillance programs at various textile plants have already afforded workers a level of protection comparable to that offered by OSHA's approach. The record shows that OSHA specifically addressed and scrutinized these studies, and concluded that their validity had largely been discredited. OSHA's judgment on this issue is sufficiently supported on this basis.
>
> Besides this careful treatment of the medical surveillance proposal, OSHA rejected the industry's proposed reliance on job transfers and respirators to protect workers suffering from acute symptoms of byssinosis on the basis of testimony in the record and express policy considerations. The industry was unable to show that job transfers would be available in sufficient number to respond to the likely prevalence of byssinosis in plants with dust levels at the 500 μg/m proposed by the industry. Further, the agency found uncontradicted testimony in the record that respirators can cause severe physical discomfort and create safety problems of their own. OSHA concluded that the industry's proposal inappropriately placed the burden of compliance on the employees. On this express policy ground, and on the basis of the evidence in the record, OSHA reasonably rejected these elements in the industry alternative.

Thus it is apparent that the court of appeals must require the agency to show that it has considered all of the evidence that it has received in its record, including any contradictory or alternative evidence presented by the industry. If the agency has failed to do so, the regulations can be invalidated on review under the "substantial evidence" standard. But, at the same time, the court will allow the agency to discredit or to reject the implications of such evidence, so long as it can show that contrary evidence is available or that it has some reason for disregarding the industry's counterproposals—presumably "such relevant evidence as a reasonable mind might accept." Indeed, OSHA can apparently reject an alternative strategy—even an alternative that arguably would be less costly—based in part on its assumption that it would be unfair to put too great a burden on employees, and not employers, in achieving compliance.

This same notion that the agency must have some basis for its decisions and that it must show that it considered all contrary evidence was carried one step further in OSHA's findings with regard to the costs of compliance with the new standards for textile mills. OSHA derived its estimate of the costs of the necessary engineering controls from two studies of compliance costs: one under contract to the agency (RTI) and one by a research institute of the textile manufacturers (Hocutt-Thomas). Yet OSHA's final estimate was far below the estimate of either study. OSHA rejected the $1.1 billion price tag on final compliance projected by RTI since on examining the study it found that RTI had assumed that new engineering controls would be required in all textile mills, even though cotton dust is not generated in 30 percent of those mills. It also concluded that RTI had overestimated compliance costs since some mills were already in compliance with the permissible exposure limits, yet RTI had assumed that all mills were currently operating at the preexisting (1,000 microgram) limit. Third, it found that the RTI study had not had available to it the more recent data used by the Hocutt-Thomas study.

At the same time, while OSHA considered the Hocutt-Thomas study more up-to-date and more realistic, it also rejected the final estimate of that study ($543 million) as well. As explained by the Supreme Court:

> First, Hocutt-Thomas included costs of achieving the existing permissible exposure limit, while OSHA thought it likely that compliance was more widespread and that some mills had in fact achieved the final standards. . . . Second, Hocutt-Thomas declined to make any allowance for the trend toward replacement of existing production machines with newer more productive equipment. Relying on this "[n]atural production tren[d]," . . . OSHA concluded that fewer machines than estimated by Hocutt-Thomas would require retrofitting or other controls. . . . Third, OSHA thought that Hocutt-Thomas failed to take into account development of new technologies likely to occur during the 4-year compliance period. Fourth, OSHA believed that Hocutt-Thomas might have improperly included control costs for synthetics-only machines, an inclusion which could result in a 30% cost overestimate.

OSHA's final estimate of the costs, therefore, assumed that the Hocutt-Thomas estimate could be reduced by at least 30 percent, making the economic feasibility of compliance with the new standards by textile mills appear much more likely than either of the two studies indicated. Over the strenuous objection of the industry, the court of appeals upheld the agency's interpretation of these two studies as "relying on the best available evidence" and based on "substantial evidence," as required by the OSHA legislation. And, again, the Supreme Court affirmed the decision of the court of appeals as not "misapprehending or grossly misapplying" the "substantial evidence" rule.

The courts were similarly concerned that the agency consider all evidence, but were at the same time willing to defer to the agency's judgment on the weighing of that evidence, in reviewing findings of the economic feasibility of compliance for the entire industry. In order to make such a finding, the agency had to review extensive and somewhat contradictory evidence concerning such matters as employment trends, energy costs and consumption levels, capital financing and its availability, and profit margins. In each case, the court of appeals reviewed the evidence in the record to ensure that the agency had considered all of the evidence and explained the basis for its findings and for its modifications or disregard of contradictory evidence. Yet, so long as there was "some relevant evidence that a reasonable mind might accept as adequate to support a conclusion," i.e., so long as the agency had what the courts regard as "substantial evidence," the judgment of the agency was upheld by the court of appeals. And so long as the court of appeals concluded that the agency had made such a review of the evidence, the Supreme Court was willing to conclude that it had not "misapprehended or grossly misapplied" the "substantial evidence" test.

The decisions in the benzene and cotton dust cases outline the principles that define the rule-making authority of administrative agencies such as OSHA. First and most fundamentally, as stated in the introduction to this chapter, an administrative agency is empowered to issue regulations or other rules or, for that matter, to do anything else, to the extent that the agency has been empowered to do so by the state or federal legislature. In the case of OSHA, the critical provisions of sections 3(8) and 6(b)(5) have been interpreted to mean that the agency is empowered by Congress to issue any standard that eliminates or reduces a significant health risk in the workplace, bounded only by the requirement that the standard is shown to be economically and technologically feasible for the affected industry. But to understand the real nature and extent of that rule-making authority, it is necessary not only to further refine the meaning of those statutory provisions, but also to understand the process by which such decisions are made, and the roles and discretion allowed to the various decision makers in that process, particularly the discretion allowed to the courts.

The courts play a dual role in the administrative process. The interpretation of the extent of the authority created by the OSHA statute is initially made by the agency, but ultimately the final interpretation of statutory language, as with any other interpretation of law, is made by the courts; first the courts of appeals, but, if the issue is further appealed, the Supreme Court. As should be clear, this role of the courts as "interpretors of law" can have a considerable effect on the agency and its decisions. At the same time, the courts play a role in reviewing the merits of the decision at hand. In the case of OSHA, the courts of appeals are empowered to determine whether OSHA has "substantial evidence" to support its decisions. The Supreme Court's role has been interpreted to be much narrower. Thus, one important observation regarding the rule-making authority of OSHA is that the agency's authority is shared, first in various formal and informal ways within the agency and the executive branch; then between the judicial and executive branches of government. Under other statutory schemes, the scope of this judicial role might be defined somewhat differently, but would be nonetheless critical to an understanding of the agency and the extent of its authority. (*See* note at end of chapter.)

It should also be noted that while the principles that establish the rule-making authority of OSHA have been defined and interpreted by the Supreme Court on several occasions, the controversy concerning the scope and nature of that authority has hardly been extinguished. Indeed, the extended legal battles over the cotton dust and benzene standards are likely to be repeated with only slight modifications each time OSHA issues a new occupational health standard. Likewise, similar battles are likely to follow any attempt by OSHA to adjudicate violations of these standards. Even some of the principles specifically addressed in the cotton dust and benzene cases are likely to be the subject of further litigation. There is a fine line, for instance, between relying on a policy of "no safe level" for known carcinogens—which the Court has read the OSHA statute not to allow—and relying on a policy of not greatly burdening employees, rather than employers, as one consideration in interpreting evidence—which the Court has apparently found within the statutory mandate. This hardly provides OSHA with a crystal clear guide to its future decision making. Nor has the judicial distinction between direct empirical evidence and empirical evidence that can be modified by assumptions sufficiently eliminated the possibility that future rule-making decisions, even those that closely parallel the reasoning of the agency in issuing the cotton dust standards, can be made while avoiding legal challenge to their evidentiary basis. Numerous other issues regarding the roles of the various decision makers and the discretion that they are allowed under the OSHA legislation remain to be litigated and, perhaps, relitigated in the future.

All this assumes, of course, that the OSHA legislation is not modified or repealed. The principle that the power of the agency to issue regulations is defined by the statute that authorized the agency also suggests that controversies over the exercise of that authority take place both before the agency and in the courts, but also on the floors of the state and federal legislatures. If the distribution of agency power is largely a legislative matter, then it is also a creature of politics. Indeed, it would be a mistake to read the chronicle of the cotton dust or benzene standards unmindful of the prevailing politics of that time or of the future. Industry representatives dissatisfied with Supreme Court decisions can shift their efforts from statutory arguments before the Court to political arguments in the halls of Congress. The Supreme Court may declare that the OSHA legislation does not require the agency to do a cost-benefit analysis, but nothing precludes Congress from amending the legislation to include just such a requirement. Just as importantly, there are a variety of ways in which a presidential administration politically predisposed to favor cost-benefit analysis can have OSHA administered in such a way that cost-benefit analysis becomes either an explicit or de facto policy of the agency.

For that matter, the possibility that a future president or agency director may be so predisposed while the current one is not (or vice versa) is a political reality the implications of which should not be overlooked.

But whether determined by political influences or by judicially interpreted principles, the importance of administrative agencies and their activities in modern state and federal governments cannot be understated. The rule-making authority of only one agency was considered in detail in this chapter. Both the complexity and the importance of administrative agencies can be understood only with reference to the seemingly endless variety of state and federal agencies, each with its own unique responsibilities and structure, presumably tailored to the specific function of the agency.

END NOTES

1. For an interpretative overview of administrative law and legal principles, see K. DAVIS, ADMINISTRATIVE LAW TEXT (3d ed. 1972).
2. A case study of adjudicatory decision making by an administrative agency— OSHA or any other—would involve very different administrative procedures than those reviewed in this chapter, but nonetheless would primarily demonstrate the same legal principle. Holding aside constitutional considerations, the procedures that must be followed and the distribution of power within the agency and between the agency and the courts would primarily be a matter of statutory interpretation. For an illustrative example, see *Mathews v. Eldredge*, cited in end notes to chapter 5.

    For a general description of adjudicatory decision making, see *DAVIS, supra*, note 1, at 194–214.
3. The interpretation of statutory provisions and the art of determining that interpretation by reference to legislative history deserve special attention.

In both the benzene and the cotton dust cases, the Supreme Court made an extensive review of the legislative history in its attempts to define the meaning of sections 3(8) and 6(b)(5) and, in doing so, provided good illustrations of the relevant considerations and their analysis. *See* 452 U.S. 490, 508–22 (1981); 448 U.S. 607, 639–52 (1980).

For general reference on statutory interpretation, see G. FOLSOM, LEGISLATIVE HISTORY: RESEARCH FOR THE INTERPRETATION OF LAWS (1972); *see also* sources cited in end notes to chapter 1.

4. The various constitutional challenges to the OSHA legislation that have been brought by employers and industry representatives, while not discussed in the text, provide further illustrations of the principles discussed in chapter 6. Moreover, they tend to support the general observation that Congress has extensive authority to regulate what is regarded as interstate commerce and that the courts are extremely hesitant to impose constitutional restraints on that authority. *See, e.g.,*, Brennan v. Winters Battery Mfg. Co., 531 F.2d 317 (6th Cir. 1975), *cert. denied* 425 U.S. 991, *reh'g denied*, 429 U.S. 873 (1976) (OSHA legislation does not violate Fourth, Fifth, Seventh, Tenth, or Fourteenth Amendment); Stockwell Mfg.Co. v. Usery, 536 F.2d 1306 (10th Cir. 1976) (OSHA legislation not a bill of attainer); Blockson & Co. v. Marshall, 582 F.2d 1122 (7th Cir. 1978) (OSHA legislation does not delegate essential legislative functions to executive branch).

But see Marshall v. Barlow, 436 U.S. 307 (1978) (statutory provision to enter employer's premises for inspection without search warrant violates Fourth Amendment).

5. In the examples discussed in this chapter, the agency's rule-making authority is subject to the "substantial evidence" test as applied by the courts of appeals. Other state and federal agencies are subject to quite different levels of judicial review. The consequent impact on the distribution of government authority between the courts and the executive branch is significant. As indicated in the text, in some situations, the statute precludes any judicial review of the agency decision whatsoever. (These usually involve very minor or informal decisions.) In a few other situations, the scope of judicial review is to make an independent judgment or "de novo" review based on the evidence in the administrative record.

More frequently, the statutorily defined standard of review will provide for broad discretion to be exercised by the agency, subject only to limited oversight by the courts. An interesting and important example was reviewed by the Supreme Court in Motor Vehicles Manufacturers Assoc. v. State Farm Mutual, 463 U.S. 29 (1983). In that case the National Highway Traffic Safety Administration (NHTSA) within the Department of Transportation had been empowered by Congress to issue motor vehicle safety standards. In making its findings, the agency is required by its authorization statute to consider "relevant available motor vehicle safety data" and to determine whether the standard would be "reasonable, practicable, and appropriate" to carry out the purposes of the statute. These standards are to be upheld on review by the courts of appeals so long as they are not "arbitrary and capricious"—a standard generally regarded as giving the agency almost unchecked discretion.

Beginning in 1967, NHTSA issued a series of standards, first requiring seatbelts to be installed in all new cars. In the 1970s, the agency considered a variety of alternatives for "passive restraints" (e.g., seatbelts that did not have to be attached by the passenger, or ignition locking devices). Under the Carter administration, standards were issued that would have eventually required either "passive seatbelts" or the installation of automatic airbags in all new cars. But, within the first year of the Reagan administration, these standards were rescinded. On appeal, the Court of Appeals for the District of Columbia held that the rescission was "arbitrary and capricious." The Supreme Court affirmed, holding that the new standard was not rational, based on a consideration of relevant factors, or within the scope of the authority delegated to the agency by the statute.

6. As reviewed in *American Textile Manufacturers Inst. v. Donovan*, the original cotton dust standards issued by OSHA included a provision requiring employers to transfer to another job employees who are unable to wear respirators, *without loss of employment or other benefits*. While upholding in virtually all other respects the cotton dust standards (and deferring to the court of appeals review of the substantial evidence for the agency's findings), the Supreme Court invalidated this requirement, holding that the agency had failed to make a finding that this requirement was related to the achievement of a safe or healthful workplace and, therefore, that such a requirement was not within the authority of the agency. Apparently the court was only convinced that OSHA had required the continuation of benefits to prevent the unfairness to the transferred employee and could not find anything in the act that gave the agency the power to prevent such inequities, only the power to prevent health risks. In the words of the Court:

> For Congress gave OSHA the responsibility to protect worker health and safety, and to explain its reasons for its actions. Because the Act in no way authorized OSHA to repair general unfairness to employees that is unrelated to achievement of health and safety goals, we conclude that OSHA acted beyond statutory authority when it issued the wage guarantee regulation.

In a footnote to this portion of its opinion, however, the Supreme Court noted that if the agency had made the finding that comparable benefits for transferred employees were necessary to encourage employees to admit that they could not use respirators, then the Court would have found the required finding of a link to a health benefit. OSHA, however, has never attempted to do so, despite this judicial "hint".

7. While the courts clearly rejected the argument that OSHA must use a cost-benefit analysis prior to issuing standards for occupational health and safety, the courts have interpreted the language of other authorizing statutes to include such a requirement. *See e.g.*, Aqua Slide 'N' Dive Corp. v. Consumer Product Safety Comm., 569 F.2d 831 (5th Cir. 1978).

8. As of Dec. 1984, the standards for cotton dust levels in textile industries can be found at 29 C.F.R. § 1910.1043, essentially those standards originally is-

sued in 1978. Under subsection (c), the maximum exposure levels are 200 micrograms per cubic meter for yarn manufacturing, 750 micrograms per cubic meter for slashing and weaving, and 500 micrograms per cubic meter for all other textile industries. The OSHA regulations stipulate that these maximum acceptable levels are to be averaged over an eight-hour period.

Subsequent to the litigation discussed in this chapter, however, knitting and hosiery manufacturers petitioned OSHA to stay the enforcement of the 500 microgram standard, contending that the levels were unnecessary and inapplicable to the knitting industry. On February 2, 1983, OSHA granted a temporary stay of the regulation as it would have been enforced against knitting and hosiery and undertook a review of the possible application of the standard in light of new studies and comments from medical experts. During the review period, the preexisting standard of 1000 micrograms (found in Table Z–1 of 1910.1000) would be in effect for knitting and hosiery.

After the revised benzene standards were declared invalid by the Supreme Court as discussed in this chapter, the regulations in 29 C.F.R. § 1910.1028 were deleted by OSHA in June 1981; the deletion left in effect the preexisting levels (found in Table Z–2 in § 1910.1000) which permit a maximum exposure of 10 parts per million over an averaged period of eight hours, a ceiling concentration level of 25 parts per million and a maximum excess level of 50 parts per million for a ten-minute period.

8

Government Enforcement of Competition: The Antitrust Laws

In the context of the delivery of health care, the regulatory authority of the government has most often been discussed with reference to direct resource allocation, cost controls, or other "command and control" regulatory measures. But the power of state or federal government is not necessarily confined to the imposition of direct government authority over the distribution of resources or the costs of services. As conservative theorists have frequently argued, government can also act to ensure that economic phenomena are governed primarily by activities in the private sector—but under properly competitive conditions. The same constitutional principles that allow the state to require certificate of need approval for hospital construction or that could allow a federal hospital cost containment program would also allow the government to undertake various activities to promote competition among providers, insurers, or others involved in the delivery of health care.

But whereas the government has been attempting to enforce and protect competition in some sectors of the American economy for nearly a century, the notion that government should be policing competition or encouraging the allocation of health care through private market mechanisms appeared to run counter to the underlying philosophy of the spending and regulatory programs that characterized public policy through the 1960s and 1970s. Indeed, most government efforts either explicitly or implicitly assumed that private competition was either unworkable or inappropriate for the delivery of health care. Health care was delivered through systems, not markets. Health care delivery was as much a social service as it was an economic activity.

The spending and regulatory programs of previous decades, however, have been subject to a number of changes in recent years, as has
their underlying philosophy. The notion that government should and
can foster competition and the "perfecting" of market mechanisms is
no longer antithetical to the political direction government policies are
now taking. This has been both a cause and an effect of increased application of the antitrust laws to the delivery of health care.

The purpose of this chapter is to review the federal antitrust laws,
the constraints that they potentially impose on health care delivery and
related activities, and the means by which antitrust laws are applied and
enforced. In doing so, this chapter will review the major antitrust decisions of the last decade that have begun to sketch out the implications
of efforts to enforce competition among health care providers, in financing and delivering services, and in determining the supply and distribution of resources. As this review will demonstrate, those implications have not yet been fully developed. The initial round of judicial
battles was primarily concerned with clarifying whether various exemptions and jurisdictional limitations on the antitrust laws were applicable
to these activities. To the surprise of many, the courts have generally
concluded that virtually all private health care providers—in most of
their activities—and most activities relating to the delivery of their services are not exempted from the purview of the antitrust laws. What is
now unfolding is the judicial clarification of the requirements and prohibitions that may be imposed by the enforcement of antitrust principles in these contexts.

It should be noted that there has been relatively little dispute
about the constitutionality of the federal antitrust laws. As was discussed in chapter 6, the power of the federal government to regulate
interstate commerce is extensive, and modern courts have been extremely reluctant to interfere with congressional discretion either in
declaring an activity within the scope of interstate commerce regulation or in determining the form or substance of appropriate regulatory
controls. Consequently, the critical issues in antitrust litigation have
been largely statutory: What activities are subject to the provisions of
the federal antitrust legislation? What practices are either prohibited or
required? Thus, as in the previous chapter, one of the primary focuses
will be on the interpretation of the wording and intent of the legislation itself, and the extent of discretion created for the various branches
of government by the mandates of the antitrust legislation. In this regard, the analysis of the procedural and substantive authority created
by the antitrust legislation could be regarded as paralleling the analysis
of the statutory authority of the occupational health and safety agencies in chapter 7. But the antitrust laws by their nature carve out a

somewhat unique role for the courts in the interpretation and enforcement of antitrust principles over and above their role as interpreters of statutory language. As discussed in later sections of this chapter, the antitrust legislation essentially requires the courts to undertake an economic analysis of an activity or industry. Among other things, in determining the scope and meaning of the antitrust laws, the courts must distinguish the differences between the performance of that industry and the theoretical dictates of economic theory and weigh both the positive and negative impact on competition of various activities and practices. Thus the courts under the antitrust legislation carry out a unique function quite unlike the judicial function in virtually any other statutory scheme, one that has caused the courts both theoretical and practical difficulties.

THE FEDERAL ANTITRUST LAWS

The enactment of the first federal antitrust legislation in the late nineteenth century has been generally attributed to popular political protest against the economic and political power of a few large corporations. The exploitive business and labor practices of the railroads, oil conglomerates, and various industrial holding companies or "trusts" (the term had both a technical and a popular meaning) apparently created a considerable political backlash which prompted Congress to enact the Interstate Commerce Act in 1887 and then the Sherman Antitrust Act in 1890. The Interstate Commerce Act was in the form of traditional government regulation, subjecting the rates and services of railroad and other interstate carriers to the control of a federal administrative agency. The Sherman legislation, on the other hand, was principally a declaration of economic policy and a proscription on certain business practices and activities.

Section 1 of the Sherman Act prohibited concerted activities (i.e., two or more competitors acting together) in "restraint of trade":

> Every contract, combination in the form of trust or otherwise, or conspiracy, in restraint of trade or commerce among the several States, or with foreign nations, is declared to be illegal. Every person who shall make any contract or engage in any combination or conspiracy hereby declared to be illegal shall be deemed guilty of a felony. . . .

Section 2 prohibited any attempt (by any one competitor) to exercise monopoly power:

> Every person who shall monopolize, or attempt to monopolize, or combine or conspire with any other person or persons, to monopolize any

part of the trade or commerce among the several States, or with foreign nations, shall be deemed guilty of a felony. . . .

The Act authorized the Justice Department to seek enforcement of these prohibitions by civil or criminal proceedings. (As most recently amended, fines up to $1 million and prison sentences up to three years can be sought in criminal proceedings.) The Act also empowered private parties injured by violations of the Sherman prohibitions to bring civil actions for damages or injunctive relief.

The Sherman Act was supplemented in 1914 by the Clayton Act and the Federal Trade Commission Act. Apparently the "antitrust" issue had continued to draw considerable political attention and developed into one of the focal issues of the preceding congressional and presidential elections. There had also been some dissatisfaction with the initial judicial applications of the Sherman Act. (One commentator has described the earliest judicial applications of the Sherman Act as "extremely conservative.")

The Clayton Act extended and added specification to the Sherman Act prohibitions by declaring illegal (although not criminal) four specific trade practices: (1) price discrimination (i.e., charging different prices to different buyers for the same product), (2) tying or exclusive dealing contracts (i.e., requiring buyers to agree not to deal with the seller's competitors), (3) corporate mergers among competitors, and (4) interlocking directorates among competitors. These specific practices were defined as illegal, however, only where the effect is to "substantially lessen competition" or "tend to create a monopoly." The Justice Department was empowered to bring civil actions seeking either monetary penalties or injunctive relief (e.g., divesture or dissolution) for Clayton Act violations.

Significantly, the Clayton Act also bolstered the private enforcement mechanism, allowing any person who can show business or property injury as a result *of anything forbidden in the federal antitrust laws* to bring a private action to recover *treble damages*, a significant incentive to private litigation.

The Federal Trade Commission Act created an independent federal administrative agency (FTC) empowered to study and issue findings (and, by later amendment, to seek judicial enforcement of those findings) identifying "unfair methods of competition" and "unfair or deceptive acts." This effectively gave the FTC concurrent jurisdiction with the Justice Department over some activities that are also subject to the Sherman Act and the Clayton Act. (For a full discussion of the various studies, investigations, and other actions that can be taken by the FTC under current law, and the means by which they can be enforced by administrative or judicial action, see references in note at end of chapter.)

Subsequent amendments have modified the scope of the Sherman and Clayton Acts and the structure and jurisdiction of the FTC; in particular, certain practices and certain industries have been given exemptions (and, in some cases, some exemptions have been modified or repealed). The modern application of the antitrust laws is also complicated by their interrelationship with a variety of other trade regulation, consumer protection, and labor legislation. (For references, see note at end of chapter.) Nonetheless, the proscriptions adopted near the turn of the century and the basic structure incorporated into the original Sherman and Clayton legislation still provide the backbone of current federal antitrust enforcement. (For a current codification of what were originally the Clayton and Sherman Acts, see 15 U.S.C. §§ 1–40 (1983); for a codification of the current statutory authority of the FTC, see 15 U.S.C. §§ 41 *et seq.* (1983).)

Some of the later amendments to the original legislation reflect the political influences that have affected the development of antitrust policy. In 1932, for example, the Norris-LaGuardia legislation clarified the exemption of many union and labor organizing activities from the proscriptions of the antitrust laws. In addition, public utilities, the banking industry, insurance companies, and various special interests, have been given at least partial exemptions as well—ostensibly on the theory that some parts of the economy are either "natural" monopolies or are already subject to state or federal regulatory programs.

Other exemptions or limitations on the scope of the antitrust laws have developed from judicial interpretations of the substantive language of the legislation. For example, some "noncommercial" activities have been considered to be exempted from the antitrust laws since they are not within the meaning of "trade or commerce." (The Supreme Court ruled in 1972 that professional baseball was not a commercial activity, although other professional sports were.) And, until recently, many legal experts interpreted the statute to require that some professional services and activities be similarly exempted (as discussed in the next section). The scope of the antitrust laws is also limited to commerce or trade in interstate commerce or in commerce with foreign nations. (There are slight differences in the definition of "commerce" under the Sherman Act and the Clayton Act.) Thus, strictly local activities have been considered exempt from federal antitrust laws. However, the modern definition of interstate commerce, as discussed below, has diminished the importance of this jurisdictional issue. (In addition, strictly local activity might be subject to the antitrust laws that exist in many states.)

At least in their broadest outlines, the antitrust laws have attempted to codify as federal policy the underlying philosophy of traditional economic theory. Unless excepted or exempted from the scope of the legislation, goods and services are to be distributed according to the dictates of competitive and private markets. The government's role as codified in this legislation is to insure that markets function properly and that market imperfections, e.g., restraints on trade or the exercise of monopoly power, are eliminated. Indeed, enthusiastic proponents of antitrust principles have argued that rigorous enforcement of antitrust laws is the ideal form of government economic regulation, promoting the welfare of the consuming public and insuring both low prices and the ideal distribution of goods and services.

But whether the antitrust laws should—or can—play such a role in the nation's economy is a subject of some debate. Certainly antitrust enforcement has been inconsistent across various sectors of the economy and over time. The rigor with which the Justice Department or the FTC pursues a particular practice or a particular industry is a somewhat political variable, changing with each new federal administration and responsive to both political pressures and prevailing economic conditions. Even an administration committed to rigorous antitrust enforcement must by necessity have limited resources and be selective in its enforcement program. Privately initiated enforcement activities clearly supplement the efforts of government agencies, but as with all private litigation, the extent of litigation is not wholly determined by the merits of the underlying legal issues.

The effectiveness of antitrust enforcement also depends on the successful application of rather vaguely stated statutory proscriptions to the complexities of various commercial and business activities. While the underlying philosophy of the federal antitrust laws is relatively clear, the specific application of the substantive provisions of the antitrust laws cannot always be determined from either the language of the statutes or their legislative history. Moreover, as noted above, the legislation requires the application of economic theory to the industry or practice under consideration, a task that is both conceptually and practically difficult. Indeed, the nearly 100 years of antitrust enforcement have presented the courts and the agencies responsible for initiating enforcement activities with as difficult and complex issues as any area of the law. In particular, the courts have had considerable difficulty articulating the principles for their economic analysis and applying those principles to various commercial and business activities brought under antitrust analysis.

It is against this background that the antitrust decisions discussed in the remainder of this chapter should be viewed. While antitrust enforcement has been applied in many sectors of the economy, until very recently antitrust enforcement in the delivery of health services was virtually nonexistent (with a few interesting exceptions; *see* note at end of chapter). Not even 15 years ago, many legal observers might have concluded that the professional services of medical care providers were exempt from the antitrust laws, or that many providers were engaged in what were essentially local activities. Even ten years ago, many providers would have argued that collective agreements among potential competitors in the delivery of health services were not only sound public policy, but that the federal government was in many ways encouraging such activities. By the 1980s, however, the enforcement of competition and antitrust prohibitions on restraints of trade and monopoly power have become part of the complicated legal environment of modern health care delivery.

JUDICIAL RECOGNITION OF THE APPLICABILITY OF ANTITRUST LAWS TO HEALTH CARE DELIVERY

The initial rounds of litigation in the 1970s that signaled the increased relevance of antitrust laws to the delivery of health care began with a series of decisions that primarily clarified the applicability of the antitrust laws to health care providers and to a wide range of service delivery and financing activities.

As noted earlier, the Sherman Act was expressly limited to acts involving "trade or commerce." Prior to the 1970s, many experts had argued that "trade or commerce" did not include the activities of the "learned professions," e.g., physicians, lawyers, and other high prestige, self-regulated professional service providers. The current Supreme Court, however, has virtually rejected the notion of a "learned profession" exemption to the antitrust laws and indicated that it would submit both the services and self-regulatory activities of professionals to antitrust scrutiny. In *Goldfarb v. Virginia State Bar*, 421 U.S. 773 (1976), the Court invalidated as price fixing the minimum fee schedules set for attorneys by the state bar, rejecting the defendant's argument that attorneys, as a member of a "learned profession," were exempt from the federal antitrust law. In *National Society of Professional Engineers v. United States*, 435 U.S. 679 (1978), the Court invalidated a portion of the ethical canons of the society that prohibited its members from submitting competitive bids, again rejecting the argument that the "learned professions" were entitled to an exemption, as well as the argument that the no-bidding requirement should be viewed as a legitimate attempt by the profession to protect the public from inferior engineering.

In both these cases, the Supreme Court indicated that in some circumstances the attempts by professional groups to self-regulate the quality of their services or the ethics of their profession might be treated differently from other economic activities. But the Court in these and later decisions left little doubt that it would view these efforts with considerable suspicion and that the exemption of the "learned professions," if extant at all, would be very narrowly defined. As the decisions discussed below confirmed, the Court's interpretation of the "learned profession" exemption left virtually all medical services and the related activities of professional associations within the definition of "trade or commerce" and subject to antitrust restrictions.

Virtually the same posture was taken by the Court with regard to the argument that health care providers were exempt from federal antitrust laws since their services did not involve interstate commerce. The few earlier decisions applying antitrust law to health care delivery had raised the possibility that even institutional providers might be viewed as engaged in strictly local activities. In *Hospital Building Co. v. Rex Hospital Trustees*, 425 U.S. 738 (1976), a proprietary corporation seeking to construct a new hospital sued several nonprofit hospitals (as well as their trustees and their adminstrators) and the local Blue Cross plan, claiming that the defendants had conspired in various ways to prevent the plaintiff from obtaining a certificate of need and from beginning construction of the facility. These activities, plaintiffs alleged, constituted both a concerted refusal to deal and a market allocation scheme in violation of Sherman Act sections 1 and 2. The *Rex* case was first heard by the Supreme Court on the defendants' claim that the affected activity was local and did not directly involve interstate commerce and, therefore, was not subject to antitrust protection. Both the federal district court and the court of appeals had agreed with this interpretation of prior case law. The Supreme Court, however, found that the proposed hospital would involve a "substantial effect on interstate commerce," albeit one that was neither intended nor direct. Applying the broad modern definition of interstate commerce—and assuming that Congress intended the scope of the antitrust laws to be as broad as their constitutional authority allowed—the Court found sufficient connection between the hospital and interstate commerce in the hospital's interstate sources of supplies, capital financing, and third party reimbursement. The case was remanded to the lower courts for a trial on the merits (discussed *infra*).

While the Court in *Rex Hospital* looked to the specific circumstances of the plaintiff's hospital in determining whether interstate commerce was involved, since that decision there has been little question that the modern definition of interstate commerce and the Court's reading of the power created by the antitrust laws is broad enough to include virtually any institutional or individual provider and that the local activity exception will no longer shield providers from antitrust liability.

Another possible exemption for many activities relating to the financing of health care was also substantially narrowed by several Supreme Court decisions in the mid-1970s refining the exemptions created by the McCarran-Ferguson legislation. In 1945, Congress enacted the McCarran-Ferguson Act expressly exempting the "business of insurance" from federal antitrust legislation to the extent that it was regulated by state law and did not involve "acts of boycott, coercion, or intimidation." Apparently Congress was concerned that the antitrust laws should not interfere with the efforts of state insurance regulatory programs; there was also concern that the determination of underwriting risks might require some amount of cooperation among competing insurance companies (e.g., sharing of data). Many antitrust experts have read this "business of insurance" exemption to cover a variety of cooperative arrangements between providers, suppliers, and health insurers which would otherwise be potential targets of antitrust scrutiny.

The Supreme Court, however, severely narrowed the apparent implications of the "business of insurance" exemption for health care financing and insuring schemes.

In *Group Life & Heath Insurance Co. v. Royal Drug Co.*, 440 U.S. 205 (1978), the Court considered—but did not decide—the validity of agreements between Blue Shield and various pharmacies under which Blue Shield policyholders would be charged two dollars for each prescription and Blue Shield would pay the pharmacy only the cost of the drug (effectively limiting the pharmacy to only a two dollar markup on all drugs sold to Blue Shield policyholders). Nonparticipating pharmacies claimed that this constituted price fixing and a group boycott against other pharmacies in violation of Sherman Act section 1. Defendants argued that the agreements were exempt as involving the "business of insurance."

In interpreting the statutory exemption, the Court looked to the legislative history of the McCarran-Ferguson legislation and the language of the resulting amendments to the federal antitrust laws and concluded that the "business of insurance" exemption should be limited in its application to only those activities that (1) involved agreements between the insurer and the policyholder and that (2) directly involved the spreading or underwriting of risks—not other activities relating to those agreements. As the Court phrased it, Congress intended to exempt the "business of insurance" and not the "business of insurers." Thus, the Court held, contractual agreements between the insurer and the providers of services are not covered by the exemption. The Court even went so far as to suggest the possibility that Blue Shield and other prepaid health plans may not be considered "the business of insurance" at all, noting that at the time of the McCarran-Ferguson legislation, Blue Shield health plans were not considered insurance under the law of many states.

More recently, the Court again affirmed its limited interpretation of the exemption allowed for the "business of insurance." In *Union Labor Life Co. v. Pireno*, 458 U.S. 119 (1983), a health insurance plan had an agreement with a state chiropractic association to review each claim for reimbursement for chiropractic services to determine whether the service was necessary and the charge reasonable. The defendant insurance company claimed that since the principal function of the agreement was to determine whether the services were in compliance with the terms of the health insurance policy (i.e., only necessary and reasonable services were covered), the agreement should be exempt from antitrust laws as the "business of insurance." Nonetheless, the Supreme Court found the *Pireno* case virtually indistinguishable from *Royal Drug* and held that the activity did not directly involve an agreement between an insurer and a policyholder, nor the spreading of underwriting of risks.

While in these and other decisions no court has gone so far as to rule that prepaid health plans or other financing schemes are wholly without the exemption, as suggested in *Royal Drug*, it is clear that the "business of insurance" exemption is to be strictly limited in its application to health insurance and health plans; as one court has interpreted *Royal Drug*, the refusal to cover a particular risk if incorporated into the insured's policy would be covered by the exemption, but other related agreements, and particularly agreements between an insurance company or plan and providers are clearly not to be exempted. That is to say, such agreements will be subject to antitrust scrutiny. Whether they will eventually be regarded as restraints on trade or exercises of monopoly power is a separate issue. It is also apparent that this limited definition of the "business of insurance" exemption is not merely a matter of statutory interpretation in the strictest sense. In interpreting the specific provisions of the antitrust laws, and particularly those provisions that relate to exemptions or jurisdictional limitations, it appears that the courts' concern is not merely to interpret the wording of the statute, but to do so in a manner that will carry out the underlying policy of the antitrust legislation to the maximum extent possible.

This attitude towards the primacy of the underlying policy of the antitrust laws has also been evident in the Supreme Court decisions applying the "implied immunity" or "implied repeal" doctrine to health care delivery and related activities. One of the inherent difficulties in interpreting the scope and application of the antitrust laws is the reconciliation of the essentially procompetitive dictates of the federal antitrust laws with the requirements and prohibitions of various federal regulatory schemes, many of which promote or require cooperative arrangements and other noncompetitive behavior among individuals or institutions otherwise subject to the antitrust laws. Where the courts are unable to separately reconcile antitrust and other congressional mandates, the courts treat any regulatory or other scheme enacted subsequently to the antitrust laws as effectively repealing the application of the antitrust laws to the extent necessary to carry out the new legislation.

Since a variety of health planning and regulatory efforts have been attempted by Congress in the last several decades, many of which encourage and some of which require noncompetitive activities, many experts had previously assumed that the "implied repeal" doctrine would provide antitrust exemption for a wide range of cooperative and joint efforts in developing resources and in financing and delivering health care services.

The most recent decisions of the Supreme Court, however, have made it clear that although the "implied repeal" doctrine may insulate some planning and related activities from potential antitrust liability, that exemption will be recognized and applied only where there is a clear and virtually unmistakable conflict between the antitrust laws and the subsequent legislation. In *National Gerimedical Hospital and Geronotology Center v. Blue Cross of Kansas City and Blue Cross Ass'n*, 452 U.S. 378 (1981), plaintiff, a proprietary acute care hospital, sought to construct a new facility without the approval of the local area health systems agency (HSA). The HSA had previously decided that it would recommend no more new beds in the Kansas City area. At the time, there was no certificate of need statute and no federal regulatory authority attached to local HSA decisions. When the hospital sought to enter into a participation contract with the state Blue Cross insurance program, Blue Cross refused to enter into the agreement based on its policy barring agreements with any new hospital constructed where there was no need for its services, relying principally on the HSA's findings.

The hospital sued, claiming that Blue Cross had violated Sherman Act sections 1 and 2, alleging a wrongful refusal to deal and a conspiracy between Blue Cross and the HSA. Defendants moved to dismiss the claims on the grounds that the national health planning legislation that provided funding for the local HSA (*See* chapter 6) implied an exemption for private actions taken in response to HSA activities. The federal district court agreed with the defendants and dismissed the action; the Court of Appeals for the Eighth Circuit affirmed.

In reversing both lower court decisions, the Supreme Court indicated that the "implied repeal" doctrine, as with other limits and exemptions, should be very narrowly drawn:

> The general principles applicable to such claims are well established. The antitrust laws represent a "fundamental national economic policy." (citation omitted) "Implied antitrust immunity is not favored, and can be justified only by a convincing showing of clear repugnancy between the antitrust laws and the regulatory system." (citations omitted) Repeal is to be regarded as implied only if necessary to make [subsequent law] work, and even then only to the minimum extent necessary.

Applying this judicial posture to the federal health planning legislation (including the "procompetition" amendments of 1979), the Court noted that at the time of the alleged violations, nothing in the legislation either compelled or approved of the actions taken by Blue Cross. The Court also noted that even if the HSA had specifically requested that Blue Cross adopt such a policy, *at the time* it would merely have been the recommendation of a private agency, albeit one that received government funding. The local HSA would not have been carrying out a federally mandated responsibility, or any certificate of need or other regulatory authority under state law. Thus the specific acts of Blue Cross were not exempted from antitrust analysis, nor would any act not required or directly encouraged by a government agency or by a private agency under express direction of federal law. (See note at end of chapter for a discussion of the "state action" exemption.)

The issue of the scope of the "implied repeal" doctrine was also raised in the *Rex Hospital* litigation, after the initial Supreme Court decision on the interstate commerce issue. At the remand trial, it was shown that the defendant hospitals and Blue Cross had formed a committee to determine the need for hospital beds in the Raleigh, North Carolina area and had sought to have the local health planning and the certificate of need agencies carry out the committee's findings (including only modest increases in the beds at the plaintiff's hospital). The defendants virtually conceded that these concerted activities might otherwise be violations of the antitrust laws, but argued that their efforts to avoid an oversupply of hospital beds in the area were protected by the "implied repeal" doctrine since they involved the kind of cooperative activities among competitors specifically encouraged by the federal and state health planning legislation. The trial court refused to apply the "implied repeal" exemption and, after a jury trial, the plaintiff was awarded $7.3 million in damages.

On appeal to the Fourth Circuit Court of Appeals, the court reviewed the various federal and state health planning programs in effect at the time of the alleged antitrust violations and agreed with the defendants that at least some participation in cooperative health planning efforts and related activities was actively encouraged. As a result, in *Hospital Building Co. v. Trustees of Rex Hospital*, 691 F.2d 678 (4th Cir. 1982), the court held that the defendants' actions should not be declared illegal "per se," but should be analyzed according to what the court characterized as a "limited rule of reason." (See next section for discussion of "per se" and "rule of reason" analysis.) In effect, the court held that the defendants should have been allowed to show that their efforts were exempted by the "implied repeal" of the antitrust laws by subsequent health planning programs:

> We think a very narrow "rule of reason" is required in order to permit defendants to show, if they can, that participation in certain planning activities that would otherwise violate § 1 might not under the circumstances have been an unreasonable restraint on trade. The appropriate rule, we find, is simply that planning activities of private health services providers are not "unreasonable" restraints under § 1 if undertaken in good faith and if their actual and intended effects lay within those envisioned by specific federal legislation in place at the time of the challenged activities as desirable consequences of such planning activities. (citations omitted)
>
> * * *
>
> The type and extent of participation in planning by health care providers that Congress envisioned in the statutes relied upon by the defendants here is not altogether clear, but it is clear that what was envisioned was merely encouraged and authorized and not mandated. (citations omitted) This suggests a fairly narrow interpretation of the range of the conduct that may properly be given an effect in derogation of normal antitrust laws.
>
> So construing the statutory authorization relied upon here we find it runs only to good faith participation in planning activities aimed at avoiding the needless duplication of health care resources in an affected area. (citations omitted) Obviously it cannot be interpreted to allow the blanket use of "planning" as a means by which some health care providers act to avoid competition by others for any other purpose or on any other justification. . . . Specifically we hold that "planning" under this special rule of reason is not "reasonable" if its purpose or effect is only to protect existing health care providers from the competitive threat of potential entrants into or expanders within the same "market."

Obviously these various jurisdictional and exemption cases have left many issues regarding the scope and applicability of the antitrust laws to be settled. While the "learned profession" exemption has been severely limited, the courts have still left open the possibility that some kinds of intraprofessional activities, particularly those concerned with the establishment of standards of quality or for ethical conduct, may be exempt from antitrust restrictions. The *Pireno* and *Royal Drug* cases have sketched out the limits on the scope of the "business of insurance" exemptions as applied to various activities related to health care financing schemes, although, significantly, in both cases the Court gave little indication of how it would rule on the merits of each case: the validity of the agreements themselves. In *National Gerimedical*, the Court firmly indicated its view of the scope of the "implied repeal" doctrine, but left open questions of how that doctrine would have been applied had the federal health planning program been fully operational at the time of the case. In this regard, the retrial of the *Rex Hospital* case, following the decision in the Fourth Circuit interpreting the scope of the "implied repeal" doctrine could be extremely important if fully litigated. (By the fall of 1984 the case had been scheduled for a second trial but had not been argued.)

What is clear from this "first round" of jurisdictional and exemption cases is the overall message. The modern judicial interpretation of the intent of Congress in enacting the federal antitrust laws requires a very narrow interpretation of any jurisdictional limitation on the scope of that legislation and of any implied or explicit exemption. (For judicial interpretations of the "state action" exemption and the exemption allowed under the *Noerr-Pennington* doctrine, also confirming this message, see notes at end of this chapter). That attitude has been applied before and to a whole range of economic activities. The major significance of these recent cases is that neither the inherent qualities of the delivery or financing of health care nor the professional status of health care providers has convinced the courts to depart from this attitude in any significant regard in applying the antitrust laws to health care and related activities.

THE SUBSTANTIVE APPLICATION OF ANTITRUST ANALYSIS TO HEALTH CARE DELIVERY

Having opened the door to antitrust scrutiny of health care financing, various arrangements among providers and insurers, and efforts taken ostensibly in compliance with health planning programs, the courts are now grappling with the difficult substantive issues regarding the application of the antitrust laws to these activities. Unlike the courts' overall attitude towards interpretation of jurisdictional and exemption issues, the overall thrust of this "second round" of decisions is harder to characterize.

The gist of substantive antitrust analysis in most cases involves the identification of unreasonable restraints on trade or competition. The general prohibition under Sherman Act section 1 literally prohibits every agreement in restraint of trade. (Many of the other provisions of the federal antitrust laws, as discussed earlier, effectively clarify what is to be regarded as a restraint of trade.) Traditionally, courts have read this language to prohibit only "unreasonable" restraints on trade, noting that in the literal sense every commercial transaction involves a restraint on competition in the market. Thus the basic inquiry required of the courts in most antitrust cases is to apply what is called the "rule of reason": the courts must analyze (1) the market(s) involved, i.e., who is selling what to whom and (2) the acts or practices involved to determine whether competition is *unreasonably* affected. The difficulty of such an analysis should be obvious. It requires the marshalling and interpretation of a tremendous amount of information—often in the face of disputed claims and allegations. It also requires the weighing of the procompetitive and the anticompetitive effects of the contested acts or practices in order to identify the net impact on competition in the market. In doing so, the court must identify both actual market conditions and those that would exist without market restraints or imperfections; thus this judicial inquiry necessarily requires the application of a considerable dose of economic theory.

An important judicial doctrine—but one that the courts claim is derived from a judicial interpretation of the statute's intent—that has been applied to make this economic analysis more manageable involves the "per se" rule. As a court proceeds with its economic investigation of an industry and of the practices or activities alleged to violate antitrust laws, if the court identifies a practice that has been traditionally and frequently shown to be unreasonable in other industries, it may proceed no further than the identification of that practice. The court will forgo the weighing of the anticompetitive and procompetitive effects of the practice under the particular circumstances. The practice or activity is considered unreasonable "per se."

As the Supreme Court justified the application of this "per se" rule in the *Maricopa County* decision (discussed *infra*), the rule may even invalidate some practices which under further examination would be found not to adversely affect competition:

Once experience with a particular kind of restraint enables the court to predict with confidence that the rule of reason will condemn it, it has applied a conclusive presumption that the restraint is unreasonable. As in every rule of general application, the match between the presumed and the actual is imperfect. For the sake of business certainty and litigation efficiency, we have tolerated the invalidation of some agreements that a full blown inquiry might have proved to be reasonable.

Classic examples of "per se" violations of the antitrust laws are price fixing, group boycotts, and market divisions among competitors. Horizontal price fixing is probably the classic example. In a case involving an allegation of price fixing, the court's economic analysis would proceed until it has identified a price fixing arrangement among competitors or, better put, the kind of price fixing that the courts regard as prohibited by the antitrust laws. At that point, no further analysis of the economic impact of that practice would be necessary; the practice would be considered illegal "per se" without a showing of an adverse impact on trade or competition. Thus the decision to adopt a "per se" rule or proceed with a rule of reason analysis can be the most critical issue in an antitrust case.

Parenthetically, it should be noted that regardless of whether a "per se" rule or a rule of reason is applied, the courts are required to make at least a threshold economic analysis of the markets and the activities or practices under examination; and, as one consequence, the threshold analysis to determine whether the "per se" rule should be applied and the subsequent analysis if the rule of reason is applied are often blurred together, sometimes inherently, other times by muddled judicial reasoning.

It should also be emphasized that if the courts do apply a rule of reason analysis, the reasonableness of a restraint on trade is adjudged entirely by the impact on competition. According to the traditional reading of the antitrust laws, the federal legislation allows only procompetitive justifications for restraints on trade. Other social objectives of anticompetitive behavior—for example, the improvement of the quality of the services rendered—are generally irrelevant in antitrust analysis. Unless exempted by Congress from the dictates of antitrust policy, restraints on trade should be measured solely by their net impact on competition.

Just how the courts will apply these principles to various aspects of health care delivery is not as yet clear. The courts must define and analyze health services, financing, and resource allocation activities in terms of relevant markets and in terms that reflect both actual and theoretical impact of competition. And they must do so in a legal environment at least partially skewed by traditional characteristics of health care delivery and the historical pattern of governmental involvement in virtually all these activities.

One of the most significant tests of the current Supreme Court's attitude towards the enforcement of substantive antitrust principles and their application to health care delivery was raised in *Arizona v. Maricopa County Medical Society*, 457 U.S. 332 (1982). In that case medical care foundations maintained by local physicians were setting maximum fee schedules which participating physicians agreed to accept in full for services to patients enrolled in health plans approved by the foundations. Each foundation also performed peer review and fiscal functions for the insurance plans. The Arizona attorney general brought an antitrust action claiming that the local medical societies, individual physicians, and the foundations were essentially fixing prices in violation of Sherman Act section 1. The defendants argued that their actions did not constitute classic price fixing and that the arrangement should be analyzed under a rule of reason. Under a rule of reason analysis, such agreements should be viewed as reasonable given the cost savings by consumers due to the maximum limits established by the arrangements and the other advantages for the health plans.

On review by the Supreme Court, a majority held that the arrangements between the foundations and the plans, even if they were, as defendants argued, maximum and not minimum price fixing, were still the kind of concerted restraint on competition prohibited by the antitrust laws and for which a "per se" analysis is appropriate.

The Court's reasoning provides an excellent illustration of both "per se" analysis and the rigor with which the Court believes competition is protected by the antitrust laws. In essence, the Court held that Congress has not given the courts the discretion to consider whether under some circumstances anticompetitive activity can be wise or fair public policy. According to the Court, the only substantive issue—unless the activity is exempted—is whether the arrangement has such a negative impact on competition as to constitute an unreasonable restraint on trade. And where that act or practice is one of several practices traditionally regarded as illegal "per se" in other markets, that negative impact on competition is to be assumed. Once the Court concluded that the arrangement constituted price fixing, the court even indicated that if the effect of the price fixing involved in the case had been in fact to lower prices, the "cost" of eliminating competition would be presumed to outweigh any advantages of the lower prices. (*See* note at end of chapter.)

Significantly, the court rejected the argument that the health care financing was so far removed from the competitive model and from other markets that the Court should apply a full scale rule of reason analysis. And it did so in terms that reflected the importance, as well as the convenience, of applying the "per se" rule:

> [T]he argument that the per se rule must be rejustified for every industry that has not been subject to significant antitrust litigation ignores the rationale for the per se rule, which in part is to avoid "the necessity for an incredibly complicated and prolonged economic investigation into the entire history of the industries, in an effort to determine at large whether a particular restraint has been unreasonable—an inquiry so often wholly fruitless when undertaken." (citation omitted)

It is instructive to compare the willingness of the Court to apply "per se" analysis under circumstances involving price fixing with the somewhat different attitude reflected in its application of antitrust doctrine under other circumstances.

In recent years, claims of antitrust violations have also been raised by physicians denied access to medical staff privileges. A physician denied admission to a hospital's staff can raise several lines of legal objections, but both private and public hospitals traditionally have been given considerable discretion in denying or limiting use of their facilities. While some courts have held that even private hospitals may have to conform to at least elementary notions of due process in denying privileges and have held hospitals to a showing of a rational basis for doing so, others have suggested that private hospitals have virtually unlimited discretion. (*See* note at end of chapter 10.) But in a number of cases in the last decade, physicians and other individual providers denied hospital privileges have raised state or federal antitrust claims, arguing that the denial of privileges constitutes, at least under some circumstances, a group boycott, tying arrangement, or other illegal restraint on trade. In a recent, important, and exceedingly complex decision, the Supreme Court both expressed its view on the restrictions imposed on hospitals by the antitrust laws and gave some further indication of the general attitude the courts should take in applying the substantive principles of antitrust laws to the delivery of health care.

Jefferson Parish Hospital District v. Hyde, 104 S. Ct. 1551 (1984), involved an exclusive contract between a private hospital and an anesthesiology group (Roux) under which the hospital agreed that any patient receiving surgery would use one of the group's physicians. As a consequence of this agreement, when another anesthesiologist applied for hospital privileges, he was denied. The physician sued in federal court claiming that this constituted a tying agreement, one of the restraints on trade traditionally recognized as prohibited under Sherman Act section 1.

Under antitrust analysis, a tying arrangement is a form of marketing where a seller insists on selling two products or services together. One product, the "tying product" is sold only if the buyer agrees also to purchase another, the "tied product." In their strictest form, tying arrangements are considered an unreasonable restraint on trade and illegal "per se." The courts, however, have been somewhat reluctant to treat all tying arrangements as illegal "per se." Only where the buyer is forced to accept the second product is the package sale regarded as an illegal "tying." Basically the seller has to be shown to have sufficient market power to force the buyer to accept a "tied" product that the buyer did not want at all, or would have preferred to buy elsewhere on different terms. Presumably, only such tying arrangements force the buyer to do something that would not be done in a competitive market and only such a forcing would either exclude existing competitors or discourage new ones, the traditional measures of competitive impact. Thus in order to hold a tying arrangement illegal "per se," the court must not only identify a tying arrangement but, in essence, the kind of tying arrangement prohibited under the antitrust laws. (As a result the distinction between the threshold analysis for application of the "per se" rule and the full analysis under a rule of reason becomes even more blurred.)

In *Jefferson*, Justice Stevens, speaking for a somewhat divided Court (four justices concurred with the decision but dissented from the reasoning; *see* note at end of chapter), analyzed the issue for the Court to decide as follows:

> In sum, any inquiry into the validity of a tying arrangement must focus on the market or markets in which the two products are sold, for that is where the anticompetitive forcing has its impact. Thus, in this case our analysis of the tying issue must focus on the hospital's sale of services to its patients rather than its contractual arrangements with the providers of anesthesiological services. In making that analysis, *we must consider whether petitioners are selling two separate products that may be tied together, and, if so, whether they have used their market power to force their patients to accept the tying arrangement.* (italics added for emphasis)

In looking at the character of two products, hospital services and anesthesiology services, the Court conceded that there were two separate products that were apparently tied together by the seller. (The hospital had argued that they were integrated services and that they should be treated as one product.) But the Court found that there was no forcing of their purchase. Looking to the market power of the hospital, the Court held that the circumstances of hospital care in the market area had not been shown to allow this hospital to exercise sufficient market power. Patients in the service area of the hospital had a number of alternatives—indeed, evidence indicated that a majority of the patients in the market area went to other hospitals; thus patients wanting to purchase the tied product elsewhere or on other terms were able to do so, and the tying arrangement did not inhibit their ability to exercise these options.

Having rejected the application of the "per se" rule, the Court went on to apply the rule of reason to the tying arrangement, i.e., to evaluate the actual competitive effects of the exclusive contract. In a surprisingly brief analysis, Justice Stevens rejected the allegation that the agreement represented an unreasonable restraint on trade:

> [A]ll that the record establishes is that the choice of anesthesiologists at East Jefferson has been limited to one of the four doctors who are associated with Roux and therefore have staff privileges. Even if Roux did not have an exclusive contract, the range of alternatives open to the patient would be severely limited by the nature of the transaction and the hospital's unquestioned right to exercise some control over the identity and the number of doctors to whom it accords staff privileges. If respondent is admitted to the staff of East Jefferson, the range of choice will be enlarged from four to five doctors, but the most significant restraints on the patient's freedom to select a specific anesthesiologist will nevertheless remain. Without a showing of actual adverse effect on competition, respondent cannot make out a case under the antitrust laws, and no such showing has been made.

Jefferson may be a good illustration of the essence of rule of reason analysis. Obviously the contract between the hospital and the anesthesiology group restrained trade and affected competition. Patients could buy the services of the hospital only if they accepted the group's physician services. But such an arrangement did not have an unreasonable effect on competition: the Court found no showing that this contract put any restraint on the market that would not be expected under normal market conditions. Patients could still buy the services of the plaintiff or any other anesthesiologist at other hospitals. Thus competitive conditions still exist in the market despite the exclusive contract. Conversely, had there been no other hospital available in the service area, the net impact on competition might have been analyzed differently or the Court might have found a forcing inherent in the mandatory tying of the two products.

CONCLUSION

In theory, a court in most antitrust cases is essentially requiredto analyze the relevant markets and to evaluate the impact on competition of various practices or arrangements. If after a threshold analysis, certain practices traditionally regarded as illegal "per se" are identified, no further economic analysis is required; but unless such a "per se" rule is adopted, the court under a rule of reason will analyze the net impact on the market(s) of the practice or arrangement to determine whether it constitutes an unreasonable restraint on competition.

It should be obvious from the cases described in this chapter that the inquiry required of the courts, particularly where that inquiry involves the economic analysis of the delivery of health care or related activities, is in practice far more complicated than this brief summary may suggest. It should be equally obvious that the courts have had considerable trouble converting the dictates of economic theory into useful analytical principles. In this regard, it is worth noting that the judicial interpretation of substantive antitrust laws has been considerably divided. On many occasions, a court has taken one judicial posture only to find that on appeal a virtually contradictory position is adopted. Even among the members of the Supreme Court there is currently considerable disagreement with regard to specific interpretations of the federal antitrust laws as well as to the overall thrust of the substantive interpretations, a marked contrast to the relatively clear direction of decisions interpreting jurisdictional and other limits on the scope of antitrust scrutiny.

For those whose interest in these cases derives primarily from an interest in health care policy, these antitrust decisions may be further complicated by the unique orientation of antitrust analysis; neither the rhetoric nor the conceptual basis of the required economic analysis may come easily to those schooled in traditional public policy analysis. Nonetheless, whatever the specific practice or arrangement drawn into antitrust scrutiny—preferred provider arrangements, cost cutting contracts, joint efforts to share services or to plan expansion—the judicial analysis under antitrust laws will focus virtually entirely on the impact of such practices or activities on what is regarded as competition in what is described as the market. The limited reimbursement arrangement in *Royal Drug*, for example, whether or not constituting good public policy when viewed in other terms or from a different perspective, is adjudged under antitrust scrutiny entirely in terms of its impact on competition. Attempts by professional groups to regulate the quality of the services provided by their peers, unless exempted from antitrust scrutiny, will be held up to comparable judicial analysis. Whether the courts can do so, and can do so efficiently and consistently raises one set of important questions. But regardless of whether such a judicial scrutiny results in better or worse public policy, the wisdom of attempting that analysis is an entirely separate question, one that is more properly directed towards Congress than the courts.

END NOTES

1. For a general introduction to antitrust law, see E. GELLHORN, ANTITRUST
   LAW AND ECONOMICS (2d ed. 1981); L. SULLIVAN, ANTITRUST (1977).
   For an analysis of the range of issues raised by the application of competitive theory to health care delivery including the relevancy of rigorous
   antitrust enforcement, see Havighurst, *Competition in Health Services: Overview, Issues and Answers,* 34 VAND. L. REV. 1117 (1982).
2. For a full description of the authority, structure, and activities of the Federal Trade Commission (FTC), see 3 TRADE REG. REP. (CCH) §§ 9500–
   9943. For a good example of the role that the FTC can play in developing
   antitrust policy, as well as some of the problems encountered in doing so, see
   the extended administrative and judicial proceedings that culminated in
   American Med. Ass'n v. FTC, 638 F.2d 443 (2d. Cir. 1981), *aff'd per curiam,*
   445 U.S. 676 (1982).
3. For several decisions that represent the earliest applications of antitrust laws
   to health care delivery, and that also document the adverse political environment encountered by early efforts to bring competition into health care
   delivery, see American Med. Ass'n v. United States, 317 U.S. 519 (1943);
   United States v. Oregon Med. Ass'n, 434 U.S. 326 (1952).
4. Another important exemption that has considerable importance for health
   care delivery and, particularly, health planning activities, involves the so-
   called *Noerr-Pennington* doctrine. The seminal decision for this judicial interpretation of the scope of the antitrust laws, Eastern R.R. Presidents Confer-
   ence v. Noerr Motor Freight, Inc., 365 U.S. 127 (1961), ruled that any
   efforts taken to urge legislative action, even clearly anticompetitive activities, were exempt from the antitrust legislation. Later decisions ruled that
   the exemption applied as well to efforts urging executive or administrative
   action by the government, as well as participation in judicial proceedings. In
   later decisions it was argued that the exemption was a proper reading of the
   intent of the antitrust laws and that the exemption of such activities was
   compelled by the First Amendment. Thus governmental "petitioning" of
   any type, despite its purpose or intent, is exempt; exceptions have been allowed only where the petitioning is shown to be a "sham"—a dilatory practice or a subterfuge for a direct attempt to inhibit competition or to inhibit
   the petitioning activities of a competitor.
   In one important interpretation of the *Noerr-Pennington* doctrine, the
   Fifth Circuit held that the attempts of physicians to urge the state board of
   medical examiners to sanction the activities of physicians cooperating with
   an abortion clinic were exempt from federal antitrust laws, as was the decision by a rival hospital to provide financial support for a lawsuit against the
   clinic. On the other hand, the same court held that writing a letter to the
   employer of the clinic's physicians claiming that they were practicing unethi-
   cally was not protected by *Noerr-Pennington. See* Feminist Women's Health
   Center v. Mohammed, 586 F.2d 530 (5th Cir. 1978), *cert. denied,* 444 U.S.
   924 (1979).

In another case, the Supreme Court held that Blue Shield's refusal to reimburse psychologists directly, in violation of a state law that required equal treatment of psychologists and psychiatrists, was not exempted under *Noerr-Pennington*, even though Blue Shield claimed it was prepared to defend itself in a lawsuit if and when the state prosecuted its refusal to obey the state law.

A *Noerr-Pennington* issue was also raised in the second *Rex Hospital* case. At the trial following the first Supreme Court decision, defendants argued that their urging of the state certificate of need agency to refuse the application of the plaintiff for new hospital beds was protected under *Noerr-Pennington*. The court of appeals held that active participation in the certificate of need process was protected, unless the defendant's conduct involved willful misrepresentations. On the other hand, the court held that if the administrative and judicial appeals of the agency's decisions were found to constitute a "pattern of baseless and repetitive claims" then the court could find antitrust liability despite the *Noerr-Pennington* protection of governmental petitioning.

Thus the Supreme Court has indicated that as with other exemptions, the *Noerr-Pennington* exemption must be narrowly interpreted and applied; nonetheless, it clearly exempts many activities relating to health care planning, litigation (at least so long as it is actively undertaken), and a wide range of lobbying efforts before both legislative and administrative bodies.

5. Another exemption of considerable relevance to participation in health planning and cost containment efforts is the state action or *Parker v. Brown* exemption. Beginning with the Supreme Court decision in Parker v. Brown, 317 U.S. 341 (1943), the courts have consistently read the federal antitrust legislation to imply an exemption for state government activities and any activities sanctioned by state government—an exemption closely paralleling the logic of the "implied immunity" doctrine. As the *Parker v. Brown* exemption has generally been interpreted, private action is exempted as state action only where (1) the statutory sanction for the activity is clearly articulated and affirmatively expressed as state policy, and (2) the private activity is actively supervised by the state itself. Thus some efforts to cooperate with state and local health planning agencies and most efforts taken under their direction should be exempted; nevertheless, the breadth of this exemption should be read in light of the apparent reluctance of the Supreme Court and other modern courts to allow broad exemptions from antitrust enforcement.

For one illustration of the "state action" or *Parker v. Brown* exemption, see Feminist Women's Health Center v. Mohammed, *supra* note 4, at 549–51.

6. For an illustration of price discrimination as prohibited under the Robinson Patman Act, and the scope of the exemption allowed under that legislation for nonprofit institutions, see Abbott Lab. v. Portland Retail Druggists Ass'n, 425 U.S. 1 (1976).

7. Another issue that could be considered either substantive or jurisdictional is the requirement under Sherman Act section 1 that the restraint of trade prohibited under the statute involve concerted action among competitors. In cases such as *Royal Drug*, it is not the limitation of reimbursement itself that is a violation of the antitrust laws, but the fact that there is an agreement among competitors to limit reimbursement and a resulting impact on competition. In this regard, it is important to note that in many of these cases the courts have been willing to look beyond a single entity and find concerted action even within one corporate institution. In Virginia Academy of Clinical Psychologists v. Blue Shield, 624 F.2d 476 (1980), *cert. denied*, 450 U.S. 916 (1981), for example, the court explicitly ruled that the local Blue Shield plan involved in that case could be viewed as the concerted effort of the individual physicians that participated in the plan's governance.

8. It should also be noted that in *Virginia Academy, supra* note 7, the court adopted a rule of reason analysis in its review of an agreement under which Blue Shield refused to reimburse psychologists unless they billed through a physician. Plaintiffs had claimed that the policy limitation was the result of a conspiracy between Blue Shield and various psychiatric professional groups and that the activities constituted a classic example of a group boycott. While concluding that the alleged conspiracy could constitute a boycott in the literal sense, the Fourth Circuit did not apply a "per se" analysis because of what it viewed as the special characteristics of the market. However, under a rule of reason analysis, the court nonetheless found that competition was impaired in the market for psychologists' services. It is worth noting that the Fourth Circuit also rejected the argument that the restriction of reimbursement of psychologists was justified since it would improve the quality of medical practice. Improvement of quality, the court held, is generally not a consideration in weighing the impact of an anticompetitive agreement.

   For a related case, see Blue Shield of Va. v. McCready, 457 U.S. 465 (1982).

9. The dissenting opinion of Justice Powell, with Justices Burger and Rehnquist, in *Maricopa County* indicates that though the majority of the Supreme Court found that the agreement between each foundation and the health plans constituted a "per se" violation, some members of the Court would have preferred a rule of reason analysis and, more importantly, would have given greater concession to the unique arrangements involved:

> I believe that the Court's action today loses sight of the basic purposes of the Sherman Act. As we have noted, the antitrust laws are a consumer welfare prescription. (citation omitted) In its rush to condemn a novel plan about which it knows very little, the Court suggests that this end is achieved only by invalidating activities that may have some potential for harm. But the little that the record does show about the effect of the plans suggests that it is a means of providing medical services that in fact benefits rather than injures persons who need them.
>
> In a complex economy, complex arrangements are commonplace. It is

unwise for the Court, in a case as novel and important as this one, to make a final judgment in the absence of a complete record and where mandatory inferences create critical issues of fact.

Significantly, the same trio of dissenters joined with Justice O'Connor and took issue with the majority's interpretation of substantive antitrust principles in *Jefferson Parish Hosp. v. Hyde*. The four justices argued that (1) "per se" analysis was inappropriate for tying arrangements and that a full economic analysis should be made in all cases involving package sales, and (2) the specific arrangements in this case should not have been analyzed as product tying but as an exclusive dealing contract; thus, in concurring with the majority, the four justices looked to the impact on different markets and to the competition between anesthesiologists as well as the competition between hospitals.

9

Malpractice: Liability for Negligence in Rendering Medical Services

All of the preceding chapters have been primarily concerned with one basic set of legal rights relevant to health and health care delivery: the legal rights that define the relationship between the government and the governed. In the first four chapters, the focus was on the relationship between the government and individual citizens with regard to the regulation of individual behavior. In chapter 5, the scope of the government's authority to fund—or not fund—social welfare programs was examined. In chapter 6, some of the same constitutional principles reviewed in earlier chapters were applied to various programs of government regulation of health facilities. Chapter 7 again examined the scope of government authority, primarily in terms of the scope and nature of authority that can be exercised by administrative agencies under their statutory mandates. The material in chapter 8 could be distinguished from the previous chapters in that the antitrust laws create relationships both between the govenment and private parties and between private parties; nonetheless the focus of the chapter was on the scope of judicial authority to enforce competition created by Congress by the enactment of the antitrust laws. Thus the basic relationship examined in virtually all of the prior material in this book involved what is regarded as public law: the legal rights defining the relationship between the government, i.e., the public sector, and certain private individuals or institutions.

In the remaining chapters in this book, the focus will shift significantly from public to private law, examining issues that involve relationships between ostensibly private entities. This chapter will be an outline of the principles that define civil liability for negligence, principally negligence in the delivery of medical care. In chapter 10, one specific problem area, the liability of hospitals for refusing to provide treatment, will be examined for the purpose of illustrating both the theoretical and the practical determinants of civil liability in greater depth.

LEGAL RIGHTS THAT DEFINE RELATIONSHIPS BETWEEN PRIVATE INDIVIDUALS: PROPERTY, CONTRACTS, AND TORTS

The principles that define liability for negligence can only be understood against the background of the whole spectrum of private law.

One broad category of legal rights that establishes relationships between private individuals or institutions and other private entities consists of private property rights. Apart from the notion of property as defined in the state and federal constitutions (which, as discussed throughout the previous chapters, define relationships between private entities and the government) the law also recognizes and provides for the protection of the private ownership of certain tangible and intangible things from interference by other private entities or the government acting in a private capacity. Ownership generally includes the right to possess and the right to control private property and the right to exclude others from doing so. And, while the law of property can be extremely complicated in its specific definition and application, in the broadest sense it makes little difference whether the private property is a tangible object, a piece of land, or an idea. Nor does the owner of the private property necessarily have to possess the property to retain ownership rights. Even when the possession is transferred to another, the original owner may retain certain rights to control the property. This book, for instance, may be owned by the person who purchases it, but the copyright and other property laws allow the author to retain control over the use of the ideas and even the format of the contents.

As with other legally defined rights, private property is recognized and enforced through the judicial system; the owner of a property right can seek judicial enforcement of the right to possess or control, or can receive compensation for damage caused to the property or by its misuse. In making such determinations, the courts will interpret private law: the common law principles inherited from judicial traditions and the statutes of the jurisdiction to the extent they have amended or supplemented the jurisdiction's common law.

Another conceptually distinct category of private law that establishes legal rights between private entities involves the law of contracts. The law has traditionally recognized that certain kinds of agreements between private entities should be legally binding and enforceable through the judicial system. Such legally binding agreements are established by a variety of human activities. They can be written or oral promises; they can be explicit agreements or merely agreements implied by individual consent. (Entering a physician's office and submitting to an examination is generally regarded as agreeing to pay the physician for the services received.) A contract can be established even by the failure to object in some circumstances. Indeed, in order for a contract to exist, there needs to be little more than two individuals who intend to be bound by their agreement, notwithstanding the difficulty of inferring what the nature of their intent actually is in some instances. Almost always, the essence of a contract is some sort of mutual exchange: one individual offers something of value or a promise of something of value for something of value—or another promise—in return.

As with property rights, contract rights are defined and enforceable through the courts, either by judicial enforcement of the agreement or, more often, by the requirement that the individual who broke the agreement compensate the other for any resulting damage.

In addition to property rights and contract rights, private law also includes a general category of law known as torts. A tort is generically defined in legal literature as "any civil wrong" or a wrong that requires the "tortfeasor" to compensate the injured party for damages. A better working definition of the concept of tort can be derived by reference to the kinds of specific activities that have traditionally been recognized as torts by the common law.

Some torts involve intentional misconduct. That is, some torts are recognized in circumstances where one person intentionally harms another. When one person acts in such a way as to put another in the "reasonable apprehension of bodily harm," the tort of civil assault has been committed and the injured party can be compensated for any resulting harm. In narrowly defined situations, for example where the conduct is regarded as malicious, punitive damages may also be awarded. If that same person acts in such a way as to cause bodily harm to the other, the tort of civil battery has been committed; again, damages, and possibly punitive damages, may be awarded to the injured party. The tort of false imprisonment occurs when one person intentionally restrains or confines another. Slander (spoken) or libel (written) are torts committed by defamation, one person relating or publishing false statements about another. In some jurisdictions, the courts have also recognized the infliction of mental cruelty and the invasion of privacy as intentional torts.

Parenthetically, it should be noted that an intentional tort may also be a crime; thus, in addition to the commission of a civil wrong giving rise to a judicial remedy for the private party, the individual's conduct may also constitute a criminal wrong, allowing the government to prosecute the wrongdoer in a separate and independent judicial action.

The more common torts, particularly in the context of health care delivery, are those committed by unintentional conduct, meaning acts that are not necessarily intended to cause harm but that are committed unreasonably or with a disregard for the consequences, or, in legal terms, by negligence. The legal concept of negligence might be loosely translated into the popular notion of "foolishness" or acts which the individual "should have known better" than to do, i.e., acts that are not—or not necessarily—intentional, but that are regarded nevertheless as wrongful. Perhaps, most critically, the notion underlying the law of negligence—that civil liability exists only where the act is judicially determined to be wrongful—is intended to distinguish circumstances where the damages caused are due to an accident or understandable mistake. Under negligence principles, an individual is not necessarily liable for causing harm to another. The driver in an automobile accident, for example, is not necessarily liable for the damage caused, but only where the driver was traveling too fast or with a lack of caution or somehow acting negligently; not for a true accident. Similarly, a physician, as later sections will demonstrate, is not necessarily liable for a poor quality outcome in delivering medical care, but only where the physician's conduct is determined to be malpractice, i.e., the negligent delivery of professional services. Indeed, the essence of the law of negligence is determining whether under the circumstances of the case the harm caused was a result of unreasonable or negligent conduct. Only under such circumstances is liability for damages to be recognized.

Understandably, this has proven to be a complicated and difficult task for the courts. Over the years, literally thousands of cases alleging negligence have been contested, requiring the judicial system to adjudicate liability in an almost endless variety of situations. In a given case, therefore, a court may be asked to define and apply the common law principles of negligence by synthesizing the opinions in dozens of previous cases; in another case at the other extreme, the court may be forced to define the principles that are applicable to a wholly unique situation which has never been previously considered. To do so, the court will in theory "read" and interpret the common law of its own jurisdiction—most negligence cases involve strictly one state's law—although, in fact, the court can choose (or ignore) interpretations of the common law enunciated in the decisions of other jurisdictions, a judi-

cial art that complicates both judicial decision making and the predicta-
bility of future decisions. (*See* discussion in chapter 10.) The judicial
definition and interpretation of applicable principles of negligence is
further complicated in some jurisdictions by the amendment or repeal
of common law principles by the state legislature.

The outline that follows is intended to emphasize that any basic
understanding of the principles of civil liability for negligence is as
much an exercise in understanding the methodology of judicial decision making as it is the understanding of specific substantive principles.
The purpose here is not to catalogue or summarize the principles of
negligence or their application to the delivery of medical care but to
outline the basic legal issues involved in determining liability in this
context and to illustrate those issues with representative examples. (Citations to more comprehensive reviews of substantive principles are included in the notes at the end of this chapter.)

NEGLIGENCE IN THE DELIVERY OF
MEDICAL CARE: THE ESSENTIAL ISSUES

While the specific interpretation of the principles that define negligence and the likelihood that a particular act or practice will give rise
to civil liability vary from jurisdiction to jurisdiction and from case to
case, across all jurisdictions and in all cases the essential legal issues that
determine civil liability for negligence remain the same. In order to recover an award for damages, the plaintiff in any negligence case must
show that the defendant had a duty to prevent or to avoid harm to the
plaintiff, that the defendant failed to live up to the requirements of
that duty, and that this failure was the actual and proximate cause of
the damage for which the plaintiff seeks recovery.

The prerequisite element of duty has been summarized by one legal critic as "a duty or obligation recognized by the law, requiring the
actor to conform to a certain standard of conduct for the protection of
others against unreasonable risks." (*See* citation to Prosser in note at
end of chapter.) In more fundamental terms, a legally recognized duty
reflects the notion under traditional interpretations of negligence that
liability does not always follow from failing to protect another from
harm; the law must first recognize that the defendant either created or
is responsible for the risk of harm, or that the defendant is in the kind
of relationship to the plaintiff that requires the defendant to protect
the plaintiff from such risks. Thus while driving a car, constructing a
building, or, in the present context, providing medical services, the law
generally recognizes that the actor has a duty to avoid harm to those

who are directly affected by his or her activities. Similarly, lifeguards, guardians of minors, merchants in some situations, and, again, providers of medical services, potentially have duties to take affirmative steps to protect certain categories of people once they have established relationships with them.

In contrast, at least under the common law as traditionally interpreted, neither a physician nor any other medical care provider nor, for that matter, anyone else has a duty to provide assistance to someone in need of medical care; unless there is an established relationship, or the condition can be attributed to the provider's actions or previous actions, there is no legal duty to provide even emergency assistance. The exceptions to this general rule are outlined in chapter 10.

Some courts have attempted to illustrate this "no duty" concept in both ordinary negligence and malpractice cases by reference to the apocryphal story (there is no American case where such circumstances have been litigated) that an innocent bystander can watch another person drown without providing assistance and nonetheless avoid liability for negligence. In theory, the bystander owes no duty to the victim, and thus, there can be no negligence, unless the bystander has somehow created the circumstances that led to the drowning or stands in a special protective relationship to the victim, e.g., the bystander is a lifeguard.

Notwithstanding this "no duty" concept, under traditional common law, both institutional and individual providers clearly have a duty to those whom they have accepted as their patients; and some courts have been willing (and almost eager) to recognize that a provider-patient relationship has been initiated even where the contact between the provider and the potential patient has been quite minimal. Thus, providers are required to conform to the standard of conduct prescribed by the law, as discussed below, in treating their patients, and they also must take affirmative steps to avoid harm to their patients. Significantly, most courts have interpreted this to mean that there is a duty to continue to treat a patient until the patient no longer needs treatment (although a few courts have suggested that a provider with "reasonable notice" can withdraw from a provider-patient relationship. *See* discussion in next chapter). On the other hand, providers who have not initiated such a relationship may not have a duty even to someone in emergent need of their services.

This common law interpretation of duty has caused some consternation, at least within the medical profession, with regard to the implications for physicians or other providers who volunteer their services at the scene of an accident. Strictly applied, the traditional notion of duty would allow a provider to ignore a roadside accident or other emergency but would recognize, once treatment is initiated, both a duty to avoid harm in providing the treatment and a duty to take steps to continue to protect the victim, possibly even forcing the provider to accept the victim as a patient or risk medical malpractice liability. Indeed, beginning in the late 1950s, state medical associations throughout the country waged a lobbying campaign in their state legislatures for a statutory amendment to the common law, fearing that the traditional notion of duty as interpreted in their jurisdiction would cause some "good Samaritan" physician to be held liable for failing to provide adequate medical treatment in an emergency, or for providing medical treatment but not accepting the victim as a patient. (Again, the story is apocryphal; no American court has ever held a "good Samaritan" physician liable for the assistance provided at the scene of an accident.) Nonetheless, "good Samaritan" laws have been enacted in virtually every jurisdiction, essentially immunizing providers from liability in rendering medical care in roadside or other accident scenes outside of emergency rooms. (*See* discussion in note at end of chapter.)

If the law recognizes that the defendant has a duty to avoid or to prevent harm to the plaintiff, the focal legal issues in any negligence case then become, first, defining the applicable standard of conduct and, second, determining whether the defendant did, under the specific circumstances of the case, violate that standard of conduct. The former is primarily a question of law, requiring the court to interpret the common law of the jurisdiction (as amended by statute); the latter is principally a question of fact-finding, requiring the jury (or the judge if there is no jury) to interpret the evidence as presented and to apply to their factual findings the legal principles explained by the judge.

In ordinary negligence cases, the legal definition of the standard of conduct involves a specification of the requirement that the defendant must prevent or avoid unreasonable risks of harm. Thus, a contractor must act as a "reasonable contractor" under the circumstances; a lifeguard as a "reasonable lifeguard." This specification of the reasonable conduct under the circumstances will generally take into consideration the training and skill of the defendant, the locality and gravity of the circumstances, and the nature of the relationship involved. In this regard, the factors that determine the standard of conduct for a physician or other provider are little different from those for anyone else. As interpreted by one court—and frequently cited by other courts and legal critics:

> A physician or surgeon, by taking charge of a case, impliedly represents that he possesses, and the law places upon him the duty of possessing, that reasonable degree of learning and skill that is ordinarily pos-

sessed by physicians and surgeons in the locality where he practices, and which is ordinarily regarded by those conversant with the employment as necessary to qualify him to engage in the business of practicing medicine and surgery. Upon consenting to treat a patient it becomes his duty to use reasonable care and diligence in the exercise of his skill and the application of his learning to accomplish the purpose for which he was employed. He is under the further obligation to use his best judgment in exercising his skill and applying his knowledge.

Thus in a medical malpractice case the jury would be instructed that a physician, in order to act as a "reasonable physician," must possess and use a "reasonable degree of learning and skill," use "care and diligence," and use "best judgment." The jury would then interpret the evidence as presented, decide the facts of the case, and apply the facts to these legal instructions. The definition of the standard of conduct for other providers of medical care, e.g., nurses, would involve similar considerations. (*See* note at end of chapter.)

It should be noted, however, that the definition of the standard of conduct in medical malpractice cases takes into account several considerations not necessarily applied in ordinary negligence cases. First, in interpreting the standard of conduct for physicians and for other categories of medical care providers, courts have traditionally added a "community practice" or "locality" rule as part of their definition of the standard of conduct. That is, in defining what a "reasonable provider" would do under the circumstances, the jury is instructed to decide what a "reasonable provider" in a similar or, in some jurisdictions, the same community would do. For a physician, one court explained the standard of conduct as:

> [T]he undertaking of a physician as implied by the law is that he possesses and will use the reasonable degree of learning, skill and experience which is ordinarily possessed by others of his profession in the community where he practices, having regard to the current state of advance of the profession. . . .

Most legal historians interpret this "community practice" rule as an allowance for the realities facing physicians and other providers in small or isolated communities. The opportunities to learn the latest procedures and techniques were not always available to a provider in such a setting. The facilities and resources of a community might also prevent the use of a procedure that might be considered standard in many other places. But while historically there was some justification for this allowance for the differences between medical practice in various communities, the notion has become less persuasive as modern transportation and communication have made medicine less of a localized activity. As a result, many jurisdictions by judicial reinterpretation of the common law or by legislative amendment have modified the "community practice" rule and a few have abandoned it altogether.

The implications of the "community practice" rule and its modern interpretation are well illustrated by a Massachusetts case.

In *Brune v. Belinkoff*, 354 Mass. 102, 235 N.E.2d 793 (1968), the plaintiff had given birth to a child in a New Bedford, Massachusetts hospital. During the delivery, the defendant, an anesthesiologist, administered a spinal anesthetic containing eight milligrams of pontocaine. As a result of the injection the plaintiff developed a permanent numbness and a weakness in her left leg.

At the trial, several Boston physicians testified that in their opinion the dosage of pontocaine was excessive and that good medical practice required an injection of five milligrams or less. Other physicians testified that eight milligrams was customary practice in New Bedford for the kind of delivery involved. The judge instructed the jury as to the application of the standard of conduct and included an explanation of the traditional "community practice" rule. The jury's verdict was in favor of the defendant. The plaintiff appealed claiming error in the judge's instructions.

The Supreme Judicial Court of Massachusetts reversed the verdict and remanded the case for a new trial based on the following opinion:

> Because of the importance of the subject, and the fact that we have been asked to abandon the "locality" rule we have reviewed the relevant decisions at some length. We are of the opinion that the "locality" rule of *Small v. Howard* which measures a physician's conduct by the standards of other doctors in similar communities is unsuited to present day conditions. The time has come when the medical profession should no longer be Balkanized by the application of varying geographic standards in malpractice cases. Accordingly *Small v. Howard* is hereby overruled. The present case affords a good illustration of the inappropriateness of the "locality" rule to existing conditions. The defendant was a specialist practicing in New Bedford, a city of 100,000 which is slightly more than fifty miles from Boston, one of the medical centers of the nation, if not the world. This is a far cry from the country doctor in *Small v. Howard* who ninety years ago was called upon to perform difficult surgery. Yet the trial judge told the jury that if the skill and ability of New Bedford physicians were "fifty percent inferior" to those obtaining in Boston the defendant should be judged by New Bedford standards, "having regard to the current state of advance of the profession."

> This may well be carrying the rule of *Small v. Howard* to its logical conclusion, but it is, we submit, a reductio ad absurdum of the rule.

The proper standard is whether the physician, if a general practitioner, has exercised the degree of care and skill of the average qualified practitioner, taking into account the advances in the profession. In applying this standard it is permissible to consider the medical resources available to the physician as one circumstance in determining the skill and care required. Under this standard some allowance is thus made for the type of community in which the physician carries on his practice.

Thus in Massachusetts the standard of practice in the community or locality in which a particular physician practices does not necessarily determine the standard to which the law holds that physician, but is only one of many circumstances that the jury can consider in determining malpractice liability. Most modern decisions have interpreted the "community practice" rule in similar terms.

Another major distinction between the definition of the standard of conduct for medical care providers and the standard of conduct in ordinary negligence cases is the limitation of the role of the jury in deciding whether the standard of conduct for a provider has been violated. In most negligence cases, the jury is instructed on the legal definition of the standard of conduct and allowed to decide, based on their interpretation of the evidence presented, whether the standard was violated. No evidence is submitted to the jury on the reasonableness of the conduct, i.e., no expert is called to give an opinion nor are witnesses allowed to give their opinions on the reasonableness of the conduct they observed. In fact, opinions as to what is reasonable under the circumstances are generally inadmissible in ordinary negligence cases. It is presumed that a jury can evaluate whether a driver or a builder or a lifeguard has acted reasonably.

In contrast, in medical malpractice and other professional negligence cases such evidence is generally required. If, for example, a physician is sued for malpractice, the plaintiff must offer testimony by at least one other physician (except in extraordinary cirucumstances) that the treatment rendered by the defendant physician was that of an "unreasonable physician." (The defendant, of course, will offer expert evidence to the contrary, even if it is only the testimony by the defendant.) The jury in such a case is essentially instructed to choose between the conflicting opinions of the experts but not to make an independent judgment based on their own opinion of whether or not the standard of conduct was violated. And if there is no expert testimony that the defendant's actions violated the standard of conduct, then the plaintiff's case may not go to the jury at all.

The implications of this concession to medical expertise should be obvious. Not only does it allow a provider's negligence to be judged in the most literal sense by his or her peers, it creates the practical difficulty for the plaintiff of finding an expert willing to offer testimony against the interests of a fellow provider; in some communities and in some circumstances this can be a practical bar to malpractice litigation.

It also serves to delegate, in large part, the fundamental judgment as to the wrongfulness of the provider's conduct, and therefore the liability for damages, to the medical profession rather than to the jury that serves that social function in most other circumstances. Whether this is justified by the inherent difficulty for a lay jury to make judgments on the quality of medical practice is an issue that is not beyond debate.

This traditional rule that the standard of conduct for a provider is to be based on the testimony of other providers does have some exceptions, as demonstrated by *Helling v. Carey*, 83 Wash. 2d 514, 519 P.2d 981 (1974).

The basic factual setting involved a woman in her late twenties who sought eye care from an ophthalmology group practice.

> The plaintiff first consulted the defendants for myopia, nearsightedness, in 1959. At that time she was fitted with contact lenses. She next consulted the defendants in September, 1963, concerning irritation caused by the contact lenses. Additional consultations occurred in October, 1963; February, 1967; September, 1967; October, 1967; May, 1968; July, 1968; August, 1968; September, 1968; and October, 1968. Until the October 1968 consultation, the defendants considered the plaintiff's visual problems to be related solely to complications associated with her contact lenses. On that occasion, the defendant, Dr. Carey, tested the plaintiff's eye pressure and field of vision for the first time. This test indicated that the plaintiff had glaucoma. . . .
> * * *
> . . . During trial, the testimony of the medical experts for both the plaintiff and the defendants established that the standards of the profession for that specialty in the same or similar circumstances do not require routine pressure tests for glaucoma upon patients under 40 years of age. The reason the pressure test for glaucoma is not given as a regular practice to patients under the age of 40 is that the disease rarely occurs in this age group. Testimony indicated, however, that the standards of the profession do require pressure tests if the patient's complaints and symptoms reveal to the physician that glaucoma should be suspected.

The trial resulted in a jury verdict for the defendant. The state court of appeals affirmed the verdict. On appeal to the state supreme court, the plaintiff argued that had she been given a diagnostic test for glaucoma earlier in her treatment, she could have arrested the disease; thus, she argued, the conduct of the defendant was not that of a "reasonable ophthalmologist" and was inadequate to protect her from harm. In essence, she argued that the standard of conduct should not be that of the defendant's peers or necessarily based on expert testimony.

Somewhat surprisingly and ignoring the traditional definition of the standard of conduct in malpractice cases, the court reversed the trial verdict:

> Justice Holmes stated in *Texas & Pac. Ry. v. Behymer*, 189 U.S. 468, 470, 23 S. Ct. 622, 623, 47 L. Ed. 905 (1903):
>
>> What usually is done may be evidence of what ought to be done, but what ought to be done is fixed by a standard of reasonable prudence, whether it usually is complied with or not.
>
> In the T. J. Hooper Case, 60 F.2d 737, on page 740 (2d Cir. 1932), Justice Hand stated:
>
>> [I]n most cases reasonable prudence is in fact common prudence; but strictly it is never its measure; a whole calling may have unduly lagged in the adoption of new and available devices. It never may set its own tests, however persuasive be its usages. Courts must in the end say what is required; there are precautions so imperative that even their universal disregard will not excuse their omission.
>
> Under the facts of this case reasonable prudence required the timely giving of the pressure test to this plaintiff. The precaution of giving this test to detect the incidence of glaucoma to patients under 40 years of age is so imperative that irrespective of its disregard by the standards of the ophthalmology profession, it is the duty of the courts to say what is required to protect patients under 40 from the damaging results of glaucoma.
>
> We therefore hold, as a matter of law, that the reasonable standard that should have been followed under the undisputed facts of this case was the timely giving of this simple, harmless pressure test to this plaintiff and that, in failing to do so, the defendants were negligent, which proximately resulted in the blindness sustained by the plaintiff for which the defendants are liable.

Such a definition of the standard of conduct in judicially determined, normative terms rather than in terms of the standard practice of the provider is rare in both negligence and malpractice cases. For that matter, this definition of the standard of conduct is no longer law in the state of Washington; following the *Helling* decision the state legislature under pressure from provider groups enacted legislation specifically requiring courts to apply a "community practice" standard of conduct in all malpractice cases. Thus, despite the *Helling* decision, as in most jurisdictions, the definition of the standard of practice and opinions as to whether it was violated are almost exclusively issues to be decided by expert opinion in cases involving medical care providers as well as many other professional services.

Even if the plaintiff can show that the defendant had a duty to avoid a risk of harm or to protect the plaintiff from such a risk, and can show that the requisite standard of conduct was violated by the defendant's actions or nonactions, the plaintiff in any negligence case must also show that the violation was both the actual and proximate cause of the harm for which damages are sought. The plaintiff is generally entitled to recover any direct loss due to medical expenses, loss of past or future income, compensation for disability, and, in most jurisdictions, compensation for pain and suffering. In some circumstances, punitive damages may also be awarded. But all recovery is premised on proof that the defendant caused the damages that the plaintiff seeks.

Actual causation is defined in most jurisdictions in terms of "but for" causation. As one legal commentator has summarized the common law, the judge should instruct the jury to find causation of damage where "it is more probably true than not the plaintiff's injury would not have occurred 'but for' the defendant's actions." (*See* citation to King in notes at end of chapter.)

In many medical malpractice cases actual causation is not a difficult issue. In others, however, such a finding can be both analytically and factually complicated particularly when the plaintiff has a preexisting medical condition or disability. For example, where it can be argued that the plaintiff would have suffered the loss or injury even if the defendant had not been negligent, the plaintiff may not be entitled to recover compensatory damages even from a negligent provider. On the other hand, any proof of additional loss or harm, any extension of recovery time, and any shortening of life (even for a terminal patient) likely would be viewed as causation of damage despite the plaintiff's original condition. The most difficult situations, of course, arise where the negligence is only one of several causative factors and the prognosis without the negligence is uncertain or poor.

The legal requirement that the plaintiff prove that the defendant caused the damages sought also requires a showing that the defendant was the proximate cause of the loss or injury. Critics have disagreed on the exact definition of proximate cause, and some argue it is more properly considered as part of the definition of the extent of the defendant's duty rather than an element of causation. But however it is theoretically defined, essentially the jury is instructed that apart from its finding of "but for" causation, it must also consider whether the defendant's conduct is sufficiently connected in time and proximity to justify a finding of proximate causation. That is to say, an act of negligence may set in motion a chain of events that eventually leads to harm, but at some point the causative link between the original negligence and the eventual harm is sufficiently strained to allow a jury to find no liability. Typically, proximate causation is illustrated by reference to circumstances where the harm to the plaintiff was unforeseeable at the time of the defendant's conduct, or where the damage to the plaintiff only occurred after several other causes intervened.

While the concept of proximate causation rarely has been applied to limit the liability of a provider for harm actually caused to the provider's patient, intriguing questions of proximate causation have arisen in professional negligence cases where the provider's negligence caused harm not to the patient but to a third party, e.g., where a misdiagnosis of a contagious disease led to the subsequent infection of the patient's family. (*See* note at end of chapter.)

To complete the outline of the essential issues in negligence cases, it should be added that even if the defendant is found to have violated the standard of conduct, and to have been the actual and proximate cause of damage to the plaintiff, the defendant may still avoid ultimate liability if he or she can prove any one of several affirmative defenses. For example, the defendant may show that the statutory or common law time limit during which the plaintiff must bring suit has expired; or that the statutory or common law of the jurisdiction has immunized the defendant from liability. Historically, charitable institutions were immune from negligence liability, although this doctrine has been abandoned in most jurisdictions. The defendant is also allowed to prove in most circumstances that the plaintiff's conduct was also negligent; in some jurisdictions, this "contributory negligence" bars the plaintiff's recovery of damages altogether; in others, the jury is instructed to apportion the defendant's liability based on the relative severity of the negligence of the parties.

As this outline of the issues in negligence and malpractice liability cases should demonstrate, even apart from the practical determinants of the initiation and outcome of litigation, the prediction of liability under any specific set of circumstances is extremely difficult and somewhat variable from jurisdiction to jurisdiction. For present purposes, it is probably most useful to analyze liability in terms of the essential legal issues and to visualize their resolution in terms of a judge "reading" the case and statutory law of the jurisdiction, defining the applicable principles, and instructing the jury on the decisions to be made and the scope of its discretion.

NEGLIGENCE LIABILITY IN
AN INSTITUTIONAL SETTING

Liability for negligence in providing medical services in an institutional setting involves essentially the same issues outlined above for determining negligence in the delivery of care by individual providers. The major differences in determining liability for negligence in a hospital or other institutional setting are primarily (1) the complications that derive from the multiplicity of potential defendants and (2) the traditional —albeit somewhat unrealistic—view of the limited role played by the institution and its staff in providing medical services.

The duty, standard of conduct, and liability for causation of damages of various physicians, nurses, and other individual providers involved in the delivery of institutional services, as well as that of the corporate entity called the hospital, must be considered separately and in terms of their specific and distinct functions, even though their liability to a particular patient may involve an analysis of the same factual setting. But at the same time, several of these providers may be found to be liable for the same damages; any or all may have violated their standard of conduct, and each may be regarded as the "but for" and proximate cause of the same harm. In such circumstances, each provider is independently liable for that harm, and the plaintiff can recover damages from any one or from all jointly. (*But see* discussion below.)

Several providers may also be liable for the same damages in an institutional setting under the principle of vicarious liability. Under the common law, employers are not only liable for their own negligence, but they are also automatically or vicariously liable for the negligence or other torts of their employees committed within the scope of their employment. This requires no finding of fault or negligence on the part of the employer. It requires only that an employer-employee relationship or its equivalent exist.

Vicarious liability derives from the reasoning that (1) the employee is acting on the employer's behalf, (2) the employer is usually exercising control and supervision over the employee's conduct, and (3) the employer is in the better position to accept financial responsibility —or to insure against it. Thus some courts have characterized it as "respondeat superior" or "let the master answer." As a result, the primary limit on vicarious liability is drawn by the distinction between employees and independent contractors. If the person employed is considered to be an independent contractor, the employer is usually not liable for the tort committed. Typically a contractor is not supervised and operates relatively independently; hence, the rationale for holding the employer liable breaks down. This distinction is a question of fact that is often disputed; the labels chosen by the parties involved to describe themselves, e.g., staff consultants or contractors or the like, are not determinative. What is crucial is their actual working relationship and the nature of the supervision and control, actually or potentially exercised.

The most important application of this principle in a hospital is in determining liability for the negligence of a physician practicing in that hospital. With the several exceptions explained below, the law has generally not held a hospital liable for the negligence of a physician on the attending staff. The attending staff of a hospital, those private practice physicians who can admit their patients to that hospital, are rarely regarded as employees of that hospital. They generally receive no direct reimbursement from the hospital. More critically, they traditionally practice relatively independently of any hospital control and supervision. Some courts have buttressed this by the claim that a hospital cannot control a physician's conduct even if it wanted to; interference with a physician's conduct toward his or her patient would be tantamount to the practice of medicine by the hospital and, under a literal reading of the law, only a licensed physician can practice medicine.

Notwithstanding this reasoning, however, a hospital is vicariously liable for the negligence of its house staff and some physicians who are actually employed by the hospital. The interns and residents in a teaching hospital are salaried employees and directly supervised in their conduct. Hospitals may also have several salaried specialists, or supervisors, not merely members of the attending staff, and the hospital may be vicariously liable for their negligence, again depending on the nature of the working relationship.

Hospitals are also vicariously liable for the negligence of nurses, attendants, and other hospital employees, at least under most circumstances.

As is a hospital, a physician is generally held to be vicariously liable for the negligence of an employed nurse or assistant whether practicing without or within an institution. A clear example is where a physician employs a private duty nurse to care for the physician's patient while in a hospital. But more complex situations arise when the negligent individual is acting under the orders of the physician but is actually employed or directly supervised by the hospital. The issue then becomes whether the relationship between the physician and the negligent individual is such that the individual is the physician's "employee," or the institution's, at the time of the negligence. Again, this is an issue of fact for the jury to decide based on the evidence regarding the specific acts and other circumstances involved.

Since several defendants can be negligent to the same plaintiff, and since one defendant's negligence may lead to the vicarious liability of another, several individual or institutional defendants may be jointly liable for the same damage to one plaintiff. This result can have considerable practical significance in determining who is sued and from whom damages are actually collected. If two or more defendants are liable for the same damage due to their separate negligence, the plaintiff can sue any one or all of them; moreover, the plaintiff can collect a judgment from any one or all of the defendants held to be liable for the damages. The choice is left entirely to the plaintiff. (But, in any event, the plaintiff can collect only the amount of actual damages, whoever pays; collection of damages is treated as the collection of an unpaid debt and involves a lawsuit separate from the original negligence litigation.) A jointly liable defendant who pays more than a proportionate share of the damage theoretically can—in a separate action—seek a proportionate contribution from all other defendants.

A jointly liable defendant who is liable solely by reason of vicarious liability of an employee will also be potentially liable to the plaintiff for the entire amount, but if the plaintiff chooses to collect the judgment from the employer, the employer can seek indemnity from the employee for the entire amount the plaintiff collects from the employer.

Thus joint or multiple liability can lead to a kind of legal "pecking order" largely determined by the ability of each defendant to pay which, in the case of medical care providers, is determined largely by the insurance coverage of each defendant. Seen in this light, each of the parties may have a different ability or willingness to litigate, to negotiate settlements, or to collect from one another, considerations that further refine the real meaning of negligence or malpractice liability and further complicate predictions of liability.

As indicated earlier in this section, an understanding of the view taken by most courts of the role of the hospital or other institutional provider in providing medical care also is critical to an understanding of the potential for liability in an institutional setting. The hospital, meaning the corporation itself, a legally recognized entity, may be liable for its own negligence, as well as vicariously liable for the negligence or other torts of its employees.

In the most literal sense, a hospital, paralleling the discussion in the previous section, may have a duty to a patient or potential patient; that duty may be defined in terms of the standard of conduct of a "reasonable hospital" to prevent or avoid harm, and any violation of that duty that actually and proximately causes compensable damage may result in the institution's liability.

The duty of most hospitals extends only to the institution's patients, although in some circumstances it may extend to those seeking admission to the institution. (*See* next chapter.) That duty to the institution's patients has been defined by most courts in terms of the traditional functions of a hospital; thus hospitals have been frequently held to have violated their standard of conduct for failing to properly train or supervise their employees. (This is entirely independent of their vicarious liability for the negligence of the employees.) Similarly, hospitals have been held liable for negligence in hiring its (nonphysician) staff, and, in a few cases, for improperly granting or continuing medical staff privileges. (*See* citations in notes at end of chapter.)

A hospital also has a duty to its patients with regard to maintaining the facility, providing equipment, and performing the other responsibilities incident to the maintenance of adequate hospital services. Any failure to act as a "reasonable hospital" in these activities would result in "corporate negligence," again independent from any corporate or institutional liability deriving from the institution's vicarious liability for the negligence of its employees.

But, until very recently, hospitals rarely have been held liable for the quality of the medical care rendered within the institution. Unless there were grounds for vicarious liability, many courts have insisted that hospitals only provide the equipment, facilities, and supporting staff for the physician, but do not directly practice or supervise the delivery of medical care. As mentioned earlier, some courts have gone so far as to read the common law to effectively prohibit any such involvement by the institution or its nonphysician employees in the practice of medicine, relying on the notion that medical care is exclusively the province of those individuals licensed to practice medicine.

While this view of the hospital and its functional role in providing medical care may have some historic justifications, it clearly understates the involvement of the institution and its employees in delivering patient care, including medical services, that characterizes the modern hospital. In a variety of ways, a hospital through its employees is both indirectly and directly involved in the medical care of hospitalized patients. Certainly there is wide discretion given to the individual patient's physician, but even the distinction between the administrative staff and the attending staff may be becoming blurred. The hospital administration sets guidelines within which attending staff must practice and, conversely, the attending staff may be very much involved in the administrative policy decisions of the hospital. Moreover, hospital bylaws, licensing standards, and the standards of hospital professional associations make it clear that the hospital is at least partially responsible for the quality of care a patient receives. Institutional programs of risk management and utilization review are prime examples.

With these changes in hospital practice, some courts have modified the traditional definition of an institution's standard of conduct and have allowed institutional or "corporate" liability in circumstances where the negligence alleged largely involved physician-administered medical care.

The landmark case that marked the beginning of a more modern view of direct hospital liability for negligence was *Darling v. Charleston Community Memorial Hospital*, 33 Ill. 2d 326, 211 N.E.2d 253 (1965).

As summarized by the Illinois Supreme Court, the case involved the following set of facts:

> On November 5, 1960, the plaintiff, who was 18 years old, broke his leg while playing in a college football game. He was taken to the emergency room at the defendant hospital where Dr. Alexander, who was on emergency call that day, treated him. Dr. Alexander, with the assistance of hospital personnel, applied traction and placed the leg in a plaster cast. A heat cradle was applied to dry the cast. Not long after the application of the cast plaintiff was in great pain and his toes, which protruded from the cast became swollen and dark in color. They eventually became cold and insensitive. On the evening of November 6, Dr. Alexander "notched" the cast around the toes, and on the afternoon of the next day he cut the cast approximately three inches up from the foot. On November 8 he split the sides of the cast with a Stryker saw; in the course of cutting the cast the plaintiff's leg was cut on both sides. Blood and other seepage were observed by the nurses and others, and there was a stench in the room, which one witness said was the worst he had smelled since World War II. The plaintiff remained in Charleston Hospital until November 19, when he was transferred to Barnes Hospital in St. Louis and placed under the care of Dr. Fred Reynolds, head of orthopedic surgery at Washington University School of Medicine and Barnes Hospital. Dr. Reynolds found that the fractured leg contained a considerable amount of dead tissue which in his opinion resulted from interference with the circulation of blood in the limb caused by swelling or hemorrhaging of the leg against the constriction of the cast. Dr. Reynolds performed several operations in a futile attempt to save the leg but it had to be amputated eight inches below the knee.

The plaintiff sued both Dr. Alexander and the hospital. The physician settled before the trial for $40,000; but the hospital, relying on the traditional interpretation of institutional liability for negligence, contested the claim against the hospital. The arguments of both sides were summarized in the (later) supreme court opinion:

> The plaintiff contends that it established that the defendant was negligent in permitting Dr. Alexander to do orthopedic work of the kind required in this case, and not requiring him to review his operative proce-

dures to bring them up to date; in failing, through its medical staff, to exercise adequate supervision over the case, especially since Dr. Alexander
had been placed on emergency duty by the hospital; and in not requiring
consultation, particularly after complications had developed. Plaintiff
contends also that in a case which developed as this one did, it was the
duty of the nurses to watch the protruding toes constantly for changes of
color, temperature and movement, and to check circulation every ten to
twenty minutes, whereas the proof showed that these things were done
only a few times a day. Plaintiff argues that it was the duty of the hospital
staff to see that these procedures were followed, and that either the
nurses were derelict in failing to report developments in the case to the
hospital administrator, he was derelict in bringing them to the attention
of the medical staff, or the staff was negligent in failing to take action.
Defendant is a licensed and accredited hospital, and the plaintiff contends that the licensing regulations, accreditation standards, and its own
bylaws define the hospital's duty, and that an infraction of them imposes
liability for the resulting injury.

The defendant's position is stated in the following excerpts from its
brief: "It is a fundamental rule of law that only an individual properly
educated and licensed, and not a corporation, may practice medicine. . . .
Accordingly, a hospital is powerless under the law to forbid or command
any act by a physican or surgeon in the practice of his profession. . . . A
hospital is not an insurer of the patient's recovery, but only owes the patient the duty to exercise such reasonable care as his known condition requires and that degree of care, skill and diligence used by hospitals generally in that community. . . . Where the evidence shows that the hospital
care was in accordance with standard practice obtaining in similar hospitals, and plaintiff produces no evidence to the contrary, the jury cannot
conclude that the opposite is true even if they disbelieve the hospital witnesses. . . . A hospital is not liable for the torts of its nurses committed
while the nurse was but executing the orders of the patient's physician,
unless such order is so obviously negligent as to lead any reasonable person to anticipate that substantial injury would result to the patient from
the execution of such order. . . . The extent of the duty of a hospital with
respect to actual medical care of a professional nature such as is furnished
by a physician is to use reasonable care in selecting medical doctors.
When such care in the selection of the staff is accomplished, and nothing
indicates that a physician so selected is incompetent or that such incompetence should have been discovered, more cannot be expected from the
hospital administration." (citations omitted)

In its various arguments the plaintiff was asking the Illinois court
to do that which virtually all previous courts had been very hesitant to
do: interpret the standard of conduct for a hospital to include a responsibility for the quality of medical care practiced by attending staff physicians. The plaintiff argued that the hospital should supervise an at-

tending staff physician's conduct in various ways, including the requirement that in certain cases consultation with a specialist be sought. The plaintiff also contended that the nursing staff, the hospital's employees, should have acted on the hospital's behalf and reported to the hospital the developments of the case once it was clear that something was wrong. Significantly, similar requirements were incorporated into the accreditation standards of the Joint Commission on Accreditation of Hospitals, state licensing standards, and even the hospital's own bylaws.

After a lengthy trial, the jury awarded the plaintiff $110,000 in damages. (The original figure was $150,000, reduced by the settlement with the physician involved.) The defendant appealed to the state appellate court and then to the Illinois Supreme Court. However, that court upheld the trial court verdict.

> "The conception that the hospital does not undertake to treat the patient, does not undertake to act through its doctors and nurses, but undertakes instead simply to procure them to act upon their own responsibility, no longer reflects the fact. Present-day hospitals, as their manner of operation plainly demonstrates, do far more than furnish facilities for treatment. They regularly employ on a salary basis a large staff of physicians, nurses and interns, as well as administrative and manual workers, and they charge patients for medical care and treatment, collecting for such services, if necessary, by legal action. Certainly, the person who avails himself of 'hospital facilities' expects that the hospital will attempt to cure him, not that its nurses or other employees will act on their own responsibility." (citation omitted) The Standards for Hospital Accreditation, the state licensing regulations and the defendant's bylaws demonstrate that the medical profession and other responsible authorities regard it as both desirable and feasible that a hospital assume certain responsibilities for the care of the patient.
>
> . . . [W]e need not analyze all of the issues submitted to the jury. Two of them were that the defendant had negligently: "5. Failed to have sufficient number of trained nurses for bedside care of all patients at all times capable of recognizing the progressive gangrenous condition of the plaintiff's right leg, and of bringing the same to the attention of the hospital administration and to the medical staff so that adequate consultation could have been secured and such conditions rectified; . . . 7. Failed to require consultation with or examination by members of the hospital surgical staff skilled in such treatment; or to review the treatment rendered to the plaintiff and to require consultants to be called in as needed."
>
> We believe that the jury verdict is supportable on either of these grounds. On the basis of the evidence before it the jury could reasonably have concluded that the nurses did not test for circulation in the leg as frequently as necessary, that skilled nurses would have promptly recog-

nized the conditions that signalled a dangerous impairment of circulation in the plaintiff's leg, and would have known that the condition would become irreversible in a matter of hours. At that point it became the nurses' duty to inform the attending physician, and if he failed to act, to advise the hospital authorities so that appropriate action might be taken. As to consultation, there is no dispute that the hospital failed to review Dr. Alexander's work or require a consultation; the only issue is whether its failure to do so was negligence. On the evidence before it the jury could reasonably have found that it was.

While many courts—including those in Illinois—have had some trouble interpreting the exact meaning of the *Darling* decision in subsequent cases, the vast majority of courts have at least followed the general lead of the Illinois court. (*See* citations in notes at end of chapter.) As most modern courts view institutional liability, the hospital has a duty to its patient that requires not only reasonable care in performing the various functions of a hospital, including the selection of physicians, but also the monitoring and controlling of the performance of physicians, regardless of the details of the physician-hospital relationship. These courts have been fairly clear in their insistence that the hospital's duty to control or monitor physician behavior is in no way comparable to the duty to supervise or control the institution's employees. Requiring consultations in some cases or requiring that the nursing or administrative staff report circumstances where the physician's conduct is clearly substandard are fairly minimal requirements; hospitals still can treat physicians as independent contractors with considerable autonomy in their practice. In essence, *Darling* and the cases that have followed it have simply refined the definition of a hospital's standard of conduct to reflect more accurately the realities of modern hospital practice; they have not created a new or unprecedented basis for liability.

It should be noted that the *Darling* definition of the standard of conduct for hospitals relies heavily on existing hospital policies and by-laws, JCAH accreditation standards, and licensing and certification standards. As such, the benchmarks for what a "reasonable hospital" would do are largely either self-determined by the institution or heavily influenced by existing industry practices. While there has been some trend in the last decade to strengthen the requirements incorporated into these standards, it would not be unexpected to find that in the future hospitals will oppose the development of even nonbinding standards by arguing that any codification of good hospital practice, e.g., JCAH standards for utilization review, may be used to increase hospital liability, citing *Darling* as a prime example.

It should also be noted that the hospital industry is not unmindful of the possibility of legislative modification of common law doctrine. Thus any real or perceived development in the case law that might potentially increase corporate liability may be subject to legislative repeal or modification.

CONCLUSION

This outline of the legal principles that define liability for negligence in the delivery of medical care is presented not as a summary or a treatise on substantive law, but as an introduction to the relevant legal issues in the determination of liability and the manner in which these issues are addressed and resolved. A full understanding of the substantive law, particularly for the purpose of predicting the potential for liability in a given set of circumstances, would require, at the least, a more detailed review of relevant legal principles and a better understanding of the intricate art of "reading" what is called the common law, its judicial interpretations, and its legislative modifications. The material in the next chapter is intended to illustrate one such in-depth examination of substantive law. The notes at the end of this chapter suggest other illustrations as well as various treatises and other works commonly used as references on substantive principles.

At least two other points deserve considerable attention for their relevance to a full and practical understanding of the law of negligence and the potential for civil liability in the delivery of medical care. First, as mentioned briefly in the introduction to this book, there are a number of practical determinants of negligence or malpractice liability that should not be overlooked, some of which have already been drawn into the discussion in this chapter. Obviously the plaintiff in a malpractice suit must rely heavily on expert witnesses. Yet provider-witnesses are often unavailable, expensive, or simply uncooperative. Even with experts to testify and, just as importantly, to assist in the preparation of a malpractice case, a fully contested malpractice trial can take a year or more to prepare and schedule, months to try, and years to complete appeals. The time and expense involved can be extraordinary. In some jurisdictions it is not uncommon for a malpractice suit to take over five years to complete.

Due to the expense of litigation, smaller claims are often impractical to pursue. Even when a large claim is at stake, some plaintiffs cannot afford to wait several years for a final award and may be forced to negotiate a settlement for less than they deserve. Moreover, while many attorneys will accept a plaintiff's case on a contingent fee basis (the attorney takes a percentage of the recovery, usually 30 to 50 percent), some will not if the potential award is small or unpredictable.

On the other hand, providers find that defending against any suit, regardless of the likelihood that the suit will be successful, can be costly. Indeed, there is a "hassle" value to even a baseless lawsuit, and consequently the provider or the provider's insurance company may be forced to defend or even settle despite their evaluation of the merits of the plaintiff's claim.

These problems in financing and preparing for negligence litigation only suggest the variety of practical determinants that must be factored into an understanding of liability or a prediction of possible liability. The potential for liability is not entirely determined—perhaps not even primarily determined—by the dictates of substantive law, however it is theoretically interpreted. Liability is determined through and by a somewhat cumbersome process of legal decision making as much as by legal principle.

Second, negligence liability and, particularly, malpractice liability must always be considered in light of the availability and coverage of liability insurance. The potential costs of liability to a provider are not restricted to the amount of the settlement or judgment; reputation, time and energy, and other "costs" have to be weighed as well. But at least in terms of the economic cost of negligence or malpractice liability, the practical issue for most providers is not the cost of being sued—most providers will never be sued—but the cost of buying insurance coverage for the potential of liability.

During the last decade, the costs of malpractice insurance, at least in some jurisdictions, have been frequently described as growing to critical proportions. Conversely, some critics have argued that the importance of the malpractice "problem" has been blown beyond real proportions by the medical profession. More importantly, critics have also argued that the actual cause of inflating malpractice premiums may not be what the providers—or the public—most commonly claim. (*See* note at end of chapter.) Nonetheless, the result has been considerable political pressure in the legislatures of most states to modify either the substantive principles determining liability or the process by which liability is determined.

The variety and range of these proposals can only be suggested here. Some states are considering legislation that would limit the contingency fee to a certain fixed maximum. Other states have tried to reduce the delays inherent in malpractice litigation or what is perceived as inequitable results by requiring that the parties to a malpractice suit go through an arbitration process and make attempts to settle the claim before a trial. It even has been proposed that this concept be expanded to require that all malpractice claims be settled through a compulsory arbitration process and not by the courts at all. Other changes in the traditional legal process that are under consideration include eliminating the role of the jury or prohibiting juries from awarding damages for such elements as "pain and suffering."

Changes in the current system for insuring against malpractice liability have also been proposed as solutions to the malpractice "problem." Some states now require that all insurance companies offering malpractice insurance in that state accept a proportionate share of all providers or a share of the bad risks. It has also been proposed that a system of "no-fault" insurance be developed for providers of medical care. Under such a scheme, anyone injured as a result of medical practice could recover from the provider's insurance company regardless of any finding of fault or negligence. The cost of this insurance might be reduced by restricting the amount a patient could recover and by reductions in the cost of the litigation and the administration now required for the determination of liability. More recently, some experts have suggested that providers and patients could contractually agree to limit potential liability, in return for some reduction in the cost of service.

It is unlikely, however, that either the substantive law defining negligence in the delivery of health care or the process for determining liability will be substantially altered in most jurisdictions. Even if there is a "malpractice crisis," there is hardly a political consensus regarding either the nature of the problem or the required solution; and perhaps more importantly, there are politically powerful interest groups, most notably the legal profession, which have a strong and vested interest that will resist any change that might adversely affect them.

END NOTES

1. Probably the most useful overview of the law of torts is found in W. PROSSER & W. KEETON, PROSSER AND KEETON ON THE LAW OF TORTS (5th ed. 1984). For an alternative source—but not as adaptable to the needs of the neophyte researcher, see RESTATEMENT (SECOND) OF THE LAW OF TORTS, §§ 299A, 328A, 457 (1965). For a narrative discussion of negligence principles as they apply to malpractice liability, see J. KING, THE LAW OF MEDICAL MALPRACTICE IN A NUTSHELL (1977).

   The best source for a description and analysis of negligence liability in an institutional setting is A. SOUTHWICK, THE LAW OF HOSPITAL AND HEALTH CARE ADMINISTRATION (1978).

2. While most of the discussion in this chapter of the standard of conduct for providers uses physicians as the primary examples, the same principles with

slight modification would define the standard of conduct for other providers.

Nurses are generally required to "exercise ordinary and reasonable care to see that no unnecessary harm comes to the patient;" this standard is generally interpreted in terms of the degree of care ordinarily exercised by other nurses in the locality involved or in similar circumstances. Annot., 51 A.L.R.2d 970 (Supp. 1984). For example, it has been held that a nurse has not followed the standard of care when he or she has failed to carry out medical orders; or carried out medical orders when he or she knows (or should know) that unnecessary harm may result; or failed to notify a physician or supervisor as to the validity of orders or treatment by the physician.

The standard of conduct for nurses, just as for physicians, is generally established by expert testimony, which may be represented by other qualified nurses in the community or, in some cases, by physicians from the same or similar communities.

The standard of conduct for hospital administrators has not often been addressed in case law. Generally, the duty of an administrator will be defined in terms of the functions and responsibilities of a "reasonable administrator," e.g., implementing and administering review procedures, evaluating staff operational procedures, or exercising reasonable care and diligence in the hiring of qualified personnel.

3. For an excellent illustration of the issue of proximate causation, as well as a discussion of some of the policy considerations that may be weighed by a court in determining whether or not civil liability should be extended to a relatively unsettled set of circumstances, see Tarasoff v. Board of Regents, 17 Cal. 3d 425, 131 Cal. Rptr. 14, 551 P.2d 334 (1976). In *Tarasoff*, the California Supreme Court held that a psychiatrist (and his employer) may be liable where he did not act to warn the victim *or take other action* after learning of a patient's intent to kill the victim. It may be relevant to the discussion of this case to note that while the California court allowed that civil liability could be found under such circumstances, the *Tarasoff* case was settled out of court for an undisclosed sum and never went to trial. Parenthetically, the patient was tried and found guilty for murder and subsequently deported.

For discussion of a physician's duty to warn third parties of possible contagious conditions of the physician's patient, see Hoffman v. Blackmon, 241 So. 2d 752 (Fla. App. 1970).

4. An outline of provider liability for rendering medical care would not be complete without some reference to "good Samaritan" laws.

Since the 1950s "good Samaritan" laws have been passed in at least 30 states, attempting at least partially to immunize physicians and other providers from liability for providing aid at the scene of an accident. A typical "good Samaritan" law allows that a provider who renders medical care or other assistance at the scene of an accident cannot be held liable for negligence in providing that assistance or for terminating assistance, as long as the provider was acting in good faith, i.e., did not intentionally cause harm to the accident victim. However, these laws vary from jurisdiction to jurisdiction in terms of the type and scope of immunity created; and, in a few states, as a kind of quid pro quo for the immunity, providers (and in some states the general public) are required to stop and render aid in a roadside accident or emergency.

But the most interesting aspect of "good Samaritan" laws is their political origin. It is apparent that in most states the immunity from liability for "good Samaritans" was enacted under pressure from medical associations and individual physicians who feared—unjustifiably—that they would run a high risk of negligence or malpractice liability if they attempted to render emergency aid to accident victims. Indeed, in some states, legislation was prompted by publicized "horror stories" about physicians who ignored people with serious injuries because of the mistaken belief that such aid created the potential for liability. As the next chapter will discuss in more detail, liability for negligence is theoretically possible in an emergency situation. In particular, a physician who renders emergency aid but subsequently leaves the scene could be accused of abandoning a "patient." But while several courts have implied that such liability is possible, the intriguing fact is that no reported case has ever found a physician liable for actions arising out of the rendering of emergency aid. Thus, though liability is possible, it is extremely unlikely, as common sense would dictate. Yet the high risk of liability for the "good Samaritan" physician is still a persistent myth and one that has made it necessary for many states to pass protective "good Samaritan" laws.

5. In addition to the potential for liability for the quality of the care provided, or for failure to provide care at all, providers are also potentially liable for failing to obtain the patient's consent to be treated. In order for consent to treatment to be valid, it must be voluntary, competent, and informed.

In the most primary sense, any unconsented-to touching, even a touching for the purpose of providing medical care, is technically the intentional tort of battery. For the requisite consent to be voluntary, it must be obtained without fraud, misrepresentation, or undue coercion. For consent to be competent, the patient must be both legally competent (i.e., of a proper age) and mentally competent. The age for consent to medical treatment and for most other purposes was traditionally defined in most jurisdictions by a particular age. However, recent Supreme Court decisions regarding the fundamental interest of privacy may mean that such fixed age standards are no longer appropriate. (*See* discussion in chapter 4.) The definition of mental competence to make decisions regarding medical treatment (or any other individual decision) varies from jurisdiction to jurisdiction, but is generally considered a medical judgment—creating something of a conflict of interest for the provider seeking consent to treatment. All jurisdictions recognize that in an emergency the requirement of consent does not bar treatment, either reasoning that the consent is implied by the circumstances or simply waived altogether in emergency situations.

For a full discussion of the requirement of consent, see G. ANNAS, L. GLANTZ, & B. KATZ, THE RIGHTS OF DOCTORS AND NURSES AND ALLIED

HEALTH PROFESSIONALS (1981) and sources cited therein.

The requirement that consent be informed is more complicated, both in terms of its legal definition and in terms of the practical implications for providers. In general, American common law (of which there is not a great deal concerning the definition of informed consent) requires that the patient be given sufficient information upon which to make an intelligent and informed choice. At the least, that information includes a discussion of the alternatives, the risks of each alternative, and the likelihood of various outcomes. But whether or not a decision is properly informed is analyzed in virtually all jurisdictions not as a failure to obtain consent *per se*, and therefore under the definition of civil battery, but in terms of the provider's duty to obtain consent; a failure to sufficiently inform the patient is therefore analyzed as negligence in performing this duty. Thus the critical questions are defining the standard of conduct for the provider, determining whether that standard was violated, and determining whether under the circumstances a violation of the standard of conduct actually (and proximately) caused damage to the patient. The implications of analyzing informed consent under negligence principles for the potential of liability are significant —but often lost on the provider community. For a good illustration of the legal principles defining the requirement of informed consent, the distinction between negligence and battery analysis, and the potential for civil liability for failing to obtain informed consent, see Cobbs v. Grant, 8 Cal. 3d 229, 104 Cal. Rptr. 505, 502 P.2d 1 (1972).

6. The Illinois courts have had some difficulty in applying the *Darling* standard. In Lundahl v. Rockford Mem. Hosp., 93 Ill. App. 2d 461, 235 N.E. 2d 671 (1968), the court of appeals made an erroneous statement of fact about *Darling* (which in turn briefly confused some jurisdictions in interpreting *Darling*), and a few subsequent Illinois cases distinguished purely medical treatment by independent physicians from the circumstances in *Darling*. The most recent decision, however, seems to have adopted the original and somewhat broader doctrine set forth in *Darling*. *See* Ingram v. Little Co. of Mary Hosp., 108 Ill. App. 3d 456, 438 N.E.2d 194 (1982).

The emerging majority in other jurisdictions applies the doctrine of corporate negligence first enunciated in *Darling* which "imposes on the hospital a non-delegable duty owed directly to the patient, regardless of the details of the physician-hospital relationship." Pedroza v. Bryant, 101 Wash. 2d 226, 677 P.2d 166 (1984). The duty has been defined as a duty of reasonable care in selecting competent physicians as members of the hospital's medical staff, in providing routine hospital services, in monitoring and controlling performance of doctors, in establishing review procedures and by-laws, and in enforcing rules, standards, and guidelines it has set or adopted. *See generally*, Pedroza v. Bryant, *supra*; Elam v. College Park Hosp., 132 Cal. App. 3d, 183 Cal. Reptr. 156 (1982); Bost v. Riley, 44 N.C. App. 638, 262 S.E.2d 391, *cert.denied*, 300 N.C. 194, 269 S.E.2d 621 (1980). *But see* Schenck v. Government of Guam, 609 F.2d 387 (9th Cir. 1979). As stated by one court:

> If a patient at a modern-day hospital has the reasonable expectation that the hospital will attempt to cure him, it seems axiomatic that the hospital have the duty assigned by the *Darling* court to make a reasonable effort to monitor and oversee the treatment which is prescribed and administered by physicians practicing at the facility.

Bost v. Riley, 44 N.C. App. at 647, 262 S.E.2d at 396.

7. For an example of hospital liability resulting from the granting of staff privileges to an unqualified physician, see Johnson v. Misericordia, 99 Wis. 2d 708, 301 N.W.2d 156 (1981).

8. For an excellent analysis of the so-called "malpractice crisis" (better termed the "malpractice premium crisis"), the underlying causes of inflating malpractice insurance premiums, and various political responses, see S. LAW & S. POLAN, PAIN AND PROFIT: THE POLITICS OF MALPRACTICE (1978).

10

Hospital Liability for Denial of Medical Care: The Access Dilemma

As the previous chapter is intended to demonstrate, a basic understanding of liability for negligence in the delivery of medical care requires at the least (1) an understanding of civil liability and how it is adjudicated and (2) sufficient knowledge of substantive legal principles to allow the identification of the relevant legal issues that will be addressed in that adjudication. Armed with this introduction, even a neophyte to legal decision making should be able to follow the progress of negligence or malpractice litigation, seek out and intelligently apply legal counsel, and even attempt to research in more specific terms the meaning and prescription of the law in any one jurisdiction.

Obviously the essence of any further understanding of the law of negligence, whether by a lawyer or a layperson, or for academic or practical application, is making some prediction of the actual potential for liability in a given set of circumstances. Ultimately, the issues, once properly identified, must be addressed in terms of the law of one particular jurisdiction and as applied to one particular set of facts. The law must be "read," meaning the case law and its statutory modifications must be interpreted and applied in such a way as to allow some prediction of how a judge will interpret the law and whether a jury, under the judge's instructions, will interpret the evidence to find liability for damages.

Only on rare occasions can such judgments be easily made. Presumably if the circumstances of a case are sufficiently similar to those in previous decisions in a jurisdiction, the courts of that jurisdiction—and juries under their instruction—should interpret and apply the law consistently with previous decisions. But more often, the nature of the circumstances in a case, and whether they do in fact and in law parallel those of previous decisions, are part of the controversy. And even where there are few evidentiary disputes (i.e., what happened, to whom, etc., is fairly clear), the case more often presents legal questions that are at least somewhat variant from previous decisions, if not wholly novel to the jurisdiction.

It is in these situations that the "reading" of the case law, the interpretation of the common law and its subsequent judicial and legislative modifications, becomes so critical but at the same time so difficult to master.

This chapter is intended to demonstrate how the common law of negligence is "read," and how it might be interpreted and applied to one critical problem that will likely pose difficult questions for both legal and health policy decision makers in the near future.

A HYPOTHETICAL

Consider the following hypothetical circumstances:

It is 1:00 a.m. The emergency room doors of a private hospital swing open and paramedics wheel in an accident victim. The emergency room staff intercepts them and immediately takes the teenaged male to a treatment cubicle. The doctor on duty and the nurses hurriedly work to stabilize the victim. He is unconscious, losing blood, and has multiple fractures. They give him oxygen and blood to bring his vital signs into a less critical range. They administer first aid to surface cuts and bruises. X-rays are taken, and they indicate that he needs surgery to clean and set his broken bones. His condition has been stabilized, but a long period of hospitalization is anticipated.

It is 2:15 a.m. The victim's parents have been contacted, and they arrive at the emergency room. A nurse meets them and informs them of their son's condition. He escorts them into the examination cubicle. The doctor on duty is with their son, and she gives the parents a rundown of his injuries. She shows them the x-rays revealing the severity of the fractures and explains that their son needs to go into surgery immediately.

The nurse then directs the parents to the admitting desk adjacent to the emergency ward. There the admissions officer begins formal admissions procedures with a series of questions:

"State the patient's full name and address, and your relation to the patient. . . ."

The parents respond to each question.

The officer queries, "Insurance coverage for applicant?"

"We're on Medicaid."

At that response, the admissions officer halts and apologetically explains the hospital's policy of not admitting patients on Medicaid.

The parents become frantic and insist upon treatment for their son. But the admissions officer remains firm. Angered and confused, the parents dash back into the emergency room to talk with the doctor. When they reach the doctor, the admissions officer is already there and is hurriedly explaining the situation to the doctor. The doctor, with a pained expression, confirms the hospital's policy on Medicaid recipients to the parents.

The patient in the hypothetical could just as easily be a woman in the initial stages of labor, someone with severe burns, or a migrant laborer with congestive heart failure. Recent headlines have provided a variety of comparable circumstances. And the hospital's reluctance to admit the patient for further treatment could result from any one of a number of practices increasingly employed by many private—and some public—hospitals: the requirement of a preadmission cash deposit or prior documentation of (adequate) insurance coverage, or a policy that all patients hospitalized be first accepted by a member of the hospital's medical staff. The underlying legal issue would be essentially the same: whether, following emergency treatment or examination, a hospital has a duty under common law negligence principles to continue to provide assistance to the patient in need of immediate treatment. (The discussion here is confined to common law obligations, and the obligations of the hospital; see note at end of chapter for a discussion of the legal obligation of the physician under such circumstances, and various statutory duties that may impose obligations on the hospital apart from the common law.) It is a sensitive and explosive issue and one that is likely to draw considerable public attention as such circumstances become more commonplace, as current economic and political trends would dictate.

Initially, it is important to acknowledge that the hypothetical situation might not result in a legal confrontation at all, or even an immediate crisis for any of the participants. In many areas of the country, the accident victim, as with any other unwanted patient, might be transferred or simply directed to the nearest hospital willing to accept Medicaid patients, likely a publicly sponsored hospital. And, if the claims of representatives of the hospital industry are to be believed, many hospitals, public or private, would relent and admit the patient for further treatment, particularly if such alternatives were not available or if a transfer would be medically inadvisable. For that matter, the hospital might decide to make exception to its "no Medicaid" policy for a number of reasons wholly apart from the potential for liability, e.g., the impact on employee or medical staff morale, public relations, or even ethical considerations.

On the other hand, in a growing number of communities there may no longer be a state or local hospital (at least one managed in the "open to all" public hospital tradition), or a private institution willing to accept unwanted transfers from other hospitals. And increasingly hospitals of all types are adopting and enforcing exclusionary admission practices to cope with both internal and external cost containment pressures. Thus it is conceivable that the hospital in the hypothetical would at least consider whether as a matter of law it can stand firm on its "no Medicaid" policy.

Whether under the common law a hospital can limit its assistance to emergency care and to the stabilization of a patient's condition and refuse to provide further care raises a legal issue which—surprisingly—has not been cogently addressed in American case law. Yet significantly, while downplaying the likelihood that any hospital would be likely to do so, in both the popular and academic literature representatives of the hospital industry have generally insisted that the common law obligation of a hospital to accept people in need of medical treatment extends only to those that represent "unmistakable emergencies;" and they have at least implied that that obligation only requires a provision of emergency services, not hospitalization or further care. At least private hospitals, they have frequently argued, are under no duty to provide further care to anyone.

A better reading of the American common law indicates that the legal issue raised by this hypothetical is a much more difficult question, and one that would be better regarded as an open question for future courts to clarify. As the sections to follow will outline, both individual and institutional providers have a duty to continue to provide care once they have initiated treatment or accepted a patient; thus once a patient is accepted or treatment is initiated, it appears fairly well settled that a court will hold a provider liable for any injury resulting from a failure to continue treatment. In addition, many jurisdictions have indicated that they require hospitals to initiate emergency care, at least to those people who present themselves as "unmistakable emergencies." But whether following the rendering of emergency services a court would recognize an obligation to provide further assistance is a question the answer to which can only be inferred from existing case law with considerable qualification.

The sections to follow attempt to trace such a "reading" of the common law. The first section outlines the general principles that de-

fine the duty of providers to continue to provide treatment once it is initiated or patient status is established. The next section reviews in detail
the existing case law relating to the obligations of a hospital after rendering emergency services.

THE DUTY OF CONTINUING CARE AND
THE LAW OF "ABANDONMENT"

As outlined in the previous chapter, American common law does not
impose a general duty to render assistance to others, even in emergency situations. The "bystander" has no legally imposed obligation to
act unless he or she has some causal role in creating the circumstances
that led to the need for assistance or unless there is some special relationship between the bystander and the person in need of assistance.
The origins of this "no duty" rule are not altogether clear; nor is the
underlying logic particularly compelling in many circumstances. (*See*
note at end of chapter.) And while the basic principle has persevered,
its harsher implications have been avoided occasionally, sometimes by
explicit modification, other times by the willingness of courts to find
that the basic factual setting is a variant on the "innocent bystander"
paradigm.

Once action is initiated, however, whether by agreement or voluntarily, the common law generally recognizes that a duty is created to
exercise reasonable care in carrying out that activity, including in some
circumstances the continuation of assistance to prevent further harm.
Thus even a wholly gratuitous undertaking can create an obligation to
continue to provide assistance, particularly where that undertaking
either creates a new risk of harm or the victim has relied to his or her
detriment upon the continuation of the assistance.

The application of these broadly stated principles of negligence to
circumstances that involve the delivery of medical care has led to a
patchwork of precedential decisions from which the more specific delineation of the legal obligations of providers is not easy to "read."
With the exception noted in the sections to follow, it is well settled that
the traditional "no duty" rule insulates private providers from liability
for refusing to render medical care to any member of the public until
the provider undertakes to provide treatment or unless what the law
regards as a patient-provider relationship has previously been established. Once a duty is recognized, however, the provider must act as "a
reasonable provider under the circumstances" and comply with the
requisite standard of conduct imposed by the law. In terms of the quality of the treatment provided, as reviewed in the previous chapter, a

physician must use a reasonable degree of learning and skill, care and diligence, and best judgment; the standard of conduct for institutional providers is defined similarly. But the common law duty of a "reasonable provider" has also been interpreted to require the continuation of treatment, as well as the provision of treatment of adequate quality, once a duty is recognized.

The definition of this continuing obligation and the delineation of the circumstances under which an individual provider might be liable for failing or refusing to continue to provide care are difficult to summarize since they have been relatively infrequently addressed by American courts. Many jurisdictions have adopted the view that once a physician-patient relationship is established, the physician cannot unilaterally abandon the patient until the physician's services are no longer needed or until the patient initiates a termination of the relationship. Most courts have defined this continuing obligation with reference to a specific spell of illness or period of treatment. The duty of continuing care apparently does not apply to the "family physician" or necessarily to any physician who provided care for a previous condition or problem. Yet the duty during a period of treatment continues even after the referral of the patient to a specialist or other physician, or at least where the referring physician retains (or should have retained) primary responsibility for the patient's care. Only a few courts have examined the separate duty of a hospital to continue to provide treatment to its patients apart from that of the treating physician. (*See* note at end of chapter.) But these cases have indicated that the duty of a hospital, like that of the physician, is measured almost exclusively by the continuing need of the patient. Legal commentators have uniformly agreed and have reasoned that the discretion of the hospital to terminate treatment parallels that of the physician.

Some courts have indicated, however, that since the basic provider-patient relationship is at least partially contractual, the duty of continuing care and the requisite standard of conduct that it requires of the provider can be modified or limited by the terms of the original agreement or undertaking or, according to a very few courts, by subsequent notice to the patient. For example, a Texas court has ruled that a physician in a small OB-GYN clinic could limit his services to normal delivery and refuse to perform a cesarean section if his patient had been given sufficient notice and explanation of this condition at the time that treatment was initiated. And, in a case that stirred no little controversy, one federal court (interpreting state law) held that a physician could even condition his care on the patient's (prior) agreement to comply with the physician's policy of sterilizing all Medicaid patients following their third pregnancy.

Only a very few jurisdictions have considered the circumstances under which a provider may, subsequent to the initiation of treatment, give notice and terminate the relationship. These cases have indicated both that the provider must have reasonable justification for doing so and that the provider must give the patient sufficient opportunity to secure an alternative source of care. Thus—in virtually the only American case which has given judicial approval to an outright abandonment of a patient in a suit against both a physician and a hospital—it was clear that the behavior of the patient made a continuation of the relationship untenable and that the patient had opportunities for treatment elsewhere. In a similar case—where the physician believed that the patient was only "sick in the head"—the court nonetheless ruled that this was insufficient justification and that the physician's termination of treatment was in violation of the physician's continuing duty. Significantly, several courts have ruled that financial considerations, e.g., the failure of the patient to pay an overdue bill (on a previous illness), are not sufficient basis for the termination of treatment. (*See* citations at end of chapter.)

Equally important, all courts that have addressed the issue have agreed that any notice of termination must give the patient adequate opportunity to find alternative sources of care. The obvious question, whether the adequacy of that opportunity is based on the actual existence of alternatives or simply an opportunity to inquire of alternatives, has not been directly addressed in any appellate case. Several legal commentators, however, have read existing case law to mean that if there is no alternative source of care and there is a continuing medical need, then a provider cannot terminate treatment simply by notifying the patient of an intent to withdraw from the patient-provider relationship.

In any event, it is clear that a provider's latitude to terminate treatment once it is initiated or once a provider-patient relationship has been established is relatively narrow. For that matter, as some of the cases to follow will demonstrate, some courts have been rather quick to find that such a relationship has been established and, therefore, to recognize a provider's duty to continue to provide treatment. At least with regard to the patients that it has accepted for inpatient status or for whom it has initiated inpatient hospital services, there appears to be little doubt that a hospital must continue to provide treatment so long as the patient needs hospital services or it will run a high risk of negligence liability for any subsequent harm to the patient.

HOSPITALS AND THE RENDERING
OF EMERGENCY SERVICES

The latitude of a hospital to decline to provide further treatment following emergency services but prior to admission to the hospital is not so easily summarized. It is even difficult to discern whether the issue should properly be framed as a hospital's refusal to accept the patient, suggesting that the critical legal question is whether the hospital has a duty to do so, or as a termination of treatment, suggesting that the critical question is whether the hospital has complied with its applicable standard of conduct, i.e., is it acting as a reasonable provider? The courts have not been particularly consistent, either in their characterization of what could be regarded as essentially similar circumstances, or in their interpretation of the applicable common law principles. Indeed, a "reading" of the case law interpreting the obligations of a hospital following the rendering of emergency services requires a synthesis of several, somewhat contradictory, lines of cases.

Hospitals and the "No Duty" Doctrine

Virtually all courts begin their examination of a hospital's common law obligation by affirming the traditional "no duty" doctrine. Until treatment is initiated, or until a provider-patient relationship is established, at least private hospitals are generally under no common law obligation to provide their services to the public. Some courts have indicated that public hospitals would have a duty to the general public, although it is not always clear whether this duty is a matter of common law or derives from the statutory authorization for the hospital. At least one jurisdiction has indicated that it may view even private hospitals as "quasi-public" and therefore impose a broader obligation on both private and public hospitals; but this is clearly a minority point of view. (*See* note at end of chapter.)

The strictest application of the "no duty" doctrine to circumstances that parallel those in the hypothetical set out at the beginning of this chapter was in *Birmingham Baptist Hospital v. Crews*, 229 Ala. 398, 157 So. 224 (1934). In *Crews*, parents took their two-year-old child to the emergency room of a private hospital for examination. The physician on duty diagnosed diphtheria and administered oxygen and antitoxin; but under a hospital policy prohibiting the admission of patients with contagious diseases, the child was denied admission for further treatment. The child died shortly after returning home. In addressing the question of whether the hospital had an obligation under the common law to continue to care for the patient, the court relied on the traditional "no duty" rule and found that the hospital had no continuing obligation to treat the child since it had not in the court's view initiated treatment or accepted the child as a patient. According to the Alabama Supreme Court:

> Defendant is a private corporation, and not a public institution, and owes the public no duty to accept any patient not desired by it. In this respect it is not similar to a public utility. It is not necessary to assign any reason for its refusal to accept a patient for hospital service. But it was shown that "it was against the rules and regulations of the hospital to admit any contagious disease, if diagnosed as such before admittance." Plaintiff's minor child had diphtheria when he took her to the hospital. It was shown to be highly contagious, and defendant owed plaintiff or the child no duty to accept her for treatment, and may have made itself liable to other patients for so doing.

Thus the Alabama court rejected the arguments that the rendering of emergency care constituted a voluntary undertaking of hospital care or the establishment of a provider-patient relationship; or that having initiated emergency treatment the hospital had created a new risk or reliance for which some continuing care might be required.

Since the 1934 Alabama decision, several courts in other jurisdictions have referred with approval to the *Crews* interpretation of the common law.

In *Le Juene Road Hospital v. Watson*, 171 So. 2d 202 (Ct. Apps. Fla. 1965), an 11-year-old boy was taken to the hospital—apparently unannounced—for an appendectomy. The boy was dressed in a hospital gown, examined, and given medication, but not formally admitted to the hospital; prior to the operation the boy was transferred to another hospital where after a delay the operation was performed. In analyzing whether the first hospital was negligent, the Florida court cited *Crews* and held that the hospital had no general duty to the plaintiff. "A private hospital is under no obligation to admit any patient that it does not desire. Harsh as this rule may sound, it is permissible for a private hospital to reject for whatever reason, or no reason at all, any applicant for medical and hospital services." The court also held, however, that the boy had been admitted—although not formally. As a consequence, the *Crews* doctrine did not apply to these facts, and, therefore, the hospital could be held liable for any harm suffered from the delay in treatment following the refusal to treat the plaintiff.

In *Joyner v. Alton Ochsner Medical Foundation*, 230 So. 2d 913 (La. App. 1970), the plaintiff was taken to the hospital's emergency room following a car accident in which he received severe injuries. The hospital staff administered emergency treatment but refused to admit the plaintiff to the hospital because he could not pay a cash deposit. He was subsequently transferred to a veterans' hospital. In holding that the hospital had no duty to admit the plaintiff, the Louisiana court also cited the *Crews* decision with approval; but, in doing so, it indicated that had the circumstances been slightly different, further treatment might have been required:

> The record reveals, that in accordance with the defendant hospital's policy and practice, *if plaintiff's condition had been such as to require immediate admission to and treatment in the hospital he would have been admitted and treated*. But his condition did not require such admission as an emergency measure. The record also reveals that the requirement of a deposit prior to hospital admission is the usual procedure among private hospitals in the area where, as here, the patient has nothing to offer for the purpose of assuring payment of hospital bills. In the absence of an immediate need for emergency hospital treatment the requirement of a deposit prior to hospital admission was neither unreasonable nor improper. (italics added)

In another Alabama case, *Harper v. Baptist Medical Center*, 341 So. 2d 133 (Ala. 1976), plaintiff was brought to a private hospital following an automobile accident. The staff physician diagnosed him as having a severed artery just below the knee. Emergency treatment was provided, but the hospital refused to admit him for surgery because he did not have hospital insurance. After a stay of about four hours, he was transferred to a charity hospital where the surgery was performed. Plaintiff subsequently suffered from a permanent foot drop, walked with a limp, and alleged that he felt constant pain. He sued the first hospital, claiming negligence both in the performance of emergency treatment and in the hospital's refusal to provide further treatment.

The *Harper* court, again citing *Crews* as controlling precedent, held that the defendant owed no duty to hospitalize the plaintiff since it had not accepted him as a patient nor created a new condition which required further treatment. (The court also questioned whether the delay in treatment brought about by the transfer of the plaintiff could be causally linked to the harm for which the plaintiff was seeking damages.)

How are these cases to be "read"? In particular, would *Crews* and the decisions that have claimed it as precedent give sufficient and compelling guidance to a modern court trying to determine whether a hospital can refuse to provide further assistance following the rendering of emergency services?

Certainly if *Crews* and, arguably, its progeny are regarded as controlling precedent, then the obligation of a hospital might be confined to the provision of emergency care in the strictest sense. At least the courts in Alabama have been fairly insistent that a hospital has no duty to provide such assistance to the patient and have been unwilling to characterize the provision of emergency services as the initiation of treatment or the creation of a provider-patient relationship. The only exception allowed by *Crews* and *Harper* is a narrow one: where the treatment itself creates a new risk that may require additional treatment. Apparently this is the Alabama courts' interpretation of the traditional exception for detrimental reliance. Thus, although the facts in both Alabama cases differ slightly from the scenario illustrated by the hypothetical, it would be reasonable to assume that any court following the apparent lead of these precedents might find that the hospital has no continuing duty following emergency services, even if it means a "harsh result."

The apparent lead of the decisions in the other jurisdictions is harder to predict. On their facts, neither *Le Juene* nor *Joyner* applied the "no duty" rule to allow a patient in need of treatment to be turned away following emergency treatment. In *Le Juene*, while indicating approval of the *Crews* holding, the court avoided that "harsh result" by holding that the preliminary handling of the case was sufficient to be characterized as the initiation of (full hospital) treatment and therefore held the hospital liable for failing to provide treatment to the patient according to traditional common law principles. In *Joyner*, the court also adopted the *Crews* definition of a hospital's duty; yet the court indicated that had the patient been in need of immediate hospitalization, hospitalization would have been required, apparently in accordance with the obligation to provide emergency services, once undertaken, in a reasonable manner. For that matter, the *Harper* decision does not apply the *Crews* "no duty" doctrine to a situation where the plaintiff is in need of immediate treatment and such treatment is not elsewhere available, but under circumstances where the hospital transferred the patient with no apparent detrimental effect on the patient.

Indeed, while a number of cases have referred with approval to the original *Crews* decision in discussing the common law obligations of private hospitals, they have done so almost exclusively as the precedential basis for the broader principle that there is no general common law duty to provide assistance to anyone. They do not necessarily condone this principle in its harsher application: allowing the refusal by a hospital to hospitalize emergency cases or condoning the abandonment of patients in immediate need of hospitalization following the rendering of emergency services.

Negligence in the Rendering
of Emergency Assistance

As indicated earlier, there have been other decisions involving the disposition of emergency cases in which the analysis has been primarily focused on whether the hospital has complied with the applicable standard of conduct in rendering emergency services. Significantly, as was suggested in *Le Juene*, these cases indicate that the failure to treat a patient in the immediate need of treatment, even where that treatment requires hospitalization, may be regarded as negligence on the part of the hospital, despite the somewhat contradictory implications of the traditional "no duty" doctrine.

In *Jones v. City of New York Hospital for Joint Diseases*, 134 N.Y.S.2d 779 (Sup. Ct. 1954), *rev'd on other grounds*, 286 App. Div. 825, 143 N.Y.S.2d 628 (App. Div. 1955), a stabbing victim received an examination and first aid in the hospital's emergency room but was subsequently transferred to a public hospital for further treatment. She died following surgery. The court held that if the transfer was for the convenience of the hospital rather than necessity (the hospital argued that no beds were available), then the hospital could be liable if the transfer causally contributed to her death. While the discussion of the hospital's obligation was predominantly factual, with virtually no discussion of the underlying legal principles (and no mention of *Crews*), the decision clearly recognized that the duty of the hospital in rendering emergency services went beyond initial examination and stabilization. In the court's words, liability could be imposed since "the deceased was denied necessary treatment . . . and, without her consent, was transferred . . . and that such transfer was a contributing factor in her death."

In *Bourgeois v. Dade County*, 99 So. 2d 575 (Fla. 1957), an unconscious man was brought to the emergency room by the police and given a superficial examination but not a complete history or x-rays. An intern, concluding that the patient was only drunk, returned him to police custody; he died in jail the next day. It was later discovered that he had broken ribs piercing his thoracic cavity. The court ruled that there was adequate evidence of negligence in both the examination and the treatment, and that the hospital could be liable if the discharge of the plaintiff had aggravated his condition. Again, the implication of the decision was that the obligation of the hospital went beyond first aid and that hospitalization would have been required had it been necessitated by the patient's condition. There was no discussion of the "no duty" rule.

A similar result was reached, although again with little discussion of the underlying principles, in *Barcia v. Society of New York Hospital*, 39

Misc. 2d 526, 241 N.Y.S.2d 373 (Sup. Ct. 1963). What the court described as the hospital's "admitting physician" (it is not clear whether or not the examination took place in the emergency room or not) refused to admit a child with symptoms of pneumonitis, following a brief examination. The child was admitted the next day but did not recover. The court indicated that the duty of the hospital on initial (preadmission) examination included both proper diagnosis and the rendering of appropriate treatment; in this case, arguably, hospitalization.

In *New Biloxi Hospital, Inc. v. Frazier*, 245 Miss. 185, 146 So. 2d 882 (1962), a gunshot victim was taken to the emergency room, bleeding profusely; he was ignored by the nurses for about 20 minutes until, on the insistence of the ambulance driver, he was briefly examined but not treated. After a second delay, he was finally examined by a doctor who, upon learning that the patient was a veteran, transferred him without treatment to a veterans' hospital. He died shortly thereafter from shock and loss of blood. The court found despite the hospital's claim of "no duty" that the hospital had undertaken to provide emergency assistance to the patient; and it defined the applicable standard of conduct in a manner that would appear to include hospitalization if immediately necessary:

> In an emergency, the victim should be permitted to leave the hospital only after he has been seen, examined and offered reasonable first aid. In undertaking to do so, a hospital must exercise due care. A hospital rendering emergency treatment is obligated to do that which is immediately and reasonably necessary for the preservation of life, limb or health of the patient. It should not discharge a patient in a critical condition without furnishing or procuring suitable medical attention.

Similarly, In *Ruvio v. North Broward Hospital District*, 186 So. 2d 45 (4th Dist. Fla. App. 1966), *cert. denied*, 195 So. 2d 567 (Fla. 1966), a Florida intermediate appellate court ruled that a hospital could be held liable for a delay in further treatment following the rendering of emergency services, if the delay was the actual and proximate cause of further harm to the patient. (Note that the *Le Juene* decision, in another Florida appellate district, was not mentioned by this court.) In *Reeves v. North Broward Hospital District*, 191 So. 2d 307 (4th Dist. Fla. App. 1966) that same court reaffirmed its attitude towards the duty of the hospital. Plaintiff was brought to the emergency room suffering from head pains. He was examined and his condition was diagnosed as hypertension. No written history was taken, although some diagnostic tests were rendered. The plaintiff became incoherent, but the attending doctor left and a second doctor relieved him; without further examination, plaintiff was discharged by the second doctor. Twelve hours later en route back to the hospital, the plaintiff died of subdural hematoma. The court held that the issue of whether the hospital had a duty to admit and treat the plaintiff was an issue of fact for the jury based on the reasonableness of the decision to discharge him from the emergency room.

The court of appeals in Alabama in *Citizens Hospital Association v. Schoulin*, 48 Ala. App. 101, 262 So. 2d 303 (1972), ruled that the misdiagnosis of a back injury in the emergency room could result in liability for failure to hospitalize the patient, arguing that *Crews* did not apply once the hospital undertakes to provide emergency treatment. (Note, however, that this appears to be a misreading of *Crews* and, in any event, the subsequent ruling of the Alabama Supreme Court in *Harper*, discussed *supra*, may have tacitly overruled *Schoulin*.)

In another misdiagnosis case, *Mulligan v. Wetchler*, 39 App. Div. 2d 102, 332 N.Y.S.2d 68 (1972), *app. dism'd* 30 N.Y.2d 951, 335 N.Y.S.2d 701, 287 N.E.2d 391 (1972), the "admitting physician" failed to diagnose acute appendicitis in a patient transferred from another hospital. (It is not clear from the decision whether this was in the emergency room.) The patient died of complications from delayed surgery. The court ruled that if the delay in treatment were a cause of the death, the hospital could be held liable.

In *Hamil v. Bashline*, 224 Pa. Super. 407, 307 A.2d 57 (1973), plaintiff with severe chest pains was taken to an emergency room, but no physician was available and he was given only cursory examination. He died shortly thereafter of a myocardial infarction. The court held that having voluntarily undertaken to provide treatment, the hospital would be liable for negligence in the performance of that treatment. No distinction was made between undertaking emergency services and undertaking hospital care. The obligation of the hospital was measured largely by the immediate needs of the patient.

In *Carr v. Saint Paul Fire and Marine Ins.*, 384 F. Supp. 821 (W.D. Ark. 1974), an action against the insurer of a county hospital, plaintiff had called ahead before arrival at the emergency room and was assured that a doctor was available; nonetheless, he was examined only by a nurse and two orderlies. At the trial, the hospital claimed that the plaintiff said he would wait until the nurse could reach his own doctor; plaintiff claimed that the nurse refused to call the doctor on call. He returned home, but died shortly after returning to the hospital. The federal district court interpreted Arkansas common law to require "that degree of care and attention as the circumstances require." Arguably this would include hospitalization if necessary.

These cases are listed here in serial fashion since they are easily misconstrued if their rulings are aggregated. None are particularly authoritative (among other things, most are intermediate appellate courts) nor, for that matter, well reasoned. Nonetheless, they demonstrate that a variety of courts have held that once emergency services are undertaken, a hospital can be liable for subsequent harm to the patient, including harm that results from a failure to receive further treatment. In most of these cases, liability apparently rests on the failure either to diagnose the need for further treatment or from some act or omission that resulted in a failure to secure that treatment, even where the treatment needed was inpatient hospitalization. Under this analysis, the critical issue was not whether the hospital had a duty to admit the patient, but whether the hospital properly carried out its duty, i.e., its standard of conduct, a duty that arose when it undertook to render emergency services.

This analytic distinction is crucial. If a court is to look to the reasonableness of the hospital's disposition of an emergency case, it is easier to predict that such a court would require the hospital either to transfer the patient (without deterioration) or to hospitalize the patient, at least if the need for further treatment is immediate. These cases certainly provide precedential basis for doing so, at least for a court inclined to be sympathetic to the plight of the patient. A court that would follow strictly the lead of *Crews*, on the other hand, might ask whether the hospital had a duty to accept the patient for hospitalization, a duty analytically separate from the duty that arises from the initiation of emergency treatment. Such a court could conceivably rely solely on the "no duty" rule and allow the harsh result of refusal to provide further assistance despite the plight of the patient. Probably the more important point is that either prediction would be speculative. Clearly, future courts have a great deal of discretion in "reading," and reading between the lines, of the common law.

The Obligation to Provide Care
in "Unmistakable Emergencies"

Both the "no duty" cases and the cases that have held liability where treatment or diagnosis is provided negligently in the emergency room should be "read" in light of the development in many jurisdictions of an important exception to the traditional "no duty" rule. As is frequently cited in this context—although sometimes in overly simplistic terms—many courts have recognized an obligation of hospitals (at least those with emergency services) to render services to anyone who presents "an unmistakable emergency." *Wilmington General Hospital v. Manlove*, 54 Del. 15, 174 A.2d 135 (1961), is usually cited as the first explicit articulation of this exception to the common law "no duty" rule.

In *Manlove*, a four-month-old infant, suffering from high fever and diarrhea, was brought by his parents to the emergency room at a private hospital after he failed to respond to medication prescribed two days earlier by the family physician. The nurse on duty denied the child any examination or treatment on the grounds that he was under the care of another physician. The child died the next day of bronchial pneumonia. At the trial, the court held that the hospital did have a duty to the plaintiff, arising out of the quasi-public character of the hospital. The court reasoned that the various public funds received by this particular hospital and the exemption of the hospital from various state and federal taxes allowed the judicial imposition of a public duty on the facility, and the failure to carry out that duty could result in liability for the hospital.

The Delaware Supreme Court, however, reversed, holding the broad "quasi-public" theory neither logical nor correct in reading the common law. On the other hand, the supreme court also rejected the hospital's argument, relying on *Crews* that as a private hospital it had no common law duty to provide assistance or protect anyone unless it undertook to do so. In the Delaware court's view, while the hospital was clearly a private institution, it did maintain an emergency room and had a well-established custom of providing emergency treatment to all who presented themselves; thus the court allowed for an alternative basis for the hospital's liability:

> But the maintenance of such a ward to render first-aid to injured persons has become a well-established adjunct to the main business of a hospital. If a person, seriously hurt, applies for such aid at an emergency ward, relying on the established custom to render it, is it still the right of the hospital to turn him away without any reason? In such a case, it seems to us, such a refusal might well result in worsening the condition of the injured person because of the time lost in a useless attempt to obtain medical aid.
>
> Such a set of circumstances is analogous to the case of the negligent termination of gratuitous services, which creates a tort liability. . . .

As a consequence of this ruling, the court remanded the case to the lower court for a full trial. In doing so, it also addressed the issue of the hospital's standard of conduct with regard to emergency services, at least in terms relevant to the factual setting of the case:

> Obviously if an emergency is claimed, someone on behalf of the hospital must make a prima facie decision whether it exists. The hospital cannot reasonably be expected to station an intern at all times in the receiving room. It therefore keeps a nurse on duty. If the nurse makes an honest decision that there is no unmistakable indication of an emergency,

and that decision is not clearly unreasonable, in the light of the nurse's training, how can there be liability on the part of the hospital?

Thus *Manlove* is virtually silent on the issue of the hospital's obligation to provide for further treatment of patients in need of hospitalization following emergency services. But it does suggest the possibility that in emergency situations where immediate treatment appears necessary and appropriate, an exception to the traditional "no duty" rule may be considered. Perhaps more importantly, in jurisdictions where the *Manlove* doctrine is recognized, it appears that hospitals do have a duty to some patients to render at least emergency services, and consequently treatment of some type must be initiated. While the implications of the cases discussed in the previous section are unclear, certainly the initiation of treatment—of any kind—makes it more likely that a continuing obligation will be recognized.

To discuss the *Manlove* decision in such detail might suggest that the case has been universally accepted as a modification of the common law and consistently followed in other jurisdictions. Neither has proven to be true. In some jurisdictions, courts that have considered similar cases have specifically declined the opportunity to state their views on the *Manlove* doctrine, finding alternative grounds for ruling on the case or holding *Manlove* inapplicable. *See, for example, Perth Amboy v. Board of Chosen Freeholders*, 386 A.2d. 900 (N.J. Super. 1978); *Fabian v. Matzko*, 236 Pa. Super. 267, 344 A.2d 569 (Pa. Super. 1975). Others have implied at least that they would recognize the *Manlove* exception but have appeared reluctant to do so if the case can be decided on other grounds. At least two courts have defined "unmistakable emergency" so narrowly as to suggest at least a partial rejection of the *Manlove* doctrine. *See Hill v. Ohio County*, 468 S.W.2d 306 (Ky. 1971), *cert. denied* 404 U.S. 1041 (1971); *Campbell v. Mincey*, 413 F. Supp. 16 (N.D. Miss. 1975). (In both cases the courts rejected arguments that women in labor presented "unmistakable emergencies.") Nonetheless, in at least a handful of jurisdictions, an "unmistakable emergency" exception to the "no duty" rule has been directly recognized and applied, although the bases for doing so have varied somewhat from jurisdiction to jurisdiction.

In *Stanturf v. Sipes*, 447 S.W.2d 558 (Mo. 1969), the Missouri Supreme Court essentially upheld the *Manlove* interpretation of a hospital's common law duty under circumstances where the hospital refused to render any treatment to a man with severe frostbite. The hospital first asked for a $25 deposit (but later, when a third party offered to pay the deposit, the hospital still refused to admit the plaintiff, apparently on financial grounds). Eventually, plaintiff was admitted to a second hospital, but both feet were amputated. The court, characterizing the circumstances as an emergency, held that the plaintiff could reasonably rely on defendant hospital's well-established custom of accepting anyone who could pay the deposit. (There was no discussion of the requisite standard of conduct or the extent of care that the hospital should have provided, although clearly the plaintiff required inpatient hospitalization.)

The Wisconsin Supreme Court also approved—at least in dictum —of an exception to the "no duty" rule in *Mercy Medical Center v. Winnebago County*, 58 Wis. 2d 260, 206 N.W.2d 198 (1973). The plaintiff was a private hospital that provided emergency treatment to a patient who was entitled under state law to medical benefits paid for by the defendant county. In holding that the county had to reimburse the hospital for the service rendered, the court indicated a very broad view of a private hospital's obligation to provide services in an emergency:

> We think . . . that today, with our society's emphasis upon a concern for the health of its citizens, private hospitals with emergency wards and facilities for emergency services have a duty to admit those in need of aid. It would shock the public conscience if a person in need of medical emergency aid would be turned down at the door of a hospital having emergency service because that person could not at that moment assure payment of the service.

In *Guerrerro v. Copper Queen Hosp.*, 112 Ariz. 104, 537 P.2d 1329 (1975), an action was brought on behalf of two infants based on the hospital's refusal to provide emergency treatment for severe burns. The Supreme Court of Arizona explicitly rejected both the *Manlove* analysis and the traditional "no duty" rule, but found a *Manlove*-type obligation implied by state legislation. "A private hospital has no duty to accept a patient or serve everyone unless a different public policy has been declared by statute or otherwise." Looking to the licensing laws of the state that required the hospital to maintain an emergency room, the court held that "the hospital may not deny emergency care to any patient without cause." (Parenthetically, the court also ruled that it would make no difference if the plaintiffs were found to be illegal aliens who had entered the country solely to obtain medical care.)

In *Richard v. Adair Hospital Foundation Corp.*, 566 S.W.2d 791 (Ky. App. 1978), the emergency room nurse twice refused to admit a child with what later was discovered to be pneumonia. The child died several hours later in another hospital. The court of appeals, distinguishing *Hill v. Ohio County* discussed *supra*, recognized a *Manlove*-type exception to the "no duty" rule and held that liability could be predicated on the refusal to admit a patient in an emergency. It remanded the case for a jury determination of whether there was an "unmistakable emergency."

In addition to these judicial recognitions of an exception to the common law "no duty" rule, many states have by legislation imposed requirements on hospitals to provide emergency services. (One commentator found that as of 1979 at least nine different jurisdictions had done so.) Thus in many, if not most, jurisdictions, a hospital may have a statutorily imposed duty to accept people in immediate need of medical care; and in doing so, a door may have been opened that cannot easily be closed.

POSSIBLE "READINGS" OF THE COMMON LAW OBLIGATIONS OF A HOSPITAL TO PROVIDE CONTINUING CARE

In order to develop a basic understanding of negligence liability, it is both necessary and appropriate to synthesize the case law, identifying the relevant legal issues and the principles by which they will be decided. More importantly, such a synthesis is ultimately the objective in developing a more sophisticated understanding of the law. It is, after all, just such a synthesis of the case law that must be applied by each court and, therefore, that must be attempted in order to predict or understand what future courts can or will do. Thus decisions should be aggregated by similar factual settings; underlying principles should be extracted from their individual applications; patterns of both reasoning and outcomes should be "read" and summarized.

But while such a synthesis may be essential, it should be attempted with considerable care. As the decisions defining a hospital's obligations following the rendering of emergency services illustrate, any summary or synthesis of this case law would, by necessity, generalize from a few individual decisions and, most likely, disguise some of the differences and the contradictions between those decisions. Moreover, any accurate "reading" of a hospital's common law obligations for the purpose of predicting what future courts do would not only be extremely difficult, it also would involve, invariably, normative as well as descriptive judgments.

As a consequence, just as it is important to develop the ability to "read" these cases and to understand the underlying principles upon which they are decided, it is equally important in doing so to avoid imposing a clarity or a consistency on the case law that simply does not exist. It is ultimately necessary and important to articulate "what most courts have decided" and "the apparent bases for these decisions." It is also critical to acknowledge that apparent patterns might as accurately be described as sketchy outlines and that any attempt to define the common law can easily blur the distinction between the "majority view," i.e., what most courts *have* decided, and "the better view," i.e., what those courts *should have* decided. As one critic has expressed it, the common law, particularly when claiming to summarize the principles of law common to all jurisdictions, can be regarded as much as a metaphor as an actual description or summary of judicial thinking.

A review of the decisions in the previous sections, for example, indicates that any summary statement of a hospital's obligation to a patient in need of hospitalization following the rendering of emergency treatment would actually involve a synthesis of a comparatively few direct interpretations of the common law as applied to this set of circumstances. In most jurisdictions, the most accurate observation—particularly for predictive purposes—might well be to conclude that the question has not been previously addressed; and, in virtually all jurisdictions, it would be extremely speculative to attempt to predict with any degree of certainty the extent to which a hospital would be risking liability for failing to provide further care. Even "reading" the case law in those jurisdictions that have decided cases involving disposition of a patient following emergency care, it should be obvious that the courts have not been particularly consistent or clear in their reasoning. In some cases, it appears that individual courts have been basing their decisions as much on their ad hoc notions of what is fair or equitable as on their interpretations of the dictates of the common law. Even those courts that have attempted to stay within the confines of traditional common law principles have shown considerable alacrity for avoiding what would be the implications of the traditional common law "no duty" rule.

Even the *Manlove* exception to the "no duty" rule, often cited as the modern or "majority view," really represents the rulings of only a handful of jurisdictions. The underlying rationale for such an exception has varied considerably across jurisdictions, further complicating any prediction of future applications or extensions of the *Manlove* doctrine. For that matter, while virtually all authorities have been quite certain in their "reading" of the continuing obligation of any provider once treatment is initiated or a provider-patient relationship is established, that principle has been enforced and applied in a surprisingly few jurisdictions, and only rarely with regard to hospital care.

The point here is not merely to emphasize the obvious difficulty of "reading" the case law with regard to this or any other issue; nor is it to dismiss as impossible any attempt to predict liability. The point is to emphasize what the case law really is—and what it is not—and what a summary or synthesis of that case law can represent. The case law must be "read," however difficult that may be. And, with some issues and in some jurisdictions that "reading" can be much clearer than in others. Ultimately the risk of liability must be predicted, even if predicted with varying degrees of certainty.

Such a "reading" or prediction should be made in the light of several observations, critical to the development of an understanding of the law and how legal principles are applied, particularly in determining civil liability. First, legal decision making, whether for determining a hospital's continuing obligation or any other issue, inherently involves incomplete information and uncertain predictions; even holding aside the economic and other practical determinants of outcomes in litigation (discussed in chapter 9), the "reading" of previous judicial decisions can at best suggest the likelihood of how the law will be interpreted by the next judge or in the next case. Simply acknowledging the uncertainty of predicting future applications of the law has obvious implications for both personal and professional behavior, particularly in reacting to the potential for liability.

Second, it should also be obvious that any summary or synthesis of the case law should be viewed quite critically, perhaps even suspiciously. Almost by its nature, any summary statement of case law tends to suggest clarity and certainty; like any good metaphor, a statement of legal principle can be an insightful or useful illustration even when it is not a literal or accurate description. One of the primary caveats in weighing the merits of any legal advice or opinion should be to emphasize the distinction between descriptions of prior case law and of relevant legal principles and prescriptions or advocacy of what that law should be. In both the popular and the academic literature, and certainly in political debates, that distinction is often lost, sometimes by inadvertence, sometimes quite intentionally.

On a more positive note, it is also important to acknowledge that the lack of clarity and the blurred distinction between "reading" what previous courts have said and what they ought to have said also allows each court considerable discretion to factor notions of public policy into their decisions. Clearly in the *Manlove* decision and in some of the decisions that have followed it the courts were explicitly modifying common law principles based on public policy considerations. In other cases, the influence of such notions can only be inferred from the court's decision. The legitimacy of judicial modification of common law principles has been extensively debated, paralleling the debate concerning the extent of the courts' role under the constitutions to oversee legislative decisions, as discussed in earlier chapters. A conservative attitude would prefer that the courts' role be defined narrowly and that modifications of the common law to reflect public policy considerations come from legislative, not judicial, discretion—as it has in a number of instances. A more liberal view of the role of the courts would hold that reformation of the common law based on public policy is properly within judicial prerogatives.

But whatever the wisdom or legitimacy of such modifications, clearly some courts make them. In the determination of liability for negligence, the definition of the obligations of hospitals, in fact, would be a prime example. As the institution has developed, and as social and political attitudes towards hospitals have changed, the judicial interpretations of the common law as applied to the modern hospital have also been modified in a number of ways. As pointed out in the previous chapters, courts have tended in the last several decades to hold hospitals increasingly responsible for the quality of the care rendered to their patients, reacting to both the technological and the organizational changes in hospital care. For these same reasons, any court reviewing the obligations of the hospital in the *Crews* decision would have to consider whether the principles applied in 1934 should be interpreted differently 50 years later. For that matter, it might even question whether the hospital fifty years later is even sufficiently similar to the institutions involved in earlier decisions to be governed by the same principles at all.

But while judicial modification of common law based on public policy considerations could lead to increased obligations for hospitals, it could also have the opposite effect. Courts in recent years have been increasingly reluctant to ascribe public responsibilities to ostensibly private institutions. Surely any private hospital would argue that any judicial expansion of a hospital's obligations to its patients or to the public is contrary to prevailing social and political attitudes regarding the autonomy of private enterprise.

END NOTES

1. For additional guidance in "reading" the common law, see references on legal research cited in notes following chapter 1.

   For background references on hospital liability and the continuing obligation of hospitals, see A. SOUTHWICK, THE LAW OF HOSPITAL AND HEALTH CARE ADMINISTRATION 185-97 (1978).
2. All of the discussion in this chapter is focused entirely on the common law obligations of private hospitals. Hospitals, both private and public, may also have obligations to accept patients arising from federal or state legislative mandates.

   Hospitals that have received Hill-Burton funds (or funds under the

1974 health planning legislation) must provide both a reasonable volume of uncompensated services *and* a community service. For a discussion of these two distinct obligations, see Wing, *The Community Service Obligation of Hill-Burton Health Facilities*, 23 B.C.L. REV. 577 (1982).

Various federal and state laws also prohibit discrimination in the provision of hospital services on the basis of race, religion, creed, color, handicap, and age (although these laws have rarely been interpreted with regard to hospital services). For background on one such legislative scheme, see Wing, *Title VI and Health Facilities: Forms Without Substance*, 30 HASTINGS L.J. 137 (1978).

It is also possible, although, again, rarely applied or enforced, that nonprofit hospitals might have either a "free care" or a "community service" obligation arising out of their exemption from federal or state taxes. For interpretations of a nonprofit hospital's obligations under its federal income tax exemption, see Rev. Rul. 69–545, 1969–2 C.B. 202; Rev. Rul. 83–157, 1983–42 C.B. 9.

Finally, it is also possible that an individual hospital might have legally enforceable obligations arising from the bylaws, charter, or policy declarations of the institution, or arising from a condition attached to the receipt of a private grant or endowment.

3. For discussion of the common law origins of the "no duty" rule, see RESTATEMENT (SECOND) OF TORTS section 314 comment c (1965); Prosser even suggests that the "no duty" rule may have evolved as a matter of convenience for courts that had enough trouble handling the "misfeasance" cases without the "nonfeasance" cases.

4. As indicated throughout this chapter, once a duty is recognized, the provider, whether individual or institutional, has an obligation to continue to provide treatment to a patient or risk liability for "wrongful discharge" or negligence in the termination of treatment. But while there have been a number of decisions holding physicians liable under such circumstances, there are very few that involve the separate liability of a hospital for "wrongful discharge." Since Meiselman v. Crown Heights, 285 N.Y. 389, 34 N.E.2d 367 (1941), the continuing obligation of a hospital to its patients has been frequently noted by legal commentators, but rarely directly addressed by the courts. *Cf.* Modla v. Parker, 17 Ariz. App. 54, 495 P.2d 497 (1972); Thomas v. Corso, 265 Md. 84, 288 A.2d 379 (1972). There are several possible explanations for this paucity of case law: (1) the long standing doctrine of charitable immunity for nonprofit hospitals was not overturned in many jurisdictions until the mid-1960s, and (2) some cases have indicated that a hospital can be insulated from liability for "wrongful discharge" if it is carrying out in good faith the explicit orders of a physician. Thus, so long as the discharge is ostensibly a medical judgment, the physician—but not necessarily the hospital—would be liable, unless the physician were an employee of the hospital.

Parenthetically, it should be noted that there are a number of decisions in which the hospital has been held liable for improper or wrongful discharge of a mental patient. *See, e.g.*, Taig v. New York, 19 A.D. 2d 182, 241 N.Y.S.2d 495 (Sup. Ct. 1963).

5. The outline of the physicians' duty of continuing care is summarized in this chapter only to illustrate the general common law principles. For cases discussing the application of these principles, see Herskovits v. Group Health Co-op, 99 Wash. 2d 609, 664 P.2d. 474 (1983); Hiser v. Randolph, 126 Ariz. 608, 617 P.2d 772 (1980); Rise v. United States, 630 F.2d 1068 (1980); Walker v. Pierce, 560 F.2d 609 (4th Cir. 1977) *cert. denied*, 434 U.S. 1075 (1978); Kraus v. Cleveland Clinic, 422 F. Supp. 310 (D.C. Ohio 1977); Lyons v. Grether, 218 Va. 630, 239 S.E.2d 103 (1977). *See also* 3 Am. Jur. P.0.F.2d 117 (1974) and Annot., 57 A.L.R.2d 432 (Supp. 1984).

6. In analyzing these cases, it should be borne in mind that not only must an institution be shown to have violated its standard of conduct, but, as in any negligence case, that violation must be shown to be the actual and proximate cause of damage to the plaintiff. In the context of rendering emergency services (or refusing to do so), this has led to some difficult problems in determining, for example, the medical consequences of delayed treatment. *See, e.g.*, Herskovits v. Group Health Co-op, *supra* note 5; Falcher v. Saint Luke's Hosp. Med. Center, 19 Ariz. App. 2d 247, 506 P.2d 287 (1973); Cooper v. Sisters of Charity of Cincinnati, 27 Ohio St. 2d 242, 272 N.E.2d 97 (1971).

7. Although many of the decisions discussed in this chapter treat the common law obligations of public hospitals as merely paralleling those of private hospitals, some courts have indicated that the duty of public hospitals is broader than the common law obligation of strictly private institutions. *See, e.g.*, Williams v. Hospital Authority of Hall County, 119 Ga. App. 626, 168 S.E.2d 336 (1969). *Cf.* Greisman v. Newcomb, 192 A.2d 817 (N.J. 1963).

In *Greisman*, the court argued that where a private hospital constitutes a monopoly on hospital services in an area, it should be regarded as a public trust, and under those circumstances a hospital would have to allow admission to the public—implying that a public hospital would have that same obligation. Thus the *Greisman* analysis would not only recognize a broader obligation for public hospitals, it would extend that obligation to at least some private hospitals. The "public trust" theory has not been raised in many other jurisdictions, and no other court has directly adopted the *Greisman* analysis.

8. The *Manlove* decision, its implications, and its application in other jurisdictions has been extensively discussed in the legal literature—far more so than the issue discussed in this chapter (which arguably could be of comparable significance both theoretically and practically). For recent reviews of *Manlove* and its progeny, see Fine, *Opening the Closed Doors: The Duty of Hospitals to Treat Emergency Patients*, 24 WASH. U. J. URB. AND CONTEMP. L. 123 (1983); Note, *To Treat or Not to Treat: A Hospital's Duty to Provide Emergency Care*, 15 U.C.D. L. REV. 1047 (1982).

9. Issues involving the discretion of hospitals to operate as wholly private institutions have also been raised by physicians seeking medical staff privileges. The resulting case law has not been entirely consistent. In some instances

courts have suggested that at least private hospitals have virtually unlimited discretion to deny, condition, or revoke medical privileges. In other cases, based on various theories, some courts have required hospitals to show at least some basis for a decision to deny privileges or to follow procedures that insure some minimum procedural fairness in the decision-making process. Curiously, however, these cases have rarely been referenced in discussions of the case law analyzing the discretion of hospitals to allow or deny admission of patients, despite the obvious parallels. *See, e.g.*, Miller v. Eisenhower, 27 Cal. 3d 614, 166 Cal Rptr. 826, 614 P.2d 258 (1980); Ponca City Hosp. v. Murphee, 545 P.2d 738 (Okla. 1976). *Cf.* Silver v. Castle Mem. Hosp., 497 P.2d 564 (Hawaii 1972). For decisions in which the challenge to the hospital's discretion has been based on antitrust laws, see Jefferson Parish Hosp. v. Hyde, *supra* chapter 8, and Liebenluft & Pollard, *Antitrust Scrutiny of the Health Professions: Developing a Framework of Assessing Private Restraints*, 34 VAND. L. REV. 927 (1981).

Table of Cases

Index

About the Author

KENNETH R. WING is Associate Professor of Health Law in the Department of Health Policy and Administration in the School of Public Health, with a joint appointment in the School of Law at the University of North Carolina in Chapel Hill. He has a J.D. from the Harvard Law School and an M.P.H. from the Harvard School of Public Health. Professor Wing has had experience outside the academic world in the California Department of Health and with the National Health Law Program. He is active in several professional organizations and has worked as a consultant for groups from the local to the national level. Professor Wing has published a number of articles in journals and contributed chapters to books; he is also the author of *Health Facility Regulation*.